Matt McMillen is a bestselling Christian author and minister of the New Covenant. His books and massive social media ministry has taught countless amounts of people their true identity in Christ. Matt's easy-to-understand biblical teachings have helped build confidence in his readers, break lifelong addictions, and find their true purpose for living: enjoying God's grace through Jesus Christ!

For more information on his ministry, visit: www.mattmcmillen.com

# 60 DAYS FOR JESUS,
## VOLUME 1

# CONTENTS

## Month 2

*"…God rewards those who diligently seek Him."*

HEBREWS 11:6

Little did I know, the *reward* is knowing Jesus, personally.

# INTRODUCTION

## 60 Days for Jesus

I was broken. Something in me needed to be fixed. I couldn't quite put my finger on it, but there was a longing for something more, something...*peaceful*. What I needed in my life the most, was peace. I thought that peace meant fun and relaxation, and it did not. I thought that peace meant financial freedom. I was wrong, once again. Maybe peace is doing what my body craves? Maybe it's refusing to deny my feelings? Wrong... again.

Little did I know, the peace I was so desperately searching for would come *through* my brokenness. The very brokenness I wanted to fix, hide, cover up, and make go away, Jesus wanted to use. So I spoke to Him about this.

"But how? How am I supposed to take all of these broken, shattered pieces, and put them back together so you can use them? YOU KNOW WHAT ALL I'VE DONE! YOU SEE ME! HOW CAN YOU POSSIBLY USE THIS FOR ANYTHING GOOD?! I AM NOT GOOD! EVEN IN MY BEST EFFORTS TO *BE* GOOD, I'M ROTTEN TO THE CORE! I CAN'T FIND PEACE!...Everything inside me is broken."

He replied with, "You are not rotten in your core, stop saying that. You are not broken on the inside either, I'm here. Inside your spirit, you are complete because of me. You are perfect just *like* me *in* your spirit, because I've given you a new spirit. Sure, your poor choices and your unrenewed mindsets are rotten, but *you* are not. Stop confusing them. Your rotten actions and attitudes might have *produced* brokenness, but *you* are not broken in any way—I'd never allow that. Matthew, no matter how many mistakes you've made, I still love you exactly as you are. I'm here with you, I'm committed to you, and I'll never go away. So give me all of those broken pieces, every single one. I want them. I'll not let any go to waste, you'll see. Just hand them over, let me use them, and let me live *through* you."

…"Okay…here…take them."

Jesus began to repair my mindset in the *middle* of my brokenness! He then *used* my brokenness *for* my purpose! The very peace I was searching for was already in me! It was Jesus! I just didn't know it yet! So little by little I began to give every broken part of my life to Jesus, as He coached me from within.

He revealed to me that He had been in me *in full* from the moment I first believed as a young boy. But now, because I finally realized my life was His life—and vice versa—our relationship started to blossom!

By me beginning to understand my identity, I had a new goal each day which was to get to know Jesus better. This action started to heal my broken feelings and mindsets. I wanted to get to know Him—not just for an hour on Sunday—but daily, even minute by minute. "Who *is* this Person living in me?" I could finally hear Him speak to me clearly, without question. Not in a literal term, but in a motivation—in an *inspiration*. From such, came His voice in my heart.

Going deeper into our relationship came forth from me forming a new habit: *waking up before the sun rose to study Him*. Of course, there is no law in this, but for some strange reason, for *me*, God kept saying, "Get up early and get to know me deeper before your day begins."

"But I'm tired!" my flesh fought back at first.

"Trust me. Study me. I'm preparing you for greater things. Go to bed earlier and you won't be tired."

So, I did, and I had no clue what would happen next! Through this daily study of Jesus, I began to journal. My journaling then turned into my ministry!

*"If I can just figure out what God wants from me, then life will be great."* This was how I thought—and I was correct! What did He want from me? He wanted me to simply *be* my heaven-ready self! He wanted me to live *out* my spiritual perfection! He wanted me to stop making choices that did not match up with my true identity as God's own child!

But this new mindset would take a lot of time to develop. Learning who I really was in Christ frightened me at times. "God, how am I supposed to live this way when I don't feel like it?"

"Stop living by how you feel. Give it time, Matthew. Give it my truth. Your feelings, attitudes, and actions will catch up as time goes on. You are learning. You are growing."

*That's* what has happened to me. I'm still *Matty Matt*, as my close family and friends call me, only now, I'm different. I'm different on the *outside* because I finally understand who I am on the *inside*. Because of my upbringing, I've never lived my life this way before. Instead, I kept trying to be someone who I wasn't. Not any longer!

Friend, the Holy Spirit wants to teach *you* the same things! He wants you to know *who* you really are in Christ! You are a holy, blameless, dearly loved child of God!

So thank you for joining me! Over the next 60 days I'll take you on a daily devotional journey of getting to know Jesus better, as well as getting to know *yourself* better! All of these devotionals can be found on my website for free, if you'd like to print them out or share them. As you read each day, don't skip ahead, and don't miss a day! Unlike some daily devotional books, I haven't put any dates on the pages, so you can start from day one!

Remember: *life is a journey, not a race.* My prayer for you is that you'll finally understand your full value to God. This will only happen by going deeper into your relationship with Him. Like any relationship, we don't want to rush ahead, but instead just spend time together, getting to know the other person one day at a time.

Your relationship with Jesus Christ was meant to be enjoyed, not *earned* through consuming more information *faster*. So take your time and savor the 60-day increments that I plan on this book series being. This is *just* volume one! At the time of me typing up this introduction, I'm already finished with day 36 on volume two!

Also, please understand these books of mine are not meant to replace your regular study of God's Word, but instead, to supplement your quiet time with Him. God doesn't want to legislate your time spent alone with Him, but His Spirit always calls us into it.

It was my devotional time each day that took my relationship with Jesus to deeper levels. This is why I whole-heartedly believe one-on-one time with God will change *your* life too. That is, if you'll give it to Him. Your time could be *any* time, and any *amount* of time, just be sure to *spend* time with God. Yes, He's in you—if you believe He is through faith in Christ's forgiveness—but He still wants some personal attention. We show *people* that we love them through time spent, this applies to our Creator as well.

I plan on *60 Days for Jesus* to be a series of books which continues until God is through using what I have to say. What an honor. I have no plans on stopping at a certain number! I know deep in my soul that these books will plant seeds in *your* soul, which will grow into something big and strong! Because of Jesus' Spirit being in us for good, He will continue to renew our minds in this lifetime, and on into eternity!

So let's go! Let's go talk about Jesus day by day! He's pretty great, you'll see! And so are you!

# Month 1

*"Ask and it will be given to you; seek and you will find; knock and the door will be opened to you." ~Jesus*

*Matthew 7:7*

# DAY 1

## WHO IS JESUS?

*"The Word became flesh and made his dwelling among us…"*

*SEE JOHN 1:14*

Why is Jesus so important? His life was lived 2,000 years ago, why are we still talking about Him? What's up with this man, whom people are lovingly obsessed over—or *hate* with all they are? Why is He such a polarizing figure and why won't He just fade away, like any other fad or story? What's the deal?

Further, why am *I*, personally, so drawn to knowing someone more and more, whom I've never met face to face? Someone whom I simply *believe* in? John chapter 1 answers all of these questions for me. It begins by telling me "He was with God in the beginning" (John 1:2). So when they (Father, Son, Holy Spirit), decided to create this universe—the very notion of *time*—they already had a relationship going on amongst themselves. This explains to me why I'm so drawn to my Creator—He, God, the Trinity, made me for an eternal relationship.

Second, it tells me "Through him all things were made; without him nothing was made that has been made" (John 1:3). This explains His infiniteness, and *my* finiteness. He always "has been." *We* have not. He has no beginning or end. We do. Everything you can currently see and feel will end, because it has a beginning.

However, your spirit is everlasting just like God. It will go on for eternity, with, or without Him. We get to choose. He doesn't choose *for* us. Hence, free will. This is what makes us like God.

So why Jesus? Why this man? Why not leave things as they were before He came? Verse 14 explains the reason, perfectly. "The Word became flesh and made his dwelling among us…"

Jesus is called *the Word*—capital W—as in, a proper noun. Why is this? I heard it once said Jesus is called the Word because He's everything God wanted to say to us! Jesus was and still is, GOD IN THE FLESH. The Word of God became flesh like us! God was now literally *speaking* to His creation, face to face!

Why is that important? Why did He do this? Why can't we just believe in and worship God without Him becoming a man? Why do we need this *personal* relationship with Him—as in, "in person"?

In my quest of nearly 35 years of life, I've determined that God became a man for many reasons, but three of them stand out to me:

1. **We needed to know what God was like in person**. Have you ever judged someone who you didn't know personally? You *thought* you knew them, just by what others have said or what you've heard, but when you finally got to know them *in person* they were completely different than what your mind was already made up they'd be like? This happens all the time. It even happened to our Creator. God saw that not very many people really *knew* Him, intimately. So He became His very own creation! The Bible says Jesus has made him known (see John 1:18). The mystery of what God would be like in person is over! Jesus showed us God in the flesh!

2. **We needed a perfect role model**. John 1:4-5 states, "In him was life, and that life was the light of men. The light shines in the darkness but the darkness has not understood it." Up until God manifested Himself in person, the world was just guessing as to who

He really was. Everyone was feeling around in the dark, trying to understand Him. Sure, the Jews had the Law of Moses which included moral and ceremonial laws (over 600 of them, not just 10). But none of that stuff made them understand God perfectly. Jesus did just that! (See Hebrews 1:3). He set the example for us by gracefully completing every law in Himself, *for* us (see Galatians 3:13). He also overrode the Law with His teachings, miracles, and life! Jesus, the human, literally became a new agreement between us and our Creator! (See Hebrews 7:22, 2 Corinthians 5:21). So now, because of this New Covenant in Christ—which had to be perfect—we have the ideal example of how to live our lives just right: WIJDTM. "What Is Jesus Doing Through Me?" (See Galatians 5:22-23, 1 Corinthians 13:4-13).

3. **We needed our sin-debt paid off with God, once and for all.** I could write a 5-page report on this, but to summarize, the grace-confused Christians will try to make you think you need to confess every single sin in order to be forgiven for them, even *after* you've accepted Christ as your Savior—and if you don't, you are going to hell. This makes no sense because there are sins we forget about and overlook all the time. They fade away into the rear-view mirror of our lives, without any confession or asking of forgiveness. So this conditional, graceless forgiveness is madness, and incorrect. Such thinking keeps you focused on your sin, rather than on Jesus' finished work *for* your sin (see John 19:30, Philippians 4:8). God had a better idea than having to worry about keeping track of our debts with Him. HE WILL PAY IT OFF! ONCE AND FOR ALL! (Hebrews 10:10). And He took it a step further, making it the easiest process ever, to be forgiven for good: admit you are sinful, admit Jesus is perfect, and then believe His sacrifice on the Cross has made you spiritually perfect...viola! (John 3:16, Romans 6:6-7, 10:9, Colossians 1:22, Hebrews 10:14). Now *that* is a loving God! A God who would die for us while we were still sinners just to make us a part of His eternal Family who are now saints! (See Romans 5:8, Ephesians 1:5, 1 John 3:1).

Of course, I'm sure if I put my mind to it, I could write an entire book on all the reasons why we needed Jesus to come to earth. But if I was forced to give one single reason as to why God got down off His throne in heaven, became a baby on His very own planet, grew up, taught us, led us, guided us, and saved us…it would be this: He wanted to show us what real love is like. That's Jesus. That's *my* Jesus. I know Him personally, do you?

**A prayer for you:** *Jesus, today I want to thank you for your life, and your death, and your life! Spiritually, I know you are the truth! Thank you for creating me for this relationship with you. Thank you for pursuing me when I ran from you, in my mind, as fast as I could. Even though you were in me the whole time, I didn't know it! Everywhere I went, you went too! Life is good now, even when my circumstances are not. Right now, I lift up all who are reading this, directly to you. For those who don't know that it's you who keeps knocking on the door of their hearts, saying, "Invite me in," reveal this to them! Show them that your way is the best way! Teach them how much you love them! Teach them how to love you! Teach them how to love others! Teach them how to love themselves! In your name I pray, amen.*

# DAY 2

## JESUS IS PATIENT WITH HIS ENEMIES

*"But I tell you, love your enemies and pray
for those who persecute you" ~Jesus*

### MATTHEW 5:44

Jesus is patient with His enemies, so *we* should be too. That's the hard part. When I first decided to really dig my heels in and get to know Christ each day, through studying His Word, reading Christian books, and allowing myself to be taught by grace-filled teachers, it was extremely difficult to change my mindset.

I WAS LOOKING TO GOD TO FIX MY PROBLEMS—not change *me*. "I'm just fine, it's everybody else who needs to shape up!" My unrenewed mindset was: *Work hard. Play hard. Love those who love me. Hate those who hate me.* And yeah, I was a saved Christian. God was in me, but I refused to allow Him to come *out* of me through my words, choices, and actions.

The fact of the matter was, I WAS HURTING! I was hurting *so* badly when I first began to dedicate a part of my day to getting to know Christ better. And because of this deep hurt caused by others (all the while overlooking *my* bad choices), I started to look up verses where God made people pay for their wrong-doings! I'd even screen-shot it!

Stuff like, "'Leave room for God's wrath, it is mine to avenge, I will re-pay,' says the Lord" (see Romans 12:19). I was like, *"SWEET! GET 'EM!"*

My thought process was, "Okay God, I'm following you now, so I need you to get so-and-so real good. Pay them back for me, get YOUR revenge FOR me, and do it quickly!"…I chuckle at this now, even typing that, be-cause it's true.

God soon taught me that He was much more interested in forming my heart, mind, and life into that of Christ's, than He was in personally settling-up debts with my enemies—as if He was my Heavenly Hitman.

Oh my goodness I wanted God to MAKE THESE PEOPLE PAY!!!!! I'd say things like, "God, you see what they're doing, how can you just let this happen?! C'MON! DO SOMETHING! Show them that me follow-ing you is better than them not!"

God simply said, "… … …Nope."

"Well…FINE! Then at least make them treat me good!"

He replied, "No. I don't *make* people do anything. I give them oppor-tunities to change, just like I'm giving you. They can choose to, or not."

"Then what's the point of me doing this?! WHY AM I SEEKING YOU? I thought you were working all things out together for my good! CAN'T YOU SEE I'M IN PAIN?! DO SOMETHING!"

"I *am* doing something. I'm working out the goodness in *you*."

"But God, it's so hard…"

"I know…you're gonna be okay. I'm showing you what Jesus went through, for you. Keep going. My power is made perfect in your weakness. I'll never leave you or forsake you. I'm teaching you how to no longer be a slave to your circumstances or the choices of people."

My friend, God is much more concerned about getting you to un-derstand how much Jesus loves you *through* the pain of doing things His way, than removing your pain, instantly. He sees the good that will eventually come from your pain, just like He saw the good that would eventually come from Jesus'. This is the exact reason why we shouldn't question God in our bad times, just like we would never question Him in our good times.

No, He doesn't cause the pain, but He allows it. He allows it to show you how to handle your problems like Jesus did—and how He still does.

You see, we naturally want to ATTACK those who attack us. Jesus doesn't do this. He is patient with those who hate Him. This is the very reason why He hasn't come back yet, He is still giving everyone a chance to turn to Him and place their faith in Him—to *believe* in Him. The Bible says that "he *waits* for his enemies to be made his footstool" (see Hebrews 10:13).

He's waiting...He's patient...

He's taking His time to come back, and to conquer *all* evil, permanently. He's giving people the chances, the *opportunities*, everything they could ever need to turn to Him. Grandma used to say, "There won't be anyone in heaven who doesn't want to be there." That could be no further from the truth. God doesn't force people, He waits. He lets them *choose* to love Him, or not.

And just *how* will people even *want* to go to heaven if we aren't properly representing Jesus? It's up to me and you to actually *show* people Christ, every day! NOT RELIGION, BUT *RELATIONSHIP*! We must use our gifts, talents, time, and resources to *show* others the love of Christ! Sometimes, we don't even have to say a word, but instead, just be available...that's it.

And part of this "showing" of Jesus includes being patient with our enemies. It includes showing love to those who don't love us. It includes overcoming evil with good, and doing our very best to walk in the confidence that *is* Christ in us!

So today my friends, please do this: Love those who hate you. How? By bowing down to them? Did Jesus do this? No, but He still had genuine love in His heart toward us. *We*, you and I, were the ones who hated *Him*! Yes! We were! Even if we don't realize it, we hated Jesus because we refused to believe that what He did was not the truth! But still, He *prayed* for us, He sacrificed *everything* for us—and then He set the example for us to follow, with grace and confidence. "But Matt you just don't understand! I'm not loving anyone who doesn't love me!" Well just imagine if Jesus had that same mindset…we'd all be doomed. But He didn't! And because He lives in you, you *can* do this too!

**A prayer for you:** *Jesus, today I ask you to show us how to love people like you do. With an unrenewed mind, this is an impossible feat. But you did the impossible all the time—AND YOU LIVE IN US! You set the standard for us and then you gave us the ability to do everything you did, because of your grace! Renew our thinking to be like yours! Help us to tap into your amazing grace to strengthen us, and to teach us how to love those who don't love us. We want to allow you to live through us, so that we can change the world with your love! Thank you, amen.*

# DAY 3

## You Can't Keep a God-Loving Man Down

*"So Pharaoh said to Joseph, 'I hereby put you
in charge of the whole land of Egypt.'"*

*GENESIS 41:41*

I wake up early each day, usually between 5-5:30 AM. But this morning, God woke me up *extra* early. He told me to get up and pray, and to read the story of Joseph. No, He didn't say this verbally, God speaks to our hearts 99% of the time. The more we walk by His Spirit, the clearer His voice becomes.

It's nearly summer here in Missouri, the sun pokes its head up about 5 AM this time of year, but *this* morning it was still dark when I let Harley out the back door. So coffee in hand, I made my way downstairs, cracked my Bible, and cracked a window. The sound of the birds at daybreak is spectacular, they are *so* excited.

So I prayed for others, and myself, and then began to read about Joseph.

Now, to be clear, I'm not referring to Jesus' earthly father, but instead, the Joseph of Genesis. A man who had something *very* special about him from the time he was young. I'm gonna skip ahead and talk about his position in Egypt, but the backstory is that his dad loved him very, *very* much—so much, that his brothers became jealous and sold him into slavery…He was a good kid, and this was not fair. Not very fair *at all*…but that's okay, because God *is* fair, you'll see.

Eventually, Joseph had become a slave in the house of an Egyptian official named Potiphar. The Bible says, "The Lord was with Joseph and he *prospered*, and he lived in the house of his Egyptian master" (Genesis 39:2).

Notice that God is *still* making crooked paths, straight, for Joseph—EVEN IN HIS TURMOIL. And because of that, his captor took notice: "When his master saw that the Lord was with him and that the Lord gave him success in everything he did, Joseph found favor in his eyes and became his attendant" (Genesis 39:3).

Joseph loved God. Even the non-believer took notice of this, and couldn't help but *promote* Joseph! Potiphar eventually put him in charge of everything he owned! (See Genesis 39:4). And when he did so, "the Lord blessed the household of the Egyptian *because* of Joseph"! (Genesis 39:5). Because of him! Potiphar *then* trusted Joseph so much that "he didn't concern himself with anything except the food he ate" (Genesis 39:6).

His captor eventually just sat back and said, "All this is yours. Just make sure I have some good meals each day." DO YOU SEE THAT?! The people around Joseph were coat-tailing his blessings from God! How amazing! God saw that the heart of Joseph was *so* dead-set on Him, that He blessed even the non-believers by proxy. Myyyyyyyyyyyyy…GOODNESS! C'mon somebody! They were skimming the good stuff!

The people in the life of Joseph were being blessed because of this God-loving man being *in* their house! And they didn't even believe in the One True God, but they *knew* that Joseph did!

Now, you would think that this is the end of the story, but no. The devil ain't gonna let that slide. You see, Joseph was a very good-looking man. The Bible says that he was "well-built and handsome" (Genesis 39:6), and Potiphar's wife took notice. One day, she came onto him very aggressively, "Come to bed with me!" (Genesis 39:7).

I gotta be honest with you, this man has my respect. Someone who *doesn't* love God would be like, "Oh yeah. This is my lucky day. This dumb man put me in charge of his house, and now his wife wants me." BUT NOPE! He didn't do that! He knew that God was watching, and that his blessings were coming directly from Him.

Joseph refused. "My master has withheld nothing from me except you, because you are his wife. How could I do such a wicked thing and sin against God?" (Genesis 39:9).

This evil, spoiled woman, was not going to take no for an answer. She kept on and kept on, telling him to come sleep with her, and Joseph just kept avoiding her until one day she grabbed him by his cloak and said, "Come to bed with me!" But Joseph ran off! The bad news is that she still had his cloak in her hand (Genesis 39:12).

Long story short, she accuses him of rape. Potiphar, FURIOUS, had him thrown in prison...a good man who loved God, just trying to do the right thing, gets framed. So, so sad...or is it?

The Bible says that "While Joseph was in prison, the Lord was with him; He showed him kindness AND GRANTED HIM FAVOR IN THE EYES OF THE PRISON WARDEN!" (Genesis 39:20-21). C'MON SOMEBODY! Do you *see* what God does for those who love Him?! What the devil uses for *harm*, God uses for our *purpose*!

"ALL THINGS WORK *TOGETHER* FOR THE GOOD OF THOSE WHO LOVE GOD AND ARE CALLED ACCORDING TO HIS PURPOSE!" (Romans 8:28).

And that prison warden liked Joseph SO MUCH, that he put him in charge of the entire prison! (See Genesis 39:22). WHAT!? HA! THIS IS SO GOOD!!!

I could keep going with this, telling you how the devil kept trying to defeat Joseph, but over the next few chapters of Genesis, he keeps getting promoted! Higher and higher, and *higher*, until eventually, he gets put in charge of the entire land of Egypt—ONLY SECOND TO PHARAOH!

> *Pharaoh then adorns Joseph in beautiful jewelry, regal clothing, and puts him in a fancy chariot, commanding everyone to respect him (see Genesis 41:41-43).*

...It is *mind-blowing* what God can do when you show Him how much you care about Him!

What ensues next, after Joseph is named VP of Egypt? A famine breaks loose in all the land. And guess what? His brothers come to Egypt to get food, and *who* is in charge of the food? Yep. Their little, happy brother, whom they thought was dead! Imagine the fear they felt when they realized it was Joseph standing in front of them!

But Joseph doesn't pounce. He doesn't have them killed. No, instead he shows them love. He said to them, "It was not you who sent me here, but God" (see Genesis 45:8). "You intended to harm me, but God intended it for good to accomplish what is now being done, the saving of many lives" (Genesis 50:20). And then he took care of them.

My friend, if you are in a battle right now, if life is hard and you are just trying to love God, take heart! Continue to stay focused on what God wants from you. DON'T GIVE UP! DON'T COMPROMISE! GOD SEES YOU! He sees you, and He loves you. He is using *all* of this—ALL OF IT—for a great, GRAND purpose, that will one day make sense! It might not make sense to you on this side of heaven, but when you finally get Home, you can sit down with Jesus and He'll tell you the story of your life—how absolutely *proud* of you He was, and still is. Keep going. He is with you.

**A prayer for you:** *God, I want to thank you for my hardships. I now know that anything you allow to happen in my life, you are using for good! Right now, I lift up all who are reading this, directly to you. STRENGTHEN THEM! Help them to understand that you see* *their situation, and that you FEEL their pain. ENCOURAGE THEM TODAY! If they've slipped off course, guide them back. Remove any guilt that they have, and help them to begin to once again TRUST you, even when it hurts. You WILL get us all to where we need to be—no matter the difficult route! THANK YOU! YOU ARE GOOD! In Christ's name I pray, amen.*

# DAY 4

## FACING THE TRUTH ABOUT YOURSELF

*"Do not conform to the pattern of this world, but be transformed by the renewing of your mind."*

*SEE ROMANS 12:2*

One of the most difficult things to do in life is to face the truth about yourself. For years I didn't want to do this, but until I did, I would never be able to enjoy my life on the level that God had planned for me. Yes, I have a ministry now, I have stories to tell because I lived them, and people look to me for advice during difficult circumstances.

But I gotta tell you, there'd be no way I'd be in this position if I never faced the truth about my own unacceptable behaviors and attitudes.

I grew up in an extremely unstable atmosphere. Addiction, adultery, and divorce began ruining my life as a little child. I was in and out of foster homes and children shelters, and when one of my parents *did have* custody of me, we moved a lot. That hurt. The close friends I made at each school or "home," I always had to say good-bye to. These uncontrollable situations caused tremendous fear and anxiety in my mind as a boy.

Fast forward to adulthood, and because of my unstable upbringing I had become a functioning alcoholic, people-pleaser, with a short fuse. To top it off, workaholism set in as I was overly-driven to show others that I *do* matter. Finally, codependency took over my life. Because of being ripped away from loved ones, friends, and family so often when I was young, I developed a terrible habit of allowing unacceptable behavior from other people just to keep them happy.

I constantly put up with being treated poorly, *used even*, because I was afraid of others leaving me alone, not accepting me, or hurting me.

This led to extreme frustration as I kept trying to change people—but I couldn't. Soon enough, my codependency turned into extreme alcohol dependency. *"Heck, if I can't change people or my circumstances, I'm just gonna change how I feel."* The bottle did this splendidly. It numbed my pain. It shoved my feelings down deep into a dark hole, and then covered them up with a buzz.

I HAD TO CHANGE MY CHOICES. God had more for me, yet there was no way I *could* change my choices, until I finally admitted that I *needed* to change my choices. So at last, I decided to allow Christ to begin living through me. This changed everything.

What ensued was a brand new peace, comfort, confidence, and a sound mind growing inside me, and sprouting *out* of me! The difficult people who used me and treated me badly, all of my uncontrollable situations, they no longer dictated my joy!

The funny thing is, hardly any of those people or circumstances changed, but instead I continued to change by letting Jesus help me make my choices each day. And little by little, I began to develop new skills (taught to me by the Holy Spirit) which I *needed* to make my life into something beautiful; something actually enjoyable—something that God had planned for me all along!

And this all began with me admitting that I didn't know how to handle a thing, on my own. I needed to change my entire mindset through God's Spirit guiding me each day. That was the truth I had to face about myself.

So today, my friends, know this: If you will face the truth about yourself God will completely change your life! What is it exactly that God wants to change? Is it an addiction? Is it you trying to constantly fix someone else who doesn't even want to *be* fixed? Is it a self-righteous, hyper-critical, graceless mindset? Is it you always giving in to your flesh's cravings? Whatever it is, just give it to God today, and His Spirit will hand you back something *so* much better.

> **A prayer for you:** *Good morning Lord, thank you for another day! What an honor it is to be able to have life! Thank you! Right now, I lift up all who are reading this who want to change. For those who need the strength to face the truth about themselves so that you can fully change their lives through your Spirit, help them. You see that they want it, now give it to them as they do this while resting in your grace! With Christ, we can do all things, INCLUDING admitting what needs to be changed in our lives. In your name Jesus, I pray. Amen.*

# DAY 5

## WHAT IS GOD LOOKING FOR?

*"God opposes the proud but shows favor to the humble."*

*JAMES 4:6*

I believe with all my heart that one of the top things God is looking for is simply people who want to make themselves *available* to Him.

God is not looking for religious zealots, or self-righteous, legalistic Christians who spout off stuff like, "Shape up and tell people about Jesus! Do it, or else burn in hell!" No way. Those people find their identity in their religion, not in their relationship with Jesus. They are confused.

God is not looking for aggressive preachers and angry "I don't sin" Christians—those who hold others' 100% forgiveness in Christ, hostage. God is also *not* looking for more people who refuse to tell the truth about Jesus finishing everything at the Cross; those Christians who won't tell the lost people of the world that our *favorable* judgment has been finalized through what Jesus did *for* us—it is finished! (See John 3:17, 19:30).

Because of Christ settling up our sin-debt with God, the only people who *will* be judged for anything they do (or don't do) are those who refuse to believe in and accept—*by faith*—Christ's forgiveness.

Yet, these types of grace-confused Christians have so much double-talk. They say polar-opposite things, such as, "Come to Jesus as you are and be *completely* forgiven!" But then the following week they refute such grace-filled teaching, and say, "Stop that or you will be judged worse than non-believers and fall right back into hell!" Which is it?…

Since *they* won't tell you the truth, I will: "IT'S FINISHED!" That's what Jesus said in His last breath on the Cross. What's most sad is that the same grace these Christians refuse to give others, they *too* will be in desperate need of.

Yes, I understand that they don't want Christians to go buck-wild with sin, neither does God—but neither do *Christians* at their spiritual core (see Romans 6:6). So this brand of conditional-grace Christianity is going about *achieving* such a goal incorrectly, which is un-truthfully and with fear. Both, *graceless-God* and *fear tactics* are broken systems. They don't work. They've *never* worked. We're not supposed to be petrified of God, but instead, we are supposed to love and respect Him, and we do this by living *from* our new hearts—*post* salvation (see Ezekiel 36:26, Hebrews 8:10).

Because of Jesus giving you a new one, your heart is no longer wicked. It is perfect *just* like Jesus, and it wants what *exactly* Jesus wants—even if the flesh doesn't, or your unrenewed mind fights it.

The Bible says that "it is the *goodness* of God that leads people to repentance" (see Romans 2:4). So no, God is not looking for graceless fear-mongers who make God look *bad*.

*This* is who God is looking for: People who will humble themselves enough to say, "Okay God, I'm willing to allow you to live through me. I've tried every other way and nothing seems to work. I know you want me to change my incorrect attitudes and actions, I *want* to change them, please help me do this." This is called humility, or, *humbleness*. Humbleness is Christianity 101, the entry level course, where it all begins. Afterwards, Christ can enter your heart, and give you a new spirit! (See Galatians 2:20).

Until you finally say, "Lord, I'm yours. Make my spirit into the image of Christ. Change everything *in* me that you want changed." Until you do this, you can't fully complete your God-given destiny.

The Bible says "God opposes the proud, but gives grace to the humble" (James 4:6). I don't know about you, but all the years I lived which were not very humble, I sure felt like God actually *was* opposing me, and that's because He was opposing my unholy actions and attitudes! So when my choices and mindsets went against my perfect spirit, a conflict was bound to happen!

But as I ignored Him each day, *because* He was in me in full, there was a longing in my heart, a *disturbance* for something so much more. God was saying, "Matthew, let's get this going. I've got some awesome plans, but you are going to have to let me use you."

Now don't get me wrong when I say, "humble yourself," I'm not telling you to become like a beat dog—absolutely not! As a matter of fact, the more humble you become by letting Jesus live *through* you, the more strength and confidence you develop! It's very strange!

People can't control you like they used to and fear doesn't grip you as often! And in my opinion, even *better*, self-pity fades away! But what's really happening in your life as you walk by the Spirit (see Galatians 5:22-23) is several oxymorons: You are learning how to live in *powerful* humility, *attractive* humbleness, and a *confident* meekness.

HOW IS THIS POSSIBLE?! Through Christ! Christ *in* you, *His* Spirit, that's who it is! (See Philippians 4:13).

So today, my friends, know this: No matter what is going on in your life, no matter *how* many problems you *think* you have or how messed up someone else has *made* you feel—please, HUMBLE YOURSELF BEFORE GOD. This is what He's looking for! Humble, confident believers, who are willing to make themselves available for Him! If you haven't humbled yourself before God just yet, you can right now. Just say, "Help me Jesus. Make me into who you want me to be!"…and then prepare yourself, because He will!

**A prayer for you:** *God, I remember when I was first trying to allow you to live through me, how it went against my mind so ferociously! I remember feeling like I was being beat up with a bag full of rocks! So I* *know this is hard, but as I've continued, you've taught me that my true strength is found in doing things your way, EVEN when it hurts! I understand this now, and it actually feels good! Right now, I lift up all who are reading this, directly to you. For those who want to humble themselves, STRENGTHEN THEM! Help them to understand your power is made perfect in our weaknesses. And when their actions and attitudes fail them, help them to understand that you NEVER give up on them, because you are IN them, forever. In Christ's awesome name, I ask these things, amen.*

# DAY 6

## HOW TO HANDLE LIFE'S DISAPPOINTMENTS

*"All things work together for the good of those who
love God and are called according to his purpose."*

*ROMANS 8:28*

How do you handle disappointments? For years, I handled 99% of my disappointments the very *opposite* way that Jesus wanted me to. Why? Because I didn't understand exactly how He expected me to react when I faced a difficult situation or a difficult person. Almost every time a disappointment happened, I would make poor choices that went against God's Spirit in me. I didn't trust His ways or myself, just yet.

The results from me doing this led me to live a frustrated, fearful, addicted, codependent life—even *after* I was saved. The good news is, Jesus had no desire for me to live like that! He wants to teach us how to handle our disappointments the proper way, *His* way.

My friend, when Jesus walked this planet He went about touching the lives of many disappointed people, people who had all but given up on life. What did He do to change this? He gave them a brand new hope! That's what He does best! He gives us hope! Hope of a fresh start of brand new attitudes and actions which match up with His Spirit in us—every single day!

Once we finally grasp the hope found in the life of Christ *in* us, only then can we grasp His grace, mercy, and love. Afterwards comes confidence! God is expecting you to be confident in Him, as well as in your true self! The Bible says, "Do not throw away your confidence; it will be richly rewarded!" (Hebrews 10:35).

God made you to be a confident person! This authentic confidence builds up your courage! Courage will steer your life in the right direction all day long *even* when disappointing situations and people head your way! Your confidence and courage comes from allowing Jesus to live *through* you! It doesn't come from being a religious nut, but instead, by simply being who you truly are inside!

Who are you? A child of God! (See John 1:12). You have strength, forgiveness, love, and enthusiasm! You have the actual Spirit of God *in* you—the Spirit of Christ Himself! (See 1 Corinthians 6:19). Jesus was very courageous despite the disappointment of being thrown through a meat-grinder and then tacked-up onto a giant cross!

Further, Jesus wasn't an enabler! He wasn't codependent! So He did everything for the right reasons! He didn't walk around saying to people, "Oh you poor thing. What can I do to help you?" NO! He told those who were caught in self-pity to "GET UP!" (See John 5:8). He said things like, "Do you even *want* to get well?! DO YOU WANT IT?!" (See John 5:6). On top of that, He wasn't a blameful, negative, critical sour-puss—so neither are we! He lives in us!

Because I didn't realize these truths, my life was not going in the right direction and I needed a desperate change. If I've been re-created in His image (see Romans 6:6-7, 2 Corinthians 5:17), then courage and confidence was mine to be had! I wanted to stop letting disappointments in my life *control* my life. Once I began to do this, God remolded me. Me, me, me, me, and…me. Not people, not my circumstances, but only me. After I began to let Him change my thought processes and choices into *who* I really was, *then* everything changed—in my mind. Which is what matters the most!

If you only knew me back then you'd fully understand! I did *not* handle my disappointments how the Holy Spirit wanted me to—or even how *I* wanted to! My old stinking thinking and the enemy acted as if they were still in charge, and they weren't! Yes, I'm still tempted to respond how I used to, but I don't—most of the time anyway. Instead, I now allow God's Spirit to guide me and by doing so little by little He's taught me how to handle life's disappointments properly—how a saint is supposed to! Every believer in Christ is a saint! (See Colossians 1:22, 1 Corinthians 1:2).

I wish I knew this all along because life is so much better! He wants to do the same for you! The people who disappoint you all the time, every unfair situation that arises, Jesus' Spirit will give you the guidance needed to be able to respond organically (see Galatians 5:22-23).

Before I began to allow Him to lead me, my life was empty, even as a Christian. It was full of frustration, anxiety, blame, sinful anger and worry, all because I kept trying to change things and people in which I had no power to change. And that's exactly what the devil wanted! I see that now! What a V8 moment! *BONK!*

If you're a Christian who ignores the devil and what he's doing in your life, then you're the same as a sheep living in a lion's den who ignores the lions around you. The fact of the matter was I had no coping skills to handle any of my disappointments because I kept ignoring God, as well as my true self. Therefore, the devil easily had his way with me.

I'm not saying stay focused on the enemy, I'm saying recognize his work. When you don't, you will live in fear. I didn't know how to handle the people and problems I faced all the time, *except* with fear. Fear would then manifest itself in bad choices, rage, addiction, self-pity, and codependency—just to name a few things it brought on.

My problem was this: rather than face my fears head on through Christ, I accepted unacceptable behavior from myself and other people all the time. Now, I'm not afraid any longer. I simply respond to disappointments in a manner that grows good spiritual fruit in my life—then I let the chips fall where they may.

*This positive mindset is natural as a child of God—it's not forced! It's having the attitude of, "I'm good! I know who goes before me! I know who makes all things new! I know who lives IN me and THROUGH me!"*

So now, when the devil tries to control me with a person's hate or an unfair circumstance, I don't worry, I don't flinch, and I don't fret. Instead, I tell him, "Go ahead and knock yourself out dummy, I'm not going there. Not today, devil."

Before I knew about his tactics—which is to attack my mind—not only did I *not* recognize my enemy, but I didn't fully trust Jesus or myself. I was running in circles discouraged each day, which resulted in me reacting with fear yet again. God has a better way for us to live! That way is through Christ! That way is through *being* our true selves! This is a process which happens day by day, year by year, so be easy on yourself! (See Philippians 1:6).

So today, my friends, please do this: Don't be like me. Don't take so long to allow the Holy Spirit to live through you! Don't wait to live out *who* you really are! Don't wait…and wait…and *wait* for your disappointments to disappear because they won't! When they leave more will head your way, but that's fine because you'll be ready! You and Jesus will *always* be ready! So simply be who He has made you to be—a confident saint who handles your disappointments properly!

**A prayer for you:** *Heavenly Father I want to thank you for waking me up today! What an amazing journey of life you've given each one of us! Right now, I lift up all who are reading this, directly to you. I ask that you begin to teach those who are constantly disappointed with their lives your Spirit's way of handling things. Give them peace in knowing your grace deeper each and every day. In Jesus' name I pray, amen.*

# Day 7

## Kill the Little Foxes

*"Little foxes spoil the vine"*

*See Song Of Solomon 2:15*

I f you are a member of PETA, the title of this devotional might have just made your blood pressure rise. But you can go ahead and take a deep breath because "little foxes" simply refers to "small sins." You know, the ones that "don't really matter"?

First off, to God, all sins are equal. The Bible actually says God sees gossip and murder the same (see Romans 1:29). As Christians, He doesn't have a sin-barometer that He judges us by because Jesus has already judged us NOT GUILTY (see John 3:17). Because we've been born of God, in our spirits we are 100% sinless as believers in Christ's forgiveness (see 1 John 3:9, Colossians 1:22). So for us, when our flesh and unrenewed minds commit sins (not our spirits, which is our identity) those sins are all the same to God.

As humans, we are not like this. We have a scale-driven judgmental mind, "eye for an eye, tooth for a tooth." But God does not work this way! For proof, read the story of the vineyard workers in Matthew 20. They all got paid the same, no matter what time of day they began working.

But that's not the topic I wanted to cover today. I needed to set up how God sees sin, so I can bring to light how very important it is that we do what He wants us to do *even* when it seems like it's no big deal—or when nobody is looking. Don't forget that God is always looking. He sees everything and knows everything, even when people don't.

Jesus said that we are all part of a "vine," which is Him. As Christians, we are individual branches each connected together through Him—the vine (see John 15:5).

So what's the deal with the foxes? Foxes sometimes *feed* on grapevines. They chew away at them, destroying its growing power. The Bible says it is the "little foxes that spoil the vine" (see Song of Solomon 2:15). No, this isn't referring to Jesus—He's indestructible, and this is pre-Cross. This verse is in reference to our purposefulness.

It's the *little* sins we allow to happen that hinders our purposefulness as believers, as a whole. This applies to the "typical" sins (lie, cheat, steal, etc.); as well as the "self-righteous" or "religious works" sins (refusing to forgive as Christ forgave you, bitterness toward non-believers, finding your identity in a church position or tithing, etc.).

Let's be clear here, I'm not simply talking about the Christian housewife who is a huge Magic Mike fan, I'm also talking about the Christian who memorizes Bible verses just so they will have ammo in their legalistic shotgun which they plan on using to *harm* others instead of helping them. *All* little sins begin to spoil the vine!

If you're still not sure what I mean, here is a list of "little fox sins" which can eventually ruin your life because the Holy Spirit *in* you will never say this is copacetic:

1. **What you watch and listen to on a regular basis**. I was blind to this for years and didn't realize it until I *really* began to allow Jesus to live through me—but, I was highly entertained by movies, TV shows, and music that did *not* match up with Him. No, I haven't shut off the secular world from my life, but instead, I've begun to be purposeful about what my eyes and ears are being flooded with on a daily basis. This is a *hidden* little fox, you gotta look for it.

2.  **Having intimate conversations with people that you shouldn't be having**. With the invention of social media, the reproduction of this little fox is at an all-time high. It's so easy to flirt with others this way and then claim it's no big deal. The little fox of inappropriate online communication has destroyed *many* families. To kill this little fox, you may have to unfollow people whom you are attracted to, or unfriend them completely if your spouse feels threatened by your social media connections. But it doesn't end there! You can easily have inappropriate real life conversations in person, over the phone, or by texts, that you *know* deep down in your spirit, you shouldn't be having. Ask God to help you recognize this little fox, kill it, and then skin it.

3.  **Gossiping**. This is a tale as old as time, blabbing our mouths to people about stuff that we shouldn't be verbalizing at all. For some strange reason, this little fox sneaks in very easily to our conversations. Rule of thumb: Is *what* or *who* I'm talking about being helped *through* my words? Am I solving a problem in a Spirit-led way, with my mouth? If not, then button it up because that little fox will zap the life out of your witness with lightning speed.

4.  **Refusing to block off time for God each day**. For years I told myself, *"I'll begin a daily devotional for God when I find time. Right now I'm just too busy."* This was a small lie, a little fox. The fact of the matter is that it's impossible to *find* any more time in the day—we all get the same amount! So instead of saying "I need more time," we must *give* our time *to* God! For me, I began to give Him this time early in the morning. It was about 2011 when I began to go to bed just a tad bit earlier (about an hour) just so that I can start getting up at 5:30 A.M. And no, I didn't make a law out of it, I just saw it as "worship," even though all I was doing was sipping coffee and reading. *This* was my designated time for God, no matter what. My devotionals don't earn me anything from God, but they allow my faith to be built up as I get to know who *He* is, better. This time spent also deepens my understanding of who I am in Christ! When I finally killed the two little foxes

of "excuses and procrastination," my entire life began to change in a positive way!

So today, my friends, know this: There are many little foxes that the enemy uses to distract you from your true identity in Christ! But as you allow the Holy Spirit to guide you, you can hunt them down, kill them, and make a nice fur coat out of them.

**A prayer for you:** *Good morning Heavenly Father, you are such a good Dad! I want to thank you for all you do for me. Please help me to begin to recognize any NEW little foxes in my life that try to sneak in on me. And please give me the spiritual concentration to get rid of those little buggers! Right now, I lift up all who are reading this, directly to you. I ask that you give them wisdom and revelation to understand what they should cut out of their life, and what they should add; the little stuff they think is no big deal. Strengthen them, help them, and comfort them! In Christ's name I pray, amen.*

# DAY 8

## GOD HAS A JOB FOR YOU TO DO

*"Now go; I will help you speak and will
teach you what to say." ~God*

*EXODUS 4:12*

As a Christian, part of your job is to teach others about Jesus with *your* life—sometimes you should even use words. However, do you ever feel like you're not good enough or qualified to tell others about God? YOU ARE NOT ALONE!

Feeling inadequate to do God's bidding is not a new thing, it began thousands of years ago with Moses. When God spoke to Moses and commanded him to go tell Pharaoh to release his people, Moses was like, "What?! No way! I'm not even a good talker, I'm not eloquent in speech *at all*. Why don't you send Aaron? He's really good at talking to people and using his mouth" (see Exodus 4).

God replied with, "Who made your mouth? I did. Now go. I will help you speak and teach you what to say" (see Exodus 4:12).

*Who made your mouth?*
*Who made your mouth?*
*Who MADE your mouth?!*

This is something that I used to repeat to myself all the time. When I decided to start my own personal ministry, I tried to talk myself out of it quite often. I was very afraid. And that's what God wants from *all* of us, a *personal* ministry. One that starts with "Jesus and me," and then goes on to infect the entire world.

For me, self-discouragement wasn't where my problems ended. The hate from close loved ones, church members, and so-called friends who didn't like that I was now "all in for Christ," they made me want to crawl into a hole and just be quiet.

"You ain't living right! Who do you think you are?! Everyone knows you're a phony! Give up! You don't have what it takes!"

Some Christians don't want you doing *too* much for God because then *they* would have to apply that same graceful effort to their own lives. So instead, they try to discourage *you* to make *themselves* feel better. They want you to stay a wall-flower Christian, so be ready for that, you'll be fine. God will actually use their hate for your eventual promotion and growth in Christ!

At first, sure, it's a huge surprise and it stings—but that goes away. You'll find your comfort in Christ, so lean on Him for strength because painful situations come to *pass*, not stay!

But besides other *people* discouraging you, the enemy will also accuse you day and night, "You're a nobody. You're not good enough to talk about God. Just shut up and mind your own business. Nobody cares."

I didn't recognize him at first because I had never really been taught about him. The teaching which I had received from the church I was attending never mentioned the devil, but instead, how much I needed to change *myself*.

So because of graceless teaching, my mindset was pointed in the wrong direction—toward *my* efforts. In return, the devil had his way with me all the time—BUT I REFUSED TO KEEP QUIET!

I *knew* there was *something* that God wanted to do *through* me, I could not deny this! I *had* to figure it out. So I kept pushing forward into His grace, I kept learning about Christ, studying the Bible, reading grace-focused books, as well as watching and listening to other teachers who I felt

God was leading me toward. I also learned who God *didn't* want me to be learning from: the self-righteous, hyper-critical, judgmental preachers. The ones who had conditional, legalistic love.

God does *not* have favorites (see Romans 2:11). *You* are just like me. I don't care what anyone else has told you, there is *something* that God has placed inside you that *He* wants to use—something irrevocable! (See Romans 11:29) That means it won't ever go away, it's set in stone!

THE BEST NEWS OF ALL IS THIS: God wants to *use* that "something" *for* Him! That gift! That talent! That ability! That *thing*! He wants you to use it to bring attention to Jesus! He wants to use it to change the lives of others—for the better—and to stock the halls of heaven with souls! He has a job for you to do, and you'll tap into that job through His grace!

So how do we begin? Here are four tips that I believe will help you, as they did me:

1. **Don't be afraid.** I could lie to you by saying once you begin to allow Jesus to live through you, you'll be so full of confidence and bravery that you'll never be scared—but that's not fair to say. Fear will *attempt* to grip your mind daily. What you must do is push! PUSH. THROUGH. Fear leads you right into discouragement. After that, you will be back to square one where the devil wants you. So simply feel the fear, recognize it as "just fear," and then, SPEAK UP AGAINST IT AND PUUUUUUSH THROUGH! Because of Christ in you, you have nothing to be afraid of!

2. **Graduate from baby-food to solid food.** In Hebrews, it says, "By this time you ought to be teachers, but you still have to be taught the elementary truths of God, all over again. You need milk, not solid food!" (See Hebrews 5:12). In context, the author of Hebrews is comparing the difference in faith in the Old and New Covenants. But still, we must graduate from being a Christian who has a "little baby" mindset of *"Gimme gimme gimme! I'm right, you're wrong!"* to eventually, being strong enough to say to God, "Even if it hurts, I'm willing to do this for you, because I love you."

3. **Don't just "go" to church**. For years I was under the incorrect impression that *attending* church made me acceptable to God—it does not. *No* action makes you acceptable to God, only faith in Christ's forgiveness does (see Galatians 3:10-11). Church is simply a place to learn and grow in Christ! If you are *going* each week, and then *leaving* each week, then rinsing and repeating with no growth, you are wasting your time. GO TO GROW!

4. **Overcome evil with good**. When I finally understood that God's Spirit in me overcomes evil with good *through* me, everything changed (see Romans 12:21). Because of the flesh and unrenewed mindsets, we can lean toward getting people back when they cause us harm. We can incorrectly think that we want to make them pay! But really, we don't. The only *real* way to defeat evil is with good! The only authentic way! This is exactly what Jesus did, so as we allow Him to help us respond when we get hurt, we can definitely get the job done as Christ, and the real you, sees fit!

**A prayer for you:** *Heavenly Father thank you for another day, I am all yours. With all the dumb stuff I've done in my past, I shouldn't even be here. Thank you for loving me and protecting me. Right now, I lift up all who are reading this, directly to you. For those who are struggling to figure out what their purpose for living is, I ask that you help them understand it's Christ IN them, living THROUGH them. Fill them up with confidence as they live Him out! GIVE THEM COURAGE! In Jesus' name I pray, amen.*

# DAY 9

## IS FEAR RUINING YOUR LIFE?

*"Don't be afraid." ~Jesus*

SEE MATTHEW 14:27

For so many years I lived in fear, and fear, when not confronted and pushed back, will ruin your life. If you don't FINALLY stand up to what, or *who*, causes you so much fear, then you will be a slave to fear your entire life.

Fear comes in two forms:

1. **A FEELING.** I say it all the time, but feelings are fickle. They come and go, ebb and flow. You can't help *how* you feel, but you can choose to allow Christ to help you *with* your feelings. You do *not* have to agree with how you feel! So when you feel fear, recognize that it's just a feeling (unless you're doing something that the Holy Spirit is telling you not to do, *that's* a healthy fear). You must also understand that whatever physical manifestations ensue, such as shaking, sweating, stammering, stuttering, or even wanting to run away from people who need to be confronted—those feelings and physical symptoms, you

can't always help. So you must learn to *not* get upset about anything you can't stop or change *physically*. Instead, move forward *despite* these things. This is called *courage*. Courage is not the absence of fear, but instead, moving forward while still feeling fear. *"We do it anyway. No matter our feelings."* And when you know *Who* lives in you, there is nothing to stop you from moving forward!

2. **A SPIRIT**. We are a spirit. Yes, we are flesh (what you can see) but we are also spirit (what you *can't* see). There *is* a spiritual realm, another dimension where activity is taking place just like in this physical realm. You'll have complete access to the spiritual realm once your physical body dies. However, your spirit is everlasting. It does not die. And because you are a spirit, evil spirits can accuse you and lie to you, causing fear. As Christians, no demonic force can possess us because Christ has *already* possessed us—but they can still *pester* us. This is why Paul told Timothy, "God did not give you a spirit of fear, but of power, love, and a sound mind" (see 2 Timothy 1:7)—that's the Holy Spirit—THE VERY SPIRIT WHO LIVES IN US!

It really doesn't matter if you are feeling fear, or if you are being pestered spiritually, you have a choice to make: *"Will I stand up to this fear, or will I keep giving in to this fear?"*

If you don't stand up to *what* or *who* keeps causing you fear, you will not be able to enjoy your life. Instead, you will base all of your choices on making sure you don't *feel* that particular fear any longer. Then, the enemy has you where he wants you as he convinces you to slip into a sin pattern to help you "cope" with that fear! You must stand up and fight back!

Ask yourself, *"What or who causes me fear, and why?"* and then bring that to Jesus to get your weapons for battle! (See Ephesians 6).

Maybe you're in a relationship which was completely built on fear. Fear of that person leaving you for someone else. Fear of them taking the kids away. Fear of ruining you financially, or socially. Fear of nobody else loving you because this person has taken advantage of you and verbally abused you for *so long* that you *think* you're not worth anything. This person whom you are afraid of, has spoken bad about you to anyone and everyone who would listen, spreading lies to keep you manipulated and fearful.

They've done their very best to destroy your reputation, in order to keep you bound and shackled, so that you'll *continue* to do as they please. You could be *very* afraid of this person, and you don't have to be!

Stand up and push through this fear! HAVE COURAGE! Stop accepting unacceptable behavior as normal! Stop being codependent! God will work everything else out, just stand up to them! STAND UP!

Maybe you have a fear of giving up an addiction. First of all, that addiction is nothing more than a way to *endure* your fear, by *changing* your feelings. JESUS WANTS IT GONE! I drank for years because of fear, and my fear was compounded because I just sat back and refused to stand up to people and situations that were *not* okay. So I know how it feels!

YOU GOTTA STAND UP FOR YOURSELF! You gotta stop giving in to fear! You gotta rattle the cage! BUT—you must do this how Christ *in* you wants you to. My friend, fear will cause you to want to reach out for your addiction every single time you feel it. Demonic lies will tell you, "You're never gonna beat this addiction. You need it for your strength!"

SO STAND UP AND PUSH THROUGH! GOD'S SPIRIT GIVES YOU STRENGTH!

Or maybe you have a fear of letting Jesus live through you. This was totally me for years. For so long I listened to legalistic Christians who refused to teach me about God's grace because they were so anti-sin. And yes, God is anti-sin as well, but it's unfair to create fear in people by withholding their complete forgiveness in Christ *hostage* because you don't *want* them to sin.

Once I finally understood that God loved me unconditionally (despite the sin of my flesh and my unrenewed mindsets) *and* that Christ paid the price for all of my sins—once—past, present, future (see Hebrews 10:10), the fear I felt was gone. Now, as God's own child, I can't act bad enough to make Him *not* love me, and I can't *be* good enough to earn or sustain His love. His love has been free from day one! (See Hebrews 7:25, John 1:12, Ephesians 1:5, 2 Timothy 2:13).

So today, my friends, know this: God doesn't want you to be fearful because fear has nothing to do with your true spiritual identity! He says it all throughout the Bible! When are you going to believe this?! What will it take? I'm here to tell you *today* to *please* stop living in fear! Yes, as you do this the world will begin to shake all around you! The people who control you with fear won't know what to do! They will fight you! You will be tempted greatly to revert right back to fear!…But don't do it. Be brave. God will work everything out for good as long as you stand up to your fears and *push through*. Do this, and *everything* changes—everything, for the better!

> **A prayer for you:** *Good morning Lord! Wow, how grateful I am for another day on your planet! Right now, I ask that you fill up these dear readers with confidence! Since you've taught me how to be confident in Christ, I want to make sure that the Christians who are living a fearful life understand there is a better way! MAKE THEM BRAVE, MAKE THEM STRONG, IN YOU! Help them to stand up to their fears to-day—the right way! Show them that this IS possible, through you! In Christ's name I pray, Amen.*

# DAY 10

## GOD DISCIPLINES HIS KIDS

*"I discipline those whom I love"* ~God

SEE HEBREWS 12:6

Nobody wants to be corrected. It goes against the grain of our mind when others try to adjust our methods of handling things. That includes me. For years, I was a Christian who ignored God's corrections nearly every single day. Each time He spoke to my heart, trying to show me how to deal with something or some*one*, I blew Him off—yes, even as a Christian. I was already saved, but still, I absolutely *refused* to allow Him to live through me. Instead, I'd let the devil have his way with nearly all of my choices.

As a Christian, I'm supposed to be growing "fruit of the Spirit" as I walk out my life *by* His Spirit (see Galatians 5:22-23). However, I had *zero* fruit, because I rarely listened to or obeyed His corrections. And because I had truckloads of excuses, blame, and self-pity, nothing good of God was growing from my life.

When people would tick me off, I'd let my unrenewed mind reign, and do my best to get them back. Even though God was saying, "Matt, I see that. Let it go. Forgive them and pray for them to come to know me deeply. I love them too."

Or if I had a really tough day at work, God would tell me in my spirit, "Just go home and relax." But instead, I'd go to the local upscale restaurant and sit at the bar, getting buzzed and blowing money like crazy. I JUST KEPT ON IGNORING HIM!

And during the times of me having the urge to "quench" my manly desires, I'd find a way to watch porn. Although God was saying, "Matt, quit that. Stop watching that junk. That is not okay. Those are my lost sons and daughters whom you are lusting over so hard. I created sex to be enjoyed by one husband and one wife." On and on, I kept ignoring His corrections!

If I had an argument with someone, or maybe a person had taken advantage of me, gossiped about me, or wrongfully accused me of something that simply was not true, I'd become fearful and then break out in a rage! The Holy Spirit doesn't approve of *that* either.

And when I did such dumb things, to top it all off I'd scramble around trying to fix the situation—or fix *them*—"making sure" nobody thought anything bad about me. It was such madness! I'm so glad those days are over.

I was a complete slave to what other people did to me all because I ignored God's corrections as they did it. Instead, I retaliated how the enemy and my unrenewed mind wanted me to. But God kept saying to me, "Matthew, I'm well aware of everything that is going on. I don't need you to do my job. Just stick to what I expect from *you*, and worry about yourself. I'll take care of the rest."

Hebrews 12:11 says, "No discipline seems pleasant at the time, but painful. Later on, however, it produces a harvest of righteousness and peace for those who have been trained by it." No, it doesn't feel good, but it is good *for* your future! God wants you to mature and grow up in your faith *through* His correction!

This is where a lot of believers fall off course and get stuck in a rut. We *love* God, we *want* to be graceful, powerful, influential Christians, but we want to do this without obedience to the Holy Spirit's guidance—and that just won't work. What is *in* us must be worked *out* of us, and this only happens through respecting our Heavenly Father's wishes (see Philippians 2:12).

Even though I'm still a work in progress, when I truly began to allow God to correct me, I'd hear a certain phrase in my heart all the time, and then I'd repeat it. Sometimes I'd say it out-loud, but mostly to myself: *"You're not allowed to do that. You weren't made for that."*

Someone would ruffle my feathers, and I'd be about 2.5 seconds away from telling them where they can buy a kite and the best place to fly it— NOPE! *"You're not allowed to do that. You weren't made for that."*

I'd be betrayed by a loved one, and I'd begin to plan my retaliation on social media—NOPE! *"You're not allowed to do that. You weren't made for that."*

I was allowing myself to actually *be* corrected. I was humbling myself to God's guidance. Oh my gosh did I feel like I was gonna die! But…I continued. When I hurt severely, I constantly looked to the sacrifice that Christ went through for *me*. That's what made it easier. If *He* can be obedient to the Father, then I can too—because He lives in me!

For example, on those days where I'd be feeling lonely and frisky, at home by myself, the devil would say, "Why don't you just go to the bathroom with your phone, it's easy, and nobody will know"—NOPE! *"You're not allowed to look at porn, Matt. You weren't made for that."*

Or if my day at work was absolutely terrible, along with the other issues in my life which seem to never change or get better, Satan would try to tempt me with the quick release of alcohol, "Just go get a 12-pack and some shots, you deserve to relax"—NOPE! *"You're not allowed to do that. Stop getting drunk. You shouldn't be drinking at all."*

*But it didn't end there. When I'd begin to feel myself hate the legalistic, ungraceful leaders at church, all the while feeling guilty because I didn't want to leave that church and be known as a "church hopper"—NOPE! "You're not allowed to hate anyone because hate has no part of you," and, "You're not allowed to feel guilty OR condemned—because you're not. YOU are the church. I live IN you, not in a building. So if you don't like it at that place, leave, and move along. I've got better things for you to do than constantly being bitter about that pastor. Forgive him and start thinking of him with love."*

On and on, I began to *allow* God to correct me—to discipline me. And although I still fail daily, I'm *so* much better than I used to be. The most assuring news is this "process" won't end until I die, or Christ comes back! (See Philippians 1:6).

As a result of me being obedient to God more often, my life couldn't possibly be any better! Not because my uncontrollable circumstances have changed (some have gotten worse), but instead, because *I've* changed *for* God! Why? Because I love Him!

So today, my friends, know this: God corrects you because He wants what's best for you. You are His child and He loves you! Good parents always correct their kids out of love. The Bible says that we are to "endure hardship as discipline, for what son is not disciplined by his father?" (See Hebrews 12:7). God loves you so much that He will never, ever, ignore you. He wants to make sure things go as smooth for you as possible by guiding and molding you each day!

**A prayer for you:** *Well good morning to you Heavenly Father! And WOW, what a beautiful morning it is! You make this planet float and spin splendidly, and you are so good at it! Thank you for this weather, and thank you for my good health today. Right now, I lift up all who are reading this, directly to you. For those who are on the fence about obeying your guidance, help them. We need your strength and your loving correction, each and every day. We are grateful for it, and we love you. In Jesus' powerful name I pray, amen.*

# DAY 11

## JESUS RECRUITS FROM HIS OPPOSITION

*"I am Jesus, whom you are persecuting"*

SEE ACTS 9:5

D o you hate Jesus? I'm sure you don't, or else you wouldn't be this far into my book. But some people actually *do* hate Jesus. This is why we must remember: Jesus recruits from His opposition.

What most new Christians don't know is that Paul used to hate Jesus with all his might! And *he* is the one who wrote most of the New Testament! Paul was a bounty hunter of Christians—he *hated* them, passionately. He actually oversaw and approved of the very first Christian being murdered for their faith, Stephen (see Acts 6).

So what happened to Paul? What made him go from the dark-side to the light-side? What was it, *exactly*, that changed His entire heart condition and mindset?...Jesus paid him a personal visit. After that, everything changed, even his name—he went from *Saul* to Paul.

Although Jesus mostly speaks to people's hearts, Paul got knocked over and then blinded for days, by Christ Himself! As usual, he was on his way to persecute more people of this new sect called *Christianity*; you know, those weird people who worship some Jew who died and supposedly came back from the dead? That one. Paul was a Jew, but he surely didn't believe in this "Messiah."

He was going to make sure he destroyed these people! His hate for them consumed his life! Cleansing the earth from these Christians had become his #1 goal!

So he and his crew were on their way to Damascus to blot out those who "love" their enemies and "forgive" everyone—however, Jesus personally interrupted his trip! "I will use this man as my chosen instrument to proclaim my name, I will show him how much he must suffer to do so" (see Acts 9:15-16).

Jesus recruited His own worst enemy *for* the gospel! The top dog, *best* hater of Christ decided to make a big change, and nobody even recognized him any longer. The Pharisees, his own people, now hated *him* and wanted *him* dead! And on the other side, the disciples, they were scared of him! They thought he was pulling a fast one on them as Paul approached the group, but his conversion was real!

After Paul met Jesus, the rest was history. Most of the verses you now read in the Bible to build *up* your faith, were written by a man who tried vigorously to tear *down* your faith. Paul's heart was changed—because he got a new one (see Romans 6:6)—and so did his mindset, as that new heart began to guide Him (see Romans 12:2). As for his body, it also began to feel what it's like to be possessed by Christ (see 1 Corinthians 6:19, Galatians 2:20, 5:22-23). He began to use the very same passion that he had to *destroy* Jesus' message, to now spread it!

Is Jesus calling *your* name? Is He constantly pulling at your heart? Yes, He is. He is everywhere. All of this stuff, this world, this creation, is His. He is holding all of it together! (See Colossians 1:17). He is like gravity, He has an effect on absolutely everything you see!

It doesn't matter what you've done or who you are, He can still use you if you let Him. Paul proved that Jesus wants to use everyone for His Kingdom purposes!

He's not waiting for you to shape up first, He's simply asking for your faith. After that, *then* your life changes organically into what *He* wants it to be! He's asking you to join Him in changing the course of *all* of humanity, forever! Join Him! Join Him, today!

**A prayer for today:** *Jesus, thank you for calling my name. Thank you for relentlessly pursuing me. Thank you for never giving up on me. Thank you for showing me that nothing can separate your love from me. Thank you for teaching me about your unconditional love, mercy, and grace. Right now, I lift up all who are reading this, directly to you. For those you are calling to do some seriously good things THROUGH you— which is all of us—let them know it's you! Give them a peek into what you have planned, and help them MOVE FORWARD! In your name I pray, amen.*

# DAY 12

## HOW TO BE A BOLD CHRISTIAN

*"Have I not commanded you? Be strong and courageous.*
*Do not be afraid; do not be discouraged, for the LORD*
*your God will be with you wherever you go."*

*JOSHUA 1:9*

I got saved as a kid because I liked the idea of Jesus—and not burning in hell for eternity—so I believed He forgave me. Big deal. So what. Other than punching my ticket to heaven, getting saved had no real impact on my life because I didn't understand what God had done *in* me. I now had the mind of Christ, but I was a wishy-washy Christian at best because I ignored Him as well as my true identity. Further, my mind was *just* beginning to be renewed so my old stinking thinking didn't want to take this Jesus thing too far.

So when I finally decided to live out my true self as a child of God, I was very surprised at how the "life long" Christians began to attack me. They came out of the woodwork. Self-professing Christians began to buck-up, as if I was in competition with them. I was shocked. Hindsight is 20/20, and I shouldn't have been so taken back. I now understand that a lot of these people don't know Jesus at all—all they really know is

Scripture memorization, church work, religion, and self-righteousness. It's really sad.

The fruit of the Spirit is love, joy, peace, patience, kindness, goodness, faithfulness, gentleness, and self-control (see Galatians 5:22-23). God's Spirit lives in me, therefore I should be growing this fruit in my life at all times—no matter if I'm being attacked by confused Christians or non-Christians.

So when my old thought patterns decide to flip out on these types of people, the Holy Spirit calms me down before I act on those ideas. "Matt, it's no big deal. Just let them talk. I know who you are." Thankfully, as I've grown in God's grace, more often than not I actually *do* just let it go.

So if you're new to this, just know that the people who don't like the fact that you're talking about Jesus so much, they *will* attack, but so what. Overlook it and move on. If they want to have a legitimate conversation, proceed. But if not, don't feel guilty about shutting them out. The enemy will use aggressive people to steal your joy so don't let him. Over time, God will use their abrasiveness to strengthen your patience and hone your gifts. Eventually they will become non-factors in your life, simply angry barking dogs on short chains who can't touch you.

However, before I began to show Jesus that I actually loved Him through my actions and attitudes, I was a Christian who still lived in hell— a self-made hell, in my mind. One reason was because I was constantly afraid of losing my salvation, which you can't. Just like you can't be un-born from your mom, you can't be un-born after your spiritual birth either. You've been born of God and the DNA mix is final! (See John 1:12, 3:6-7, 1 John 3:9, Ephesians 1:5).

If that weren't the case then the Cross wasn't all it was cracked up to be and we are right back to *attempting* to earn our positions with God. We're back to the broken "rewards system" of the Old Testament, which is now obsolete (see Hebrews 8:13).

What's funny is, if you're not Jewish, none of that Old Testament "obeying commandments and laws" applies to you. You're a Gentile, an outsider. You're not even part of God's original chosen people to carry *out* those commandments and laws. Instead, you are just reading a history book and applying old recorded events to your own moral inventory. It doesn't work that way. We have a new Covenant on this side of the Cross! (See Hebrews 8:6).

Only what Jesus did *at* the Cross allows you to be a part of God's family (see Galatians 3:28). So no matter how many rules you think you're obeying properly (there are 613 in all, not just 10)—all you're really doing is running out onto the court in the middle of someone else's basketball game. If you're not Jewish, you can't play. You're a spectator. Only Coach Christ can draft you onto His team, by grace through faith (see Ephesians 2:8-9).

This brings us to the fact that our salvation through Christ was paid in full, finished, and complete—once for all time! (See John 19:30, Hebrews 10:10, 1 Peter 3:18). We get forgiven *once* of past, present, and even future sins! Yes, even future sins! Remember, *all* of your sins were in the future when Christ died. He is not bound by time, we are. Further, God doesn't require us to keep asking for forgiveness—we're already forgiven. *Asking* never forgave anyone anyway, only faith in perfect blood does (see Hebrews 9:22, John 3:16). And even more, *continual* asking is neurotic. We can relax because we've been perfected in spirit once for all time! (See Hebrews 10:14).

Even the Jews before Christ's sacrifice, they got an entire *year* of forgiveness at the Day of Atonement. They never asked God, "Will you forgive me?!" each time they broke the Mosaic Law because they knew only blood could cover up those sins. Jesus, however, actually takes *away* our sins, rather than cover them up! (See John 1:29, 1 John 3:5).

As you begin to understand the truth of Christ's final sacrifice, and your true identity as a reborn saint, you will organically become bold! Here's more on how to do just that!

1.  **Refuse to live in fear**. First and foremost *stop* being afraid of God. As a believer in Jesus' forgiveness you are saved! You are His child! Yes, He understands you will mess up in your attitudes and actions, that's why He sent Jesus here to do what you can't. But *never* be afraid of God! Instead, listen to His Holy Spirit and be your true self!

2. **Let God use your past**. For me, it's addictions, among many other things. I let God use this former weakness of mine to help others. I *could* look back on my past and cringe. I could deny it, or worse, try to hide it. I could even try to minimize it but God doesn't want that. He wants me to talk about it with honesty and clarity, and then point to His grace as to the reason why I am who I am today. I finally understood this when I read 2 Corinthians 12:9: *"Then He said to me, 'My grace is sufficient for you. My power is made perfect in weakness.' Therefore I will boast all the more gladly about my weaknesses, so that Christ's power may rest on me."*

3. **Don't compare yourself to others**. Being bold in who God made *you* to be will be impossible if you do this: *strive to be exactly like other people.* This is a trick of the enemy because you *can't* do this! Yes, be inspired and learn from others, but be yourself! God likes you and wants you to be you! Being yourself is imperative to living boldly because you are the best version of you! You are awesome!

4. **Do something!** Be willing to allow God to live through you each day. When you do this it attracts Satan's attention greatly, so be ready. He's not so much worried about you being a child of God if you're not active. To get at you, whatever or *who*ever you place your trust and confidence in, the devil will hold it over the flames—but you'll be fine. Just keep going! Keep making yourself available for good works, take action, and be bold! You'll accomplish this feat in the best way possible by simply being yourself and resting in God's grace!

**A prayer for you:** *Heavenly Father, you are such a good God! Please continue to teach me more and more about your grace, and give me boldness as you do! Right now, I lift up all who are reading this, directly to you. So many of them feel weak, but the truth is they're strong! Teach them who they are as believers, and what Christ has done for them! Then help them to live it out! In His name I pray, amen.*

# DAY 13

## CHURCH "ATTENDANCE" IS NOT IMPORTANT TO GOD

*"Do you not know that you are God's temple
and that God's Spirit dwells in you?"*

*1 CORINTHIANS 3:16*

After reading the title of this devotional, you might be mad. RELAX. Don't throw your hat on the ground and stomp on it just yet. Let me explain.

I love church—the building—yes. But, I *am* "the church" and so are you, if you've accepted Christ's forgiveness! However, me attending the building or gathering no more makes me acceptable to God than dressing up a monkey in a three-piece suit, handing him a Bible and a tambourine, and then setting him on the front row, makes *him* acceptable to God. Our hearts have to be right, no matter *where* we are at. *This* is what's most important to God, our hearts. Does Jesus dwell there? Is it brand new? (See Ephesians 3:16-19, Romans 6:6-7, Galatians 2:20, 2 Corinthians 5:17, Colossians 2:9-10).

Every Sunday morning millions of people get ready for church. They put on their best clothes and head off to a geographical location to learn about God and worship Him. But really, it doesn't matter *where* the actual church-going Christian is physically. God is much more interested in us understanding what kind of church *we* are—you and I. Luke even penned what Paul said about this, in Acts 17:24:

> *"The God who made the world and everything in it is the Lord*
> *of heaven and earth and <u>does not live in temples built by</u>*
> *<u>human hands</u>"*

Friend, *we* house His Spirit at all times (see 1 Corinthians 3:16, 6:19)—but do we show the world who Jesus really is *through* us? Or are we thinking that God is giving us a gold star for driving our rears to the nearest church building and sitting there for an hour? I thought this way for years.

And really, all we have to do is try "going to church" for so long until we grasp that our appearance there isn't going to fix our lives or fulfill us. Church attendance can be important, yes, I'm not downplaying that, but so many Christians have made it the end-all-be-all. They've made a law out of going there.

"You skipped church?!" *GASP* "Are you still a Christian?! Wait until I tell so-and-so!"

This mindset of "grace based on building attendance" is ludicrous. Christ destroyed the need for an actual building to be able to have access to God. When He was crucified, a 3-foot-thick veil was torn from top to bottom, which led to the most holy place of the temple! (See Matthew 27:51). So now, as New Covenant believers, because of Christ's blood we have complete access to God every second of the day! (See Ephesians 3:12, Hebrews 4:16).

Nobody is better than you! And nobody is worse, either, because they go to church, or don't go to church. Church *going* means nothing if we don't allow ourselves to *be* the church—to live it out! Once we believe, we literally become a place where Jesus lives and dwells with love, truth, and confidence!

In the book of Hebrews it says "we are his house" (see Hebrews 3:6). WE ARE. You and me. All of us Christians *together* all throughout the world, we form *the Church* because Jesus lives in us! We are the body of Christ! He is the head and we are His hands, feet, and mouth! When you read the word *church* in the Bible this is what it's referring to—us! NOT A BUILDING!

You might ask me, "So Matt, are you against going to church?" Well heck no. Go to church! But go for the right reasons! Go to grow! Don't go to earn anything from God—or worse—to think you're better than those who *don't* go. Some of the meanest acting, most unloving people I know are faithful church-goers *because* of this incorrect mindset. They say such things as:

"Well…if they don't go to church then they just ain't Christian."

"BACKSLIDERS! You better get back into church if you don't want to go to hell!"

Or you ask them, "Are you a Christian?" and they'll reply with, "Yeah, I go to church."

For so many years, before I came to understand God's grace, my response would have been, "So what! You don't show it! Show me Jesus! If going to church makes me like you, then you can keep it! I don't want to be like you at all!"

Friends, we gotta have change. We gotta change the way the world looks at us church-going Christians! Church attendance means nothing if we don't allow Christ to live through us. If we refuse to do this, then why are we going? We may as well sleep in or go fishing—or whatever. Be *willing* to allow the Holy Spirit to live through you! Be *being* the Church! LET HIM OUT OF YOU!

So today, my friends, know this: I'm all for church. Go. Please go. Find one and get plugged in. You are a vital part of the body of Christ! But never find your identity in that building—or in what you do *for* the building. Find your identity in who lives in you! Why? Because *you* really are, His Church.

**A prayer for you:** *Lord, thank you for allowing me to be born in a country where I can speak freely about you—for the most part anyway. Each Sunday, countless amounts of people go to buildings to worship you and be taught about you. Today, I lift up every preacher and teacher all throughout the world, directly to you. Touch their minds and help them understand who you really are, as well as who they really are. Help them to teach their listeners about your love, grace, and truth. Use their words to mold this generation into people who love you, respect you, honor you, and allow you to live through them—organically. Thank you. In Christ's name I pray, amen.*

# DAY 14

## HOW TO FINALLY OVERCOME ADDICTIONS

*"Because he himself suffered when he was tempted,*
*he is able to help those who are being tempted."*

*HEBREWS 2:18*

I'm in recovery for alcoholism. I finally got sober on May 8th, 2014. Now, unless you knew me *closely* before I quit, you would have had no clue that I was tempted greatly by the quick release of a buzz. That's all an addiction really is: giving *in* to a temptation on a regular basis.

With the stress of running a thriving business, codependent relationships in which I was accepting *completely* unacceptable behavior, all the while trying to make sure I live up to an impossible public perception, getting drunk was one of the temptations I gave in to almost daily.

*"It's no big deal. It's legal. Plus, if I quit drinking completely, people would think I have a problem."*

These were a few of the excuses I used in order to keep giving in to what Satan wanted me to give in to, which was, "Poppin' a top at beer-thirty, baby! Yeah!" This always turned out badly (at least 90% of the time). So in order to try to overcome my binge-drinking, I began to study everything I could get my hands on to get rid of this thing. I didn't want it, but I could *not* seem to shake it!

I wasn't your typical drunk. I say this humbly, but I was extremely successful. So, with me being a "Type A personality" I would *attempt* to apply my strong work ethic toward my goal of sobriety. Over the years, during short-lived bursts of sobriety, I've watched every episode of *Intervention* (while jealous each time I saw the person's sobriety date, or sad because they relapsed). I've studied secular books of successful former-alcoholics, trying to skim off their secrets. I've watched every movie I could find on alcoholics or alcoholism, or *anything* that had to do with how to get sober and *stay* sober. I've tried "programs" and I've gone to groups—still, nothing worked!

Every time I thought I had it beat—BAM—I was tippin' them back *again! "WHY, CAN'T, I, QUIT?!"* I was a complete slave to *this* particular temptation! Eventually, my unrenewed mind had succumb to my alcoholism—the coaxing of the devil made it even worse, "Matt, it's just who you are, you stupid drunk. You are *weak.*" Shame then gripped my life, then depression, then fear and anxiety. Heck, I remember even recording videos of myself *while* drunk, just to show my *sober*-self how ridiculous I looked—NOTHING WORKED!

Friend, what I had to do was realize that God loved me even while stuck in an area of darkness that He didn't want me at. I had to understand that if I *never* quit drinking, I was still *perfect* in my spirit (see Romans 6:6, Galatians 2:20, Colossians 1:22). A severe conflict was going on inside me because drunkenness would never match up with Christ *in* me. My drinking never ran Him off, instead, it *grieved* Him. That's why *I* was grieving too, each time I did it (see Ephesians 4:30).

But the grace-confused Christians taught me the opposite of this fact. They said, "If you were *really* a man of God, you would *never* give in to that bad habit!" SUCH CRAP! If you only *knew* how many Christians are in the bondage of alcohol, drugs, porn, legalism, sex-addiction, and many more vices which do *not* match up with the Holy Spirit in them, it would blow your mind.

However, because I was taught these lies, I felt hopeless. *"What's the big deal? I already blew it."* Their method took no pressure off of me, it only made things worse. The harping of a self-righteous, overbearing preacher who says, "STOP DRINKING! BE HOLY! YOU AIN'T LIVING RIGHT!" only compounded my problems and made me start to resent church people as a whole—the *very* people whom I thought would help me.

So what did I do? I kept seeking answers from Jesus *as* a Christian who struggled with drinking, day by day, month by month, and year by year, and then finally the Holy Spirit gave me an epiphany: "You are going to have to get uncomfortable if you want to stop drinking." *"What?...Okay...I get it! EUREKA! To beat this temptation, I gotta get uncomfortable!"*

I devote a full chapter to my drinking testimony in my first book, *True Purpose in Jesus Christ*, but the secret to beating an addiction—to overcome *any* temptation—is this: *get uncomfortable!* You're not going to stay in a state of being uncomfortable, but this is where it begins as your mind starts to be renewed. You get uncomfortable when you begin to *feel* what you are currently feeling, and then ask God to help you *deal* with those feelings authentically as a saint. He helps us deal with our feelings by teaching us who we really are: holy.

I understand this is not the answer that everyone wants, we want a magic pill or a magic *trick* to be performed on us, "I want to be delivered! I want the taste of alcohol *gone!*" Some people in sobriety claim that's what happened to them, they got "delivered." I thought that too, until I drank again. "I guess I need to get delivered again! It just didn't take the first time!"

It's not about being delivered or having the "taste" for it removed, it's about having your mind renewed by the Spirit of God *in* you. God is not a drunk, and He lives *in your spirit*. Therefore, when your flesh is tempted to taste that ice-cold beer, or your mind says, "I'm stressed. I need a drink," your spirit—the real you—says, "Why do you think that?" Then He explains why you really *don't* want to taste it, and why you really *don't* need it.

So today, my friends, know this: The Holy Spirit will guide you into sobriety by teaching you your identity in Him. First, He will teach you how to get uncomfortable as well as realize it's okay to *feel* uncomfortable. And second, you will learn how to handle your uncomfortable feelings by

Him teaching you the difference between your "who" and your "do." The divorce between your "who" and your "do" *must* happen, if you want to get sober in a restful state. As a Christian, spiritually, you *are* a perfect child of God, that's your *who*, a perfect spirit. Your *do* is your attitudes and actions. Realizing this great separation will change everything about your life, including the status of your sobriety. Why? Because you'll *know* that getting drunk all the time is just not who you really are.

> **A prayer for you:** *God, I know you remember the battles I went through with my drinking, but you were there in me, the whole time. Thank you. You've always been so good to me, even when I made bad choices. Thank you for your mercy, grace, and unconditional love. Right now, I lift up all who are reading this, directly to you. For those who want to quit drinking, help them. Help them to realize they can't QUIT, but they CAN begin a new life of allowing you to live through them! They can do ALL THINGS through Christ, He will strengthen them! Amen!*

# DAY 15

## DOES GOD LOVE ME WHEN I MAKE MISTAKES?

*"Nothing can separate us from the love of
God which is in Christ Jesus."*

*ROMANS 8:39*

The short answer to the title of this devotional is, "YES!
ABSOLUTELY!" God's love for you is not based on your performance—good *or* bad. He loved you with an everlasting love even before you placed your faith in Jesus! (See Romans 5:8). God will never stop loving you, ever! But, a debt has to be paid off with Him, a sin debt. God can have *nothing* to do with sin.

However, God knew that we *would* sin even before He created this planet (see Romans 8:29). So what would be His answer to take care of our sin problem? It's not a what, but a *who*, it's Jesus. For Christians, the debt which *had* to be paid off with God is now gone! Jesus did what we could never do, and now, by our faith in Him we have access to a clean slate, PAST, PRESENT, AND FUTURE (see Hebrews 10:10, 1 Peter 3:18).

Yes, even though your flesh still commits sins, and your unrenewed mindset might have sinful thoughts, God still loves you and you are going to heaven (see Philippians 1:6). Hard to understand, I know—but true! The Bible actually says, "God remembers your sins no more!" (See Hebrews 8:12). He *chooses* not to remember your wrongdoings! It also says, as long as Jesus lives you will *stay* saved! (See Hebrews 7:25). That's unfathomable because Jesus won't die again!

And that's what God's love for us is, unfathomable. We *can't* understand His love in our finite minds, especially when we keep messing up. We think that He will leave us or He won't love us anymore. Friend, you don't have the ability to make God *not* love you—even if you hated Him.

There is a lot of false teaching out there which goes like this: "God pulls away from those who sin and from those who 'fall back' into a sin pattern." This is not true, and it creates tremendous fear for Christians. This demonic lie makes us think that God's love is conditional or that it's contingent on our excellent behavior. There could be nothing further from the truth! We've been *infused* into Christ! (See Colossians 3:3).

So if we are *in* Jesus, actually inside Him, spiritually (just like a ring is inside of a ring-box) where we go, Jesus goes too, and vice versa. NOTHING CAN SEPARATE US FROM HIM! NOTHING! NOTHING! NOTHING! OH...AND NOTHING! (See Romans 8:38-39).

Jesus said He will be with us always, even to the end of time (see Matthew 28:20). He didn't say, "I'll be with you always until you sin really bad, then I'm out." He didn't say, "I'm gonna stay in you, spiritually, and you in me, that is, until you miss three Sunday morning church services in a row or refuse to witness to the guy on the park bench. Shape up! Or I'm done with you!"

NO! He didn't say that! This conditional-grace is madness and not how God has things set up! ONCE YOU HAVE CHRIST THROUGH ACCEPTING HIS FORGIVENESS—BELIEVING IT AS TRUE FOR YOUR SIN—YOU CAN'T LOSE HIM!

The grace-confused Christians who find their identity in what they do and don't do *for* God will hate this idea because they *don't* admire Jesus' finished work—He's a footnote. Instead, they find their identity in adding their works *to* His. Everything they do is *not* based on what Jesus already *has* done, like it should be.

They want to add to the Cross, but they can't. They want to make sure they don't lose their spot with God, but they can't. No matter how much time they spend in Bible school, doing volunteer work, or singing in the choir, *nothing* will make God love them *more* than He does right now at *this* very moment in time. The same goes for you and me.

So today, my friends, know this: God loves you no matter what you do. He didn't *start* loving you because of your good behavior, and He won't *stop* loving you because of your bad behavior. He loves you because you are His child. So believer, learn more about who you are, and then be yourself. To this, you were called.

**A prayer for you:** *Heavenly Father, thank you for teaching me that nothing I do can earn your love, and that you love me exactly as I am. Thank you for sending Jesus here to remove my sin for good, so we could finally be together forever. Right now, I lift up all who are reading this, directly to you, those who might be afraid of you. Please teach them you have no desire to punish them, but that their sins have to be forgiven through Christ. Teach them that Jesus did this for them completely, and for free. I now understand that we can't do anything to earn your love, or to lose it, but I know we CAN grieve your Holy Spirit with our actions and attitudes. Help us not to do so by teaching us more about who we truly are! In Christ's name I ask all these things, amen!*

# DAY 16

## ANGELS ARE REAL

*"Do not forget to show hospitality to strangers, for by so doing some people have shown hospitality to angels without knowing it."*

### HEBREWS 13:2

I know I talk a lot about the devil and his little peons, *demons*, and I do so because I want you to be aware of them and their tactics. These tactics, if ignored, will destroy your life. It's a goal of mine to shake up the soul of every Christian to start being aware of who really hates them the most: the real, present, demonic force, of Satan and demons.

However, just like the demons are real, angels are real too! Let's not forget about them! All throughout the Bible, angels are talked about. They are used by God to send messages directly to people, they are used to *protect* people, and as Christ stood on trial before Pilate and the Pharisees, angels are used as a threat by Jesus.

Angels have an uninterrupted relationship with God, they are completely in-tune with His will. They worship Him day and night, and have a soft-spot for us humans, as God's created *beloved* beings. They know we are weak because of our flesh and mindsets, and they help us out all the time with our weaknesses. They even minister to us and serve us spiritually (see Hebrews 1:14).

Years ago, my grandma had an angel appear to her as she swept the kitchen floor, late at night, praying.

Let me give you some background on my grandma: she is a saint, who married a monster. Nobody caused this sweet lady more unnecessary pain than my grandfather. Grandpa was an alcoholic, an abuser, a philanderer, and just about the exact *opposite* of Grandma.

Grandma said she married him because *he* said if she didn't, he would kill himself. In her loving innocence, she actually believed him. The terror that my grandfather caused, not just my grandma, but also my dad, uncle, and aunts, was something out of a horror movie—but, they still had Grandma. Just like Grandma stepped up in my own personal childhood, to make a nightmare better, she did the same for her own kids as well. She never gave up.

Grandpa didn't want anything to do with God, and he didn't want Grandma going to church because he said she would "find another man" or "blow money." Fact of the matter was, that's what *he* thought about all the time, not Grandma. Grandma couldn't care less about the attention of other men, or money. She cared about Jesus, and what *He* wanted from her.

She told me a story about how one Sunday morning as she was getting ready for church, Grandpa said, "I'll kill you before you go to church!" He went in the other room, got a gun, came back and pointed it at her. She told me that she prayed to God, "I'm ready if you want me to come home. I don't want to go, but I'm ready." Grandpa lowered the gun, and said, "I'm not gonna kill you today, but I'm gonna kill you tomorrow." Grandma said she didn't come home that day, instead she stayed at a friend's house.

IF YOU ONLY KNEW THE NIGHTMARE THAT MY GRANDPA WAS, AND WHAT MY GRANDMA PUT UP WITH, IT WOULD BAFFLE YOUR MIND! HER COMMITMENT TO HER WEDDING VOWS, TO GOD, AND TO HIM, IS MIND-BLOWING!

I've asked her many times, "Why didn't you just leave him?" She said she planned on it quite often and then one night, she had a dream that Grandpa died and went to hell. After that, she completely removed the word "divorce" from her mind. She said she *knew* that God wanted her to stay, and that He had a greater purpose for her pain.

Had she left, you would not be reading this right now.

Instead of leaving, she used his hate for good. She committed herself to loving someone who was unlovable, just like Jesus does. Grandpa's loathing of my grandma made her know God better, and deeper. And now, that's been passed on to later generations. She didn't run from the devil, she fought him head on, and she has a legacy for it.

So as Grandma swept the kitchen floor, late that night in the 1960s, praying for Grandpa (no telling what he was out doing, probably at a bar), and her kids, an angel appeared before her.

The story I've heard a hundred times is, "I looked up—it was the brightest thing I've ever seen! It was transparent and covered the entire wall! It was beautiful!" Frightened, Grandma gasped out loud, "No Lord, not now!" thinking, in her own words, "The angel had come to take me home"—and just like that—it disappeared.

Now if you ask her about this event, she'll tell you that she knows the angel had a message for her. She'll say that she wishes she didn't respond how she did, because she wanted to know what it had to say...she'll find out when she gets to heaven. I'm very curious as well.

So today, my friends, know this: Jesus said, "Blessed are the pure in heart, for they will see God" (Matthew 5:8). My grandma has a pure heart, as do all believers in Christ, but because of just how *deep* her dependency on Him ran, she got to see an actual angel. I don't know anyone who has a deeper relationship with God, than Granny Mac. She never gave up on what He wanted her to do—she loved *Him* and her family too much. She allowed Christ to live through her on such a grand scale, that her pain was rewarded with a view of heaven while still here on earth. She is an inspiration to me. I want to see angels too, don't you?

**A prayer for you:** *God, I know there are people reading this who are on the brink of giving up on a relationship that you've brought together— IT'S HARD ON THEM. We know that a strand of three is not easily broken, and that every relationship needs Jesus to be strong. You match people up all the time with extremely opposite characteristics so they have to look to you for help. I'm asking that you teach us how to love others, even to the point of a Christ-like sacrificial state. But at the same time, give us the strength to stand up to unacceptable behavior FEARLESSLY, with love, truth, and peace. I know this is possible. Thank you for your Holy Spirit and for placing angels all around us! We love you so much! In Jesus' name I pray, amen.*

# DAY 17

## YOU HAVE THE SAME POWER OF CHRIST

*"Until now you have not asked for anything in my name. Ask
and you will receive, and your joy will be complete." ~Jesus*

*JOHN 16:24*

Do you realize you have power in you? Yes, *you* have access to the
same power as God! This is the strange part of Christianity because it's difficult to wrap our minds around such a statement. Even if you
are already enjoying a deep relationship with Jesus (you "get" His grace,
and you understand your spiritual perfection) admitting that you have actual power requires a child-like faith.

I can try to encourage others all day long. I can even point to the
organic ways of the gospel which will help improve the quality of their
life—which is realizing we have Christ's life (see Colossians 3:4). But when
I go so far as to tell people they have God's power *in* them, sometimes even
I get a small batch of butterflies trickle into my stomach.

Why is this? First off, it's weird. But if you really think about it, all
of this is weird. This world, this life, us breathing air, on and on. Life is
strange as can be, but it was God's idea so it is good!

Second of all, we must understand that on our *own* we have *no* power, nada! (See John 15:5). We humans are completely powerless even if we think we're loaded with it—by whatever means (money, status, etc.). But the good news is this: every Christian has access to the power of God through our simple faith in Jesus Christ!

Jesus said that He has given us power (see Luke 10:19). I repeat, Jesus said that He has given *us* power! We gotta stop overlooking that! He also said we will do even *greater* things than Him! (See John 14:12). So how do we tap into this power? By simply being yourself. If you believe Jesus has saved you, you have all the power you could possibly ever need, right now, in your spirit.

Our God works miracles every second of the day and He lives in *you*, believer! The greatest miracle of all is love! (See 1 Corinthians 13:13, John 3:16). When you love, you are being your true self in the purest form. THIS IS THE POWER OF GOD IN YOU BECAUSE YOU BELIEVE IN JESUS! YOU. HAVE. POWER!

Say it, "I HAVE POWER…I HAVE POWER!"

And this supernatural power in you is coming directly from the Holy Spirit—your Savior's Spirit, Jesus.

So today, my friends, know this: Whatever you are facing or *who*ever you are facing, please stop reacting with fear or timidity. Instead, begin to react with the power of Jesus Christ! React with confidence! Tap into His power today, at all times, by simply saying "Jesus." He's right there, inside you.

**A prayer for you:** *Heavenly Father, thank you for giving me the honor of living out another day on your planet. You are good. You are sovereign. I also want to thank you for my job, for my home, and for my family's good health. Thank you for this ministry you've given me as well. What a privilege it is to talk about you to so many people. Right now, I lift up all who are reading this, directly to you. You see their hearts, you see their situations, you see their lives. In Jesus' name*

*I ask that you help them. I'm asking that you let them know about the power inside them! Make them bold through the enormous power of the Holy Spirit! Teach them how to get rid of defeated, negative attitudes, through the confidence of Christ! I'm also asking that you break addictions and heal broken relationships! Show them how much POWER they have in them because of you! Amen.*

# DAY 18

## DO YOU LIVE BY HOW YOU FEEL?

*"For we walk by faith, not by sight."*

*2 CORINTHIANS 5:7*

God created us to be emotional. There is nothing *wrong* with our feelings, but they are extremely unpredictable—you can't count on them. The ripple of our emotions were never meant to dictate the direction of our lives, but instead, our trust in God is.

All throughout your day, there will be opportunities to *allow* your emotions to rule you. You could be shocked by what a loved one said about you, or what they did. You could be tremendously hurt by a nasty, untrue rumor. You could then become frustrated, trying to defend yourself or plead your case. You might also have the chance to become furious over a dirty house, or you may *even* have the opportunity to have lustful, intimate feelings toward someone who shows you attention—who is *not* your spouse.

Whatever it may be, your feelings were never meant to guide your choices, but instead, God's *Spirit* is.

Hate is a feeling we develop toward those whom we allow ourselves to loathe. Extreme fear, depression, or even anxiety can pop up on the inside of us, and override the medication that was supposed to help stop those feelings. Then we are even *more* fearful, depressed, and anxious because the pills didn't work.

Soon enough, we can begin to allow our feelings to lead our lives—not to a good spot—but instead, down a path of making choices that God does not approve of; choices that do not match up with our perfect spirit.

So what do we do? Should we just fly by the seat of our fuzzy feelings? Or should we "follow our hearts"? That's a very popular saying. However, the problem with following our hearts is this: if Christ doesn't live *in* our hearts, our hearts will lead us into a lot of trouble, eventually into severe pain (see Jeremiah 17:9).

What we must do is begin to make choices that match up with the Holy Spirit's guidance. This is how you will enjoy your life *despite* how you feel. Emotions—your feelings—do not define you. As Christians, when we have an emotion, that emotion isn't sinful, it just is what it is. Now, if we make a poor choice based on that emotion, that's another story. This is why we must walk by God's Spirit in us, who will always lead us into peace (see 2 Corinthians 5:7, Galatians 5:22, 23).

So today, my friends, know this: We must begin to allow Jesus to help us make the right choices *about* our feelings. If we don't, then we will be "tossed back and forth like the waves of the sea" (see Ephesians 4:14). Jesus knows how we feel, and even better, He always wants to help us *with* our feelings. Just ask Him to, and He will!

**A prayer for you:** *Heavenly Father I want to thank you for teaching me how to NOT live by my feelings. Because of your Spirit guiding me, I'm learning how to stand up to unacceptable behavior, which I've been giving in to for years because of fear. But you've taught me that fear is just a feeling! Right now, I lift up all who are reading this, directly to you. For those who struggle with allowing their feelings to lead their lives in the wrong direction, help them begin to let YOU lead them! Through your Holy Spirit, I ask that you give them wisdom, strength, confidence, and hope—all day long! Bless them in every area of their lives! In Christ's name I pray, amen.*

# DAY 19

## WHAT ARE YOU THINKING ABOUT?

*"We take captive every thought to make it obedient to Christ."*

SEE 2 CORINTHIANS 10:5

Your thoughts will destroy your life—if you let them. For years, I didn't realize that my thought life dictated how my day would go. I'd wake up every morning like a sheep being led to the slaughter. As soon as a thought popped into my mind, I'd agree with it as truth.

Each and every thought that the enemy put in my mind (along with my own incorrect *learned* thinking) would immediately ruin the day before it even began. Unbeknownst to me at the time, I didn't realize just because I had a thought which created fear, anxiety—or made me want to give in to sin—I didn't *have* to act on it, or even pay any attention to it.

As I began to grow in the knowledge of God's grace through prayer, Bible study, and good Christian books, Jesus opened up my mind to what I *should* be paying attention to:

"Whatever is true, whatever is noble, whatever is right, whatever is pure, whatever is lovely, whatever is admirable—if anything is excellent or praiseworthy—<u>think about such things</u>" (Philippians 4:8).

"Well Matt, that's easy for you to say! I can't help what I think!"…No, you're right, not always. But you *can* begin to recognize the thoughts that *are* true, pure, lovely, admirable, excellent, or praiseworthy, and then *think* (focus on, pay close attention to) about such things. It's all about what you *choose* to focus on—so begin to focus on the good stuff!

If we are going to get the most out of this life, we must have our minds transformed and renewed into that of Christ's! (See Romans 12:2, 1 Corinthians 2:16). This happens by paying close attention to our thought life.

We must consciously and consistently *guide* our thoughts toward Holy Spirit thoughts, which are: love, joy, peace, patience, kindness, goodness, faithfulness, gentleness, and self-control (see Galatians 5:22-23). So when a thought hits you that doesn't match up to this, SPEAK UP AGAINST IT! Correct it! Here are some examples:

**Incorrect thought:** "This person is *never* going to change! Give up on them! They keep hurting you! They don't appreciate you! They don't even love you!"

**Corrected thought:** "This is where I feel like God wants me to be. God can change the heart of any person, if they let Him. I'm staying faithful, I'm praying for them diligently, and I'm trusting that God is using this unfair situation for a good, future purpose."

**Incorrect thought:** "You'll never break that addiction! You are weak without it! Don't even try!"

**Corrected thought:** "No, I *can't* break this addiction, on my own. But through Christ's strength *in* me, I can do anything! And *He* says that He loves me just as I am. So *He* will help me defeat this addiction as I learn more about my perfect spiritual identity *in* Him. Today is a new day which He's given me to enjoy, eventually I will beat this *through* Him, and then He'll use my painful testimony to help many people who struggle with the same things."

**Incorrect thought:** "If God is so good, why does He let bad things happen to you?"

**Corrected thought:** "God loves me more than I can possibly understand, and *because* of His great love for me, He doesn't even have the *ability* to allow any harm to come my way without a greater *future* purpose. It's my job to simply relax in His grace and allow the Holy Spirit to teach me how to react to unfair situations how He wants me to. After all, Jesus' crucifixion was very unfair, but He knew that it was for an amazing future purpose! So I'll trust Him even when it hurts because I know He still loves me and something *good* is in the works—even if I never get to see it."

So today, my friends, know this: Don't just ignore your incorrect thoughts, correct them! When you allow the Holy Spirit to correct your thinking, you are allowing yourself to be molded into the image of Christ! You may even have an incorrect mindset of being hyper-critical, self-righteous, or graceless. You might look down on others who don't do the "Christian things" like you do—*that* is incorrect thinking as well, so we must correct it! It's like Grandma used to say, "Matthew, you can't stop the crows from flying over your head, but you don't have to let them make a nest in your hair"—she's right! No, we *can't* stop the thoughts that hit us, but we can *choose* to not agree with them, and then correct them *through* Jesus' Spirit!

**A prayer for you:** *Heavenly Father, thank you for giving us your mindset. Please begin to make it even more clear WHAT exactly you want us to do for each situation in our lives. Continue to mold OUR lives into YOUR life, through our thought life! Keep the devil far from us and reshape our minds into being peaceful, confident, and loving. You can do this! I know you can! You can do all things, so thank you in advance! In Christ's name, amen.*

# DAY 20

## WHY DID JESUS HAVE TO DIE?

*"There is no greater love than to lay down
one's life for one's friends." ~Jesus*

*JOHN 15:13*

At the time of me writing this, yesterday was Good Friday. So, what exactly *made* Good Friday so good? An innocent man was beat into a hamburger-like state, spat on like he was the worst pedophile in human history, and then literally *nailed* to a giant cross. That doesn't sound so good to me. How could we *possibly* call such a day, *Good* Friday? Faces of Death Friday sounds more appropriate! How in the Sam Hill was yesterday good for Jesus?!

It wasn't. It was good for us. It was good for everyone *except* Jesus. It was *our* Good Friday—not His.

So that begs the next question: Why was it good for us? Why did we even need Jesus to do what He did? I'll get to that in full detail in just a minute, but here are the CliffsNotes:

Good Friday—the day Jesus was sacrificed—was good for us because Christ took the entire brunt of our sin problem head on, and *removed* this problem *from us* once and for all, therefore giving us the opportunity to become spiritually perfect *exactly* as God is, by grace through faith (see John 1:12, 1:29, 1 John 2:2, Hebrews 9:28, 10:10, Romans 6:6, Colossians 1:22, Ephesians 1:5, 2:8-9). And now, post-Cross, every human being has free access to this sin-punishment pay-off through our faith in Him as the Messiah because *only* the blood of the Messiah could save us by *removing* our sin with God forever *rather* than covering it up. The event at the Cross finalized an agreement with the Father and the Son—not us—we are simply the beneficiaries *to* that contract, which did not go into effect until Jesus' death occurred. As a result of this promise between God and God, we will stay saved forever from the very moment we believe Jesus forgave us because Jesus will never die again. We literally become reborn *in* our spirits—the everlasting part of us—as our old spirit dies *with* Jesus, and is resurrected *as* a perfect creation while still here on planet earth in non-perfect bodies (see Hebrews 6:17-19, 7:25, 9:15, 9:22, John 3:16, 19:30, 1 John 3:9, 2 Corinthians 5:17, Colossians 3:3, Galatians 2:20, 3:28, 2 Timothy 2:13).

The Bible says all have sinned and fallen short of the glory of God—that is, all of humanity, as a whole—this is not referencing Christians (Romans 3:23). However, Jesus never sinned, so He never fell short. This is what made Him the perfect sacrifice for us. The Bible also says the wages of sin is death, but God's free gift is eternal life in Christ (see Romans 6:23).

So Good Friday is *good* because of Jesus' loving sacrifice for us. Now, "all are justified freely by his grace through the redemption that came by Christ Jesus (at the Cross)" (see Romans 3:24, my note added).

So when I got home from work yesterday evening I decided to watch *The Passion of The Christ*. It was Good Friday, what better a day? Also, I wanted to watch it because it is so gruesome. This sounds a tad bit sadistic but that brutality Jesus went through *reminds* me of just how much He *cares* for me—in turn, it reminds me of just how much *I* should care for the people who hurt *me*.

I've seen this movie six or seven times since originally seeing it at the theatre in 2004, and each time I watch it, I can't help but cry. When it was first released, I sobbed in my seat, then after it was over I walked out the movies *baffled* as to what I just witnessed. "Wow…" Now when I watch it, I even try *not* to cry, but I can't help it. It's beautiful. It's barbaric. It's my Jesus.

To know that was for me, for *my* eternal salvation, it moves my soul every time! What *pain* Jesus went through for me—and for *whosoever* believes in Him! *You* are a whosoever! (See John 3:16). That pain was for *all* of humanity, not just for a select few.

But to be honest with you, this was years in the making for me—actually *caring* about Christ. I wasn't always like this. At first, sure, I loved Jesus, but at the same time I resented Christians. I know that sounds stupid to say, but so many legalistic, unloving, self-righteous Christians had misrepresented what Jesus had finished *for* me (on Good Friday), that I didn't even want to be in the same room with them. They wanted me to be like *them*, and I wanted to be like Jesus.

Although I had been saved since I was a kid, when I was new to *truly* allowing Jesus to live through me—that is, actually caring about what He wanted from me—it was difficult. Because of my unrenewed mindsets, I disliked religious people on a very deep level. I loathed those who found their identity in their church works and so-called *lack* of sin.

Letting Jesus "live through them" was *not* what these people were doing, yet, they advertised that they were. It's no wonder why so many of the lost won't give Jesus a chance. It's because of the conditional-love, grace-confused Christians. Nobody wants anything to do with that except for other Christians who act the same way.

The devil used them to attempt to make me feel like I actually *could* lose my salvation—as if Jesus' finished work on the Cross wasn't suffice if I didn't "straighten up" like them, so that I could *complete* my salvation. This was total horse-crap. They should have been walking around with shovels.

To top that off, my mind wasn't very mature in Christ because I was still learning about His grace and biblical truths *of* that grace. As a result, I still had tons of fleshy sin in my life, stuff which was very difficult to give up. My "Christian drinking" and my "innocent" porn habit was not matching up very well with my newly-in-charge perfect spirit. Especially now that I realized I *wanted* to allow Him to guide me each day.

I also wanted to keep my daily marathon sessions of video game playing just as it was—while ignoring my family—that wouldn't work either. Furthermore, the enemy and my angry, unrenewed thought pockets wanted to hang on to hate toward my enemies, "I'll get you back! You'll see! Mess with me? Ha! You're crazy! I *will* win!"

Oh, but it doesn't end there. I still held with a death-grip, my absolute *refusal* to give up control of every situation in my life! And I stonewalled against forgiving those who had hurt me so terribly! "No freaking WAY am I forgiving you!"

I could hold a grudge with the best of them! My old mindsets did *not* want to give these things up—and more! Jesus, however, wanted to reform and reshape the landscape of my life, but my attitude was:

"Why should I?! Why should I like you church people?! You self-righteous, cliquey jerks! All you do is make me feel worse! Why should I stop drinking?! It's the only thing that helps me relax! Why should I stop looking at porn?! I'm not getting any satisfaction any other way! Nobody appreciates anything I do! Everyone uses me! Why should I forgive THEM again, and again, and AGAIN?! Why should I chaaaaaaaaaaaaaaaaaange?!"

"Do it for me."

"What?!...."

Jesus was speaking to my heart, "Do it for me, please. Trust me. I see your pain, I *feel* your pain, and I know how deeply it hurts. I'll use it for a great purpose, but you must hand that pain *to* me. Make these changes because they match up with *me*, and I live *inside* you. Trust me, I have a better plan for your life, a peaceful plan. I'm going to use this unfair stuff for good, and yes, it *will* get worse at times but I'll still be here."

"Really?"

"Yes. I'll show you."

"Okay, Jesus. I'll do it. Help me."

"I will. I already am helping you. I've been helping you your whole life."

My friend, Jesus knew that Good Friday would become good for Him as well, but only *after* He paid off our debt with God. So He knows the benefits of painful sacrifice and He wants to teach us the same. It is in our actions that *show* Him our appreciation of such.

We don't change our lives for Jesus to earn a spot in heaven, or to keep ourselves from losing our spot either. We change our lives because we appreciate Him, because we love Him, and because He wants us to finally live *out* the perfection we've received in Him, on Good Friday.

**A prayer for you:** *Jesus, I want to thank you for what you've done for me at the Cross. I can never pay you back, but I will still show you my gratitude forever. Today, I ask that you touch the hearts of everyone reading this who still have doubts about what you've done. Please make it perfectly clear to them that your sacrifice 2,000 years ago made them spiritually perfect in the eyes of God—ONCE they believe that it has. Open up their minds to your grace and let them understand how easy you've made access to heaven for us. Help them to remove any incorrect mindset of legalism, and old Jewish commandments or laws. Instead, help them to understand your New Covenant by grace through faith. Thank you for dying for us, and thank you for coming back to life to prove to the world that you truly are the Son of God! Amen.*

# DAY 21

I DOUBTED JESUS' RESURRECTION, AS A CHRISTIAN

*"Stop doubting and believe." ~Jesus*

SEE JOHN 20:27

Today is Easter! Jesus has risen! Hallelujah! How exciting!...Or is it? Or should I say, *was* it? Was this day, approximately 2,000 years ago, exciting? Nope! Not at first. It was a day of doubt. The disciples *doubted* Jesus came back to life.

As I woke up this morning, I wanted to read each account of Jesus' resurrection in the Bible, from each gospel. The overall feel was shock and skepticism by those who were closest to Him. After personally listening to Jesus for so long, how could this amazing event have snuck by them? Was He not clear? Or did they think He was simply speaking in hyperbole? Either way, they didn't expect Him to come back to life.

Had they known this was going to happen they would have celebrated on Friday, invited their family and friends over for a nice dinner on Saturday, camped outside of the tomb that night, and then fallen asleep with smiles on their faces like kids on Christmas Eve.

The disciples had no *clue* Jesus would be walking out of that tomb! They didn't get it when He said He'd destroy the temple and build it again in three days! (See John 2:19). He was referring to Himself!

When you really think about it, if it weren't for this one final act—the Messiah rising from the dead—nobody would be talking about Him today. He would have been listed off in history as a madman who said weird stuff like, "Eat my flesh, drink my blood" (see John 6:56). I mean, to an unbeliever that's crazy talk!

But He was speaking *spiritually*. Nobody around Him fully understood that just yet. His final miracle would open up the supernatural eyes of everyone for the rest of all time. Truth be told, it was His miracles which solidified who He really was. Without miracles, Jesus would have been the most insane cult leader the world has ever seen.

Every miracle Jesus performed He did so for one main reason: so we would believe that He was, and is, the Son of God.

Sure, there were many other sub-categorical reasons for His healings, His molecule-shiftings, water-walkings, and constant displays of verbal authority over the elements. But His number one reason for performing miracles was so there would be no doubt that He is God in the flesh! He knew we'd be reading about His phenomenons today, and He wants us to believe *today*!

However, on the original Easter morning, all of the disciples along with Jesus' mom and Mary Magdalene, they were doubtful. These people were shook to their core when they found out Jesus had come back to life! He outdid *Himself* with this latest miracle!

You would have thought Jesus' friends would be expecting this to happen, but no. Jesus had to actually get on to them for their doubt! (See Mark 16:14). When I found this out it gave me hope in my own doubts of such an unfathomable event. It's hard to believe!

If the very closest people to Jesus had a difficult time believing that He came back to life after three days, then I'm in like Flynn. It's difficult to grasp in our minds! But He did it!

Jesus showed off His power over death to prove that *what* He said while here on earth was the truth. We must have a definite truth! Without a specific truth, anything goes. Without an *exact* truth, Hitler had a truth, and ISIS has a truth as well. Without a rock-solid truth to go by, who's to say that what those monsters did and still do is not truth?

"Matt, that's easy! Nobody with any good truth would do such terrible things!"

Says who? What are you basing your truth on? A self-made truth? Friend, we *must* have a precise truth. Without an unequivocal truth, truth from our Creator, truth from the One who created life...well...anything goes, anything. All bets are off. We can all make up our own truth. Without a definitive truth, the very word *truth* contradicts itself. It becomes an oxymoron.

But wait, we do have a truth! Jesus said that He is "the way, *the truth*, and the life!" (See John 14:6). All we have to do is believe this truth to *receive* this truth! It's not about what we do or don't do, it's about faith! Christ completed all the action required to tap into this truth *at* the Cross on Good Friday! That's the truth! The truth is Jesus! Without Him, we'll never know God, and we'll never fulfill our God-given destinies of becoming one with Him forever!

So today, my friends, know this: Christ rose from the dead to finalize a truthful new agreement with the Father, and all believers have become the beneficiaries! (Hebrews 6:16-20, 8:13, Ephesians 2:8-9, Romans 10:9). This agreement was sealed up forever through Jesus' blood! But He's not bloody anymore! He has risen! This is the truth! Stop doubting, and believe!

**A prayer for you**: *Heavenly Father, thank you for your kindness to us through Jesus' sacrifice. Thank you for sending Him here to show us what you're like in person. You are good, you are loving, you are forgiving, and you are powerful! Right now, I lift up all who are reading this, directly to you. For everyone who is doubting, let them know Jesus will forgive them if they just believe He has! With the same power used to raise Christ back* *to life, I also ask that you break mental strongholds, addictions, destructive sin-patterns, self-righteousness, and legalism. I'm also asking for you to heal relationships, bodies, and minds! As the world celebrates Jesus' resurrection, we also celebrate the truth! In His name I pray, amen.*

# DAY 22

## JESUS WANTS YOU TO TELL OTHERS ABOUT HIM

*"Go home to your family and tell them how much the Lord
has done for you, and how he has had mercy on you." ~Jesus*

### SEE MARK 5:19

"As Jesus was getting into the boat, the man who had been demon-possessed begged to go with him. Jesus did not let him, but said, 'Go home to your family and tell them how much the Lord has done for you, and how he has had mercy on you'" (Mark 5:18-19).

The man Jesus was speaking to had one foot in the boat *with* Jesus, and he was ready to go! But Jesus stops him and looks up with a smile, "Ah, ah, ah, stay here. Tell people about me." And why did this man want to go with Jesus? Because Jesus had just changed his entire life!

After suffering a lifetime of personal torment and public ridicule, this man had all but given up on living an abundant, happy, or even *normal* life. But then, he had an encounter with Christ! Jesus freed him!

The Bible doesn't say his name, but this person went from being a madman "cutter," with a Tourette's-like Syndrome, to someone at complete peace.

Mark recorded the local people's reaction after Jesus had His way with the man's severe problems, "When they came to Jesus, they saw the man who had been possessed by the legion of demons, sitting there, dressed and in his right mind; and they were afraid" (Mark 5:15).

The townspeople were bamboozled! "Isn't this Crazy Joe from up in the hills?! What happened to him?! Why's he so relaxed?!" They had never seen him in such a state! Before, they couldn't even chain him up because he was too strong and whacked-out! (See Mark 5:4). And now, look at him…cool as a cucumber. OH THE THINGS JESUS DOES IN PEOPLE!

This is the exact reason why he was trying to get *into* the boat with Jesus—HE WANTED TO GO WHEREVER CHRIST WAS GOING! He was *so* thankful to Jesus for finally setting him free! So much so, that he didn't want to leave His side. But Jesus said, "No. Stay here and tell everyone what I've done for you."

I'm sure he was heartbroken at the time, but I bet this man never shut up about how awesome and *amazing* Jesus really is. I want to do the same, don't you?

**A prayer for you:** *Heavenly Father I want to thank you for sending Jesus here. Thank you for showing me what you are really like. Right now, I lift up all who are reading this directly to you. Help them to know the truth, that Christ has the ability to change everything about us as long as we are willing to let Him come and live in our hearts. Once we finally do this, His unconditional love and never-ending grace changes us from the inside out. Thank you Jesus! Amen.*

# DAY 23

## WHEN YOU WANT TO GIVE UP ON GOD

*"Be strong in the Lord and in his mighty power."*

*EPHESIANS 6:10*

Are you weary? One of the devil's primary goals is to make Christians weary. If he can wear out your flesh—with severe temptations and troubles—as well as wear out the parts of your mind which are not yet renewed—through stresses and frustrations—he can *then* get you to make choices based on fear or sin *rather* than relying on your Creator as well as your *own* true identity. The gist to that run-on sentence is this: our enemy wants us to give up on trusting God and he doesn't want us to know who we truly are.

Thankfully, we only *think* we want to give up on God, but deep down we don't. Such a thought is coming from our old mindsets and is not the truth. Because we've been born into God's family—and this is permanent—we have a natural bend to trust God at all times. When we don't, we have forgotten who we are (see 2 Peter 1:9).

However, Satan's desire is to force you into saying, "This Christian stuff doesn't work, so I'm just going to _____ because I don't see God doing anything." He wants you to become destroyed mentally, physically, socially, economically, and emotionally, all by trying to convince you that you should *not* do what God wants you to do—or what your *true* self wants to do. His intent is to wear you down, and wear you out!

BUT WE ARE NOT WITHOUT HOPE! Christian, God wants to use your difficult situations to work *out* what's already *in* you—HIM!

Imagine if Michael Jordan with all of his amazing basketball skills never played one minute in the NBA. That talent on the inside of him would be wasted! So just *how* did his spectacular abilities come out of him! By facing the world's greatest competitors! It was when he battled the Bad Boys of the Pistons—the Champions—he was beat to a pulp! But no matter how many times he was defeated by them, that defeat didn't change the greatness on the *inside* of him! Instead, it brought it out!

When Mike went up against Magic and the Lakers, Charles Barkley and the Suns, Shawn Kemp and the Glove, Stockton and Malone, it was in these upper-echelon levels of competition that the best—which was *inside* him—was brought *out* of him! The cream always rises to the top! But if MJ never faced these extremely strong nemeses, that greatness would have never come to complete fruition!

It was *through* his supreme difficulties a legend was made! This is why James said:

> *"Consider it pure joy, my brothers and sisters, whenever you face trials of many kinds, because you know that the testing of your faith produces perseverance. Let perseverance finish its work so that you may be mature and complete, not lacking anything. (James 1:2-4)*

GOD ALLOWS DIFFICULTIES TO PULL THE BEST *OUT* OF YOU! YOU AREN'T SITTING ON THE BENCH ANY LONGER OR WATCHING FROM THE CROWD! You are ready! Christ is in you *in full*—this very moment! You have all you need to persevere, so let's gooooooooooooo!

Here are some other key verses for your strength when you *think* you can't keep going:

- "We are *more* than conquerors through Him (Jesus) who loved us!" (Romans 8:37)
- "Rejoice in the Lord *always*. I say again: Rejoice!" (Philippians 4:4)
- "Don't be anxious about anything, but in *everything*, by prayer, petition, and thanksgiving, present your requests to God." (Philippians 4:6)
- "Do *not* become weary in doing good, because at the proper time we will reap a harvest *if we don't give up!*" (Galatians 6:9)

The key words are: IF WE DON'T GIVE UP!…If we don't give up… *If*…we don't give up.

My friend, don't give up! Results *will* come, so you must begin to enjoy the journey! Try to remember that the greatest return you can ever get from doing things God's way is forming a deeper level of trust in Him. Once the foundation of that trust is built, *then* major changes happen—in your mind! God is not so much concerned about removing your difficult circumstances (or removing difficult people) as He is in changing your level of trust in Him. He wants that foundation firm! And the solidifying component of that foundation is poured *in* by allowing Jesus to live *through* you—at all times!

So today, my friends, know this: Imagine if Michael Jordan never played in the NBA. Instead, he decided to bag groceries at the local supermarket for the rest of his life. Just imagine that. There would have been such greatness on the inside of him, but it never would have been worked out of him for all of us to enjoy. This is exactly what happens when we don't allow Jesus to work through us during life's most difficult challenges—when we quit doing what is natural as holy people. Yes, greatness *is* within us! It's Jesus combined with us! But we gotta let Him come out of us by seeing every single challenge the enemy sends our way as an opportunity to grow in Christ! We must work *out* the greatness that has already been worked in! To this, all of us saints were called!

This is exactly what happens when we don't allow Jesus to work *through* us during life's most difficult challenges—when we quit. Yes, greatness *is* within us—it's Jesus! But we gotta let Him come *out* of us by seeing *every single challenge*—that the enemy sends our way—as an opportunity to *grow* in Christ! We must work *out* what has already been worked *in*! JESUS!

**A prayer for you:** *Heavenly Father, thank you for the revelation of understanding the strength we get from your grace. Because of such grace, we need not question you in the hard times just as much as we need not question you in the easy times. You are loving, sovereign, perfect, and good! And best of all, you live IN us! Help us all to realize this TRUTH more and more each day! And help us to understand that you work THROUGH US to change the world for the better! We love you, and we feel honored to be used by you. Amen.*

# DAY 24

## How to Take Off Your Masks for God

*"With unveiled faces we can see and reflect God's glory."*

*See 2 Corinthians 3:18*

Some years ago, when the Holy Spirit kept on pestering me about becoming who *He* wanted me to be—on the outside—I had on many masks. Although my spirit was perfect because of my faith in Jesus, as is every Christian's spirit (see Romans 6:6, Galatians 2:20, Colossians 1:22), I still wore masks which covered up this perfection. I had on tightly, many masks:

- A *Do not disturb my life, I'm busy* Mask
- A *Clean-cut, fake, social media* Mask (Boy, did that one come smashing to the ground.)
- *I'm a successful business owner, so look to me for advice on success, I know it all* Mask
- *I don't want to take this Christian thing too far and be weird* Mask
- *What will people think of me if I start my own ministry?* Mask
- *Codependent, closet alcoholic who is in severe denial* Mask
- *I better be good and start doing more for God or else I'm going to hell!* Mask

- *Deep fear of loved ones hurting me* Mask
- *Deep anger for never being appreciated* Mask
- *If I don't get the approval of EVERYONE, I'm not good enough* Mask

On and on, I wore many masks as a Christian. God, however, wanted to *remove* my masks—ALL OF THEM—even to the point of severe discomfort. Removing our masks exposes us, and that's where the uneasiness begins. *"Am I REALLY not like this?"*

So just *why* would God want to do such a thing (expose us) if it causes us so much pain? Because those masks aren't our *real* identity, Jesus is! Those stupid masks actually *restrain* Christ from living *through* us, fully!

Further, Jesus wore no masks, He was completely transparent. This is why we've never read about Him being afraid, or frustrated trying defending Himself—and also, why He was so loving. It's because He *knew* who He really was! God wants us to live the same way!

As a creation who is spiritually perfect on the inside, yet at the same time, we have flesh (which *can* still sin), and a mind (which is constantly growing in maturity *towards* our spiritual perfection), we can *start* to become transparent like Jesus by separating our "who" from our "do."

Our *who* is "spiritually perfect child of God" (see John 1:12, Ephesians 1:5, Hebrews 10:10,14). Our *do* is our actions. In order to separate these two it will require severe humility because we have to learn that our identity is *separate* from our actions. But once we stop confusing our *who* with our *do* (or intermingling them) we can finally drop the masks we wear each day, therefore, exposing Christ in us.

Every time we are tempted to raise a mask back up to our faces, in order to get back on track with our true identity in Christ, we must refocus on who we really are *in* our spirits! (Remember, in our spirits, we are perfect children of God). This is why Paul said, "When we remove the veil (a mask) from our faces we can understand the glory of Christ within us!" (See 2 Corinthians 3:18). If you are having difficulty understanding what *the glory of Christ within you* means, this might help:

Let's say you are walking along a country road and you glance over at a farm with a barn out front. There are some animals grazing, horses, cows, goats, and you also notice some chickens pecking at the ground—but suddenly you stop dead in your tracks. You squint your eyes and are taken back as you witness a huge, beautiful bald eagle walking around *with* those chickens, and it's pecking at the ground too! Bamboozled, you say, "What in the world?! That eagle is acting like it's a chicken! Why would it be doing such a thing?!" The only logical conclusion would be that it has *forgotten* that it is an eagle! Freaked out, you even run over towards it, trying to make it fly away—but nope! It scampers off with the rest of the chickens!

That bald eagle has lost sight of its true identity, but its actions doesn't make it *not* a bald eagle! God did not create this majestic bird to be down on the ground messing with these weak, small-minded chickens! IT WAS MADE TO SOAR! IT WAS MADE TO SEE THE COUNTRYSIDE FROM THE AIR! IT WAS MADE TO BE THE MOST REGAL BIRD ON THE PLANET!...But, some how, some way, it has lost sight of *who* it really is.

Who knows, maybe it was raised by one of those little KFC critters, so it has never known that it actually *is* an eagle. Or maybe, the chickens had a meeting *with* the eagle, and convinced it that it's not really an eagle after all! Do you know any chickens like that?! FRIEND, YOU ARE AN EAGLE! YOU *ARE* AN EAGLE! NO MATTER WHAT THEY SAY, YOU WERE MADE TO FLY HIGH IN CHRIST! As a believer, He *is* your identity!

We must come to our senses and begin to realize the perfection which comes from within! Christ Himself! HE *HAS MADE* US HOLY, FOREVER—PAST TENSE! Your spirit *is* perfect just like Him! (See Hebrews 10:10). This supernatural epiphany will only happen when we shift the focus off of our behavior and attitudes, and onto our identity in Him!

The changing of incorrect behaviors and attitudes is simply a byproduct of finally understanding our true spiritual perfection. This *shift* in our thinking and choices will never happen organically until we begin to remove "fleshly masks" and "unrenewed mindset masks" which do *not* match up with our spiritual identity in Christ.

Do you not realize that you, as a Christian, are not close to Christ or following Him? I know these are very popular sayings, and even I have used them many times, but God has given me a deeper revelation of our relationship with Him as I've grown in the knowledge of His grace. Trying to be "closer" to God, or attempting to "follow" Him, is pre-Jesus-thinking. That is a mindset of effort, which was *before* the Cross. As New Covenant believers, it doesn't work like that any longer—we've become one *with* Jesus, which is so much better! (See 1 Corinthians 6:17).

This is why Jesus told His disciples to *follow* Him, and David kept asking God to *come close* (see Matthew 4:19, Mark 1:17, Psalm 34:18, 51:11). But as for us, on *this* side of the Cross, we have a better deal! We have a better covenant! *We* are actually hidden *inside* of Jesus! We've been placed *into* Him, FOREVER, ONCE, BY GRACE, THROUGH FAITH! (See Colossians 3:3, Romans 6:6, Galatians 2:20, Ephesians 1:13, 2:8-9).

Understanding this truth *despite* any of our incorrect attitudes and actions (which do not match up with His perfection in us) requires a lot of humility. "God, how are you still with me?! HOW?! I keep messing up!" Or on the flip-side, "God, how are my countless good works not earning me anything with you?! HOW?!"

This notion of God staying faithful to us, even when we are not faithful to Him, *is* the gospel! (See 2 Timothy 2:13). The gospel is based on a promise between the Father and Son—not us. We are simply the beneficiaries *to* that contract. We didn't create it, and we can't sustain it, so we simply say, "Thank you!" and enjoy it, as we know that we *will* stay saved as long as Jesus lives! (See Hebrews 6:16-20, 7:25).

Believing this allows us to come to the point of actually *agreeing* with the Holy Spirit and finally saying, "You know what? You're right. I *wasn't* made for this. I *am* spiritually perfect because of the Cross. I'm *not* supposed to be wearing these masks. God, please help me understand this more and more."

That's humility. That's saying, "I agree with God when He says I'm perfect in spirit." The wonderful news about becoming humble in this manner is that God shows *grace* to the humble! (See James 4:6). So when we humble ourselves to the point of saying, "Teach me who I am in you!" Christ then doles out a power from within you *called* grace. Grace is not simply how you are saved, but it is also how you live! Grace is a God-given power which gives you the ability to do all things *through* Christ, whom you are hidden inside of! (See Titus 2:11-12, Philippians 4:12-13).

Admitting that you are spiritually perfect doesn't even feel right to say, let alone think—and that's because as eagles we've been taught the opposite by the chickens. We've been taught so much non-gospel in our churches of, "Try harder!" "Do better!" "Be a promise keeper!" (We always fail terribly at that one because God is the only true promise keeper.) "Prove you are saved!" "Prove you are a Christian!" "Give more money *to* God, to get more money *from* God!" (As if you can buy God's favor—what a joke!) "Act, talk, walk and *be* like us chickens! We know who you *really* are! You aren't an eagle, *you* are a chicken too!" FRIENDS, WE MUST STOP BELIEVING THE LIES OF THE CHICKENS!

Instead, we must start believing the *truth* about our real *spiritual* identity! We must begin to admit the fact that we are already complete and heaven-ready, right now! Yes, at first, it almost feels like heresy, but this is the truth! This is *why* Jesus died—to make us just like Him—*in* these bodies! Paul tells the Colossians that *through* Christ's body they were *completely reconciled* with God—not just partially, and not when they die! He even takes it further and let's them know they are "holy, blameless, and blemish-free!" (See Colossians 1:22). What kind of chicken would say that? They wouldn't! They are too busy messing around with stupid stuff that doesn't matter while focusing on the ground!

BUT WE ARE EAGLES! WE LOOK UP! WE TAKE OFF! WE SOOOOOAR! We *don't* shrink back! We are spiritually-perfect people who wear no masks! Our identity in Christ shines through us *brightly* for all the world to see!

**A prayer for you:** *God, thank you for teaching me my identity in Christ—it has changed everything. Right now, I lift up all who are reading this, directly to you. Please begin to reveal the difference between their WHO and DO. Give them peace, strength, and confidence as they finally begin to understand what you've REALLY done for them at the Cross! Help them to soar high as the eagles they are while giving them courage to begin removing their masks! In Jesus' name, amen.*

# DAY 25

## How Do I Defeat Satan?

*"Get out of here, Satan." ~ Jesus*

*SEE MATTHEW 4:10*

"YOU'RE A LOSER!"
"YOU'LL NEVER AMOUNT TO ANYTHING!"
"YOU'RE A DRUNK!"
"YOU'RE A CHEAT!"
"YOU'RE A DRUG ADDICT!"
"YOU'RE THE SAME AS YOU'VE ALWAY BEEN!"
"YOU'RE A PHONEY!"
"YOU'RE A BAD PARENT!"
"NOBODY LOVES YOU!"
"YOU'RE A HOT HEAD!"
"YOU'RE AN IDIOT!"
"YOU'RE GETTING WHAT YOU DESERVE!"
"YOU'RE A TERRIBLE CHRISTIAN!"

...These are common phrases from Satan. Sometimes these words come as thoughts, and at other times they come from people who are heavily influenced *by* Satan. So what should we do about it?

WE MUST RECOGNIZE HIS VOICE AND *SPEAK BACK*! DO *NOT* AGREE WITH HIM!

I was on a morning jog the other day, and all of a sudden I had a *really* bad thought which came out of nowhere. It was totally out of character so I said to myself, "Where is *this* coming from?" Almost immediately the Holy Spirit spoke up and said, "That's not coming from you. That thought is coming from the enemy. Ignore it."

I was like, "Yep! You don't stand a chance devil, get lost. I'm not going there," and I kept on running. I had made the *correct* choice by agreeing with Christ *in* me, and *disagreeing* with the thought that the devil had placed in my mind. I could have *easily* agreed with it, and then chased it down for the rest of the day—but nope! Instead, I spoke back with the truth!

Trespassing into our thought life is *not* a new strategy for our enemy. He even tried the same barrage on Jesus in Matthew chapter 4. However, each time he lied to Jesus, Jesus spoke back! Notice that Jesus didn't argue with him, but instead, He spoke the *truth* to this trouble-making idiot. The devil *hates* the truth. He will attempt to use everyone around you—especially those who want nothing to do with Jesus—to try to get you to believe *his* lies.

What are his lies? Any thought that makes you feel worthless, not good enough, furious, depressed, anxious, used, overlooked, self-righteous, better-than, stuck in your past, fearful, greedy, lazy, jealous, condemned, unloved, unliked, hated, resented, codependent, addicted, or *not* completely forgiven—*these* are the lies from our enemy *or* from one of the demons who do his bidding.

The Bible says "we are not battling against flesh and blood, but against spirits and principalities of the heavenly realms" (see Ephesians 6:12). There *is* a spiritual world, just the same as there *is* a physical world. If you are a Christian who doesn't realize this, allow me to dump a cold bucket of water on your face, "WAAAAAAAAAAAKE UP! MY GOODNESS! PLEASE, WAKE UP!"

Right now, as human beings, we are in the middle of both the spiritual world *and* the physical world because we are both spirit *and* body. The devil is constantly walloping our physical lives *through* the spiritual world. He is doing everything he possibly *can* do, in order to *lure* you into doing things his way. He is evil! And sometimes he makes his evil look like a great option! In addition, he wants to *compound* his evil by baiting you into reacting with even *more* evil!

Paul knew this about Satan and that's why he told the Roman Christians to "overcome evil with good" (see Romans 12:21). For me, this was life-changing even though at first I fought it! In the beginning, I didn't *want* to overcome evil with good—I WANTED TO GET PEOPLE BACK! The sin of my flesh and my unrenewed mindsets did anyway; but not the real me.

"What?! You mean I'm supposed to be kind to *them*?! Are you serious?! How could you ask this of me when you know what they've done?! God, how could you *possibly* expect me to put up with such pain and *not* attack them back?!"

He replied, "Look to the Cross, and stay focused on what Jesus did, for *you*."

"BUT IT'S NOT FAIR! I DON'T DESERVE THIS! IT HURTS SO MUCH!"

"I know it does. You'll be fine, just give it time. I'm strengthening you *through* this. You have all you need to pass these tests, my grace is sufficient for you."

Friend, as we begin to fight the devil how God wants us to, rather than by our old methods (fighting evil with evil), eventually we begin to understand *our* value as well as the value of *others*. So when we *do* have a battle, we don't fight with gossip or hurtful retaliations. Instead, we fight like this: "I love you, but I'm no longer putting up with this as normal—your choices are *not* okay. A change must happen in your actions and attitudes because you are effecting my life, and the lives of others, very negatively. Healthy changes *will* happen, or our relationship will not be the same. Please take my requests seriously, because that's exactly what they are."

This is just one example of how to overcome evil with good, and as you can see, God's fighting style is so much better than us throwing a sinful fit as we attempt to *force* healthy changes in the actions and attitudes of others. Confrontations *are* coming, so expect them and don't back down!

*As* you confront, simply allow the Holy Spirit to guide your thoughts and words during those confrontations. If you feel yourself starting to react by the sin of your flesh *or* by a section of your unrenewed mind—stop. Just be quiet. Nothing good will come from you at that point. Let your emotions die down and cool off. Regroup, stop confronting, and forgive yourself quickly.

But remember: Plan on confronting again *later*. And next time, allow the Spirit to guide you *into* that confrontation *deeper*. He is with you, so listen for Him. But more than anything, *never stop confronting the unacceptable behavior of others which impacts YOUR LIFE negatively*. Jesus confronted people all the time—out of love—and they too didn't always like it.

So as you learn how to confront people with respect (both for them *and* for you) you'll begin to notice yourself organically growing *Fruit of the Spirit*, which is: love, joy, peace, patience, kindness, goodness, faithfulness, gentleness, and self-control! (See Galatians 5:22-23). From that point on, as you continue to water that fruit by walking in God's grace, you will naturally and *easily* defeat Satan on a regular basis! HE STANDS NO CHANCE AGAINST YOU BECAUSE CHRIST IS *IN* YOU!

**A prayer for you:** *Father, I want to thank you for the gift of Christ's power within me. Because of Him, Satan is already defeated for good! That's EXACTLY what happened at the Cross! He knows his days are numbered, and that's why he attacks us—BUT WE HAVE OVERCOME SATAN BY FAITH IN CHRIST'S BLOOD, AS WELL AS BY OUR TESTIMONIES! Right now, I lift up all who are reading this, directly to you. Help them begin to recognize the lies that are coming from hell, and give them the grace to combat those lies with the truth of their spiritual perfection! In Jesus' name I pray, amen.*

# DAY 26

## DOES GOD REALLY WANT TO USE ME?

*"The gifts and calling of God are irrevocable."*

*ROMANS 11:29*

From start to finish, the Bible is clear: *God wants to use people for His plan.* It took me a long time to understand why He would do this, but as I've grown in the knowledge of His grace, I now know that His deep desire to work hand-in-hand with us is based on His passion to form relationships. God is a God of relationships—loving, *eternal* relationships. This is the ultimate reason why we were created: relationship.

Truth be told, our Creator was already enjoying at least one relationship before He even formed the foundation of this planet—a relationship with Himself. The Father, Son, and Holy Spirit always *have been* in a relationship, and always *will be* in a relationship. They have no beginning or end.

They are not bound by time, space, or matter, but instead, God (all three together) *created* the very notion of time, space, and matter for us. They did this so that we could have a physical beginning and end, and then we can decide whether or not we would like to go on to live with them forever in heaven. *We* decide if we go to heaven, God doesn't. Nobody gets *sent* to hell. Instead, hell is simply a place reserved for those who reject Jesus' free forgiveness.

But let's back up just a step. How do we know that God always *has been* in a relationship? For proof of the Trinity's pre-earth connection, we need only to look to the very first chapter of the first book in the Bible. In Genesis 1:26, God says, "Let *us* make mankind in *our* image, in *our* likeness." That's plural!

So if God created you in His image, that in itself should make you feel spectacular! YOU LOOK LIKE GOD! Oh, but it doesn't end there! The Bible also says that as a Christian you have *gifts of the Spirit* (see 1 Corinthians 12). YOU ARE GIFTED! Some how, some way, YES, you most certainly are!

To be clear, as a believer in Jesus, love is your greatest gift! Love is not only meant to be received *from* God, but it's also meant to be given away *as* your gift! (See 1 Corinthians 13). However, you do have other gifts in the drop-down menu *from* your unconditional love. This unconditional love is a supernatural love that Jesus has permanently placed in you. Your gifts and talents sprout up from this love, which God can use to help others know Him better—as well as *themselves* better (see Ephesians 2:10, 6:24, Romans 5:5, 12:2).

The problem is, the devil wants you to think there's nothing gifted about you. But remember, he's a rotten, ugly, stupid liar, so don't believe it! You *must* learn to stand up to him when he places such erroneous thoughts in your mind! TALK BACK! Tell him, "I AM GIFTED! I AM TALENTED! GOD WANTS TO USE ME FOR A WONDERFUL PURPOSE AND I KNOW HE WILL!" Jesus talked back to that fibbing twit, so we should too.

Friend, there *is* something special about you. I don't care what you've been told, there's something that God wants to use *through* you to increase the population of heaven and to help people enjoy their lives while still here on planet earth! If you're not sure what your gifts are, here are some tips to help bring them out of you. They *are* there, we just gotta get them to come out!

1. **Focus on what you enjoy.** If you get great pleasure and satisfaction from performing a particular activity, ask God to help you use that activity to bring attention to Jesus! And then brace yourself, because He will!

2. **Don't try to be like someone else.** Why? Because you're not! And you can't be! Plus, you're not supposed to be! Worst of all, you'll live a frustrated life if you *try* to be! Even if you have a particular role model, God does not want you to be exactly like them. *Please*, embrace who *you* are, and be proud of it! THIS IS SO IMPORTANT! God is not interested in copies of His creations, but instead, the originals!

3. **Exercise your gift! Use it!** When it comes to your gifts, the old adage, "Use it or lose it," is a lie. You're never going to lose it. Instead, it will be buried inside of you, even at your grave. Your gifts will never go away because God has personally placed the seeds of those gifts inside you! Now, it's your job to *allow* Him water those seeds by listening to His Spirit each day, so that eventually those gifts can sprout up and out for all the world to enjoy!

4. **Don't give up on your gift because of criticism.** This is one of the devil's greatest weapons, which is simply discouragement—RECOGNIZE THAT! Remember, your identity is not in your gift anyway, it's in what Jesus did for you at the Cross! So allow criticism, consider it, bring it to God, and then keep your confidence in what can never be destroyed or criticized: God's unconditional love for you in His Son, Jesus Christ!

**A prayer for you:** *Heavenly Father, I want to thank you for allowing me to use my gift of writing each day, what an honor. Thank you for using me! I ask that you continue to use my words to help others come to know your grace on an even deeper level! I also ask that you help these dear readers to develop their own gifts in such a way that even when hard work is involved, they still enjoy it because they love you so much! Reveal that you really DO want to use them to bring even more people into an eternal relationship with you! In Jesus' name I pray, amen.*

# DAY 27

COMBINE FAITH AND ACTION TO CHANGE YOUR LIFE

*"If I could just touch his clothes, I will be healed."*

MARK 5:28

D o you ever get around people, Christians even, who seem to only have bad things to say? They are always negative or down-in-the-mouth? You hesitate about asking them, "How was your weekend?" or "How are you doing?" because you know they'll have a long list of how terrible everything is? Something is *always* wrong. Someone is *always* treating them unfairly. They are *always* sick, and *always* in a bind. If they didn't have anything negative to talk about, their mouth would stay shut most of the time. Know anyone like that?

These types of people can easily drain you if you're not careful. Even worse, if they *are* a Christian, non-Christians witness them being full of self-pity, negativity, and blame, which results in them thinking, *"If that's how it feels to be a Christian, then I don't want anything to do with it."* They are misrepresenting Christ with their extremely poor attitudes!

THEY ARE POWERLESS—BY *CHOICE*! THEY TAKE *NO* ACTION *WITH* THEIR FAITH!

Sure, they're Christian, saved even—our salvation is not contingent on our attitudes (good *or* bad). But still, they sit around mopey, saying stupid things like, "Well I guess if God wants me to have that, then He'll give it to me. If not, then I'm all outta luck."

NO! YOU'RE WRONG! YOU GOTTA GO AFTER IT! YOU GOTTA GET UP AND *MOVE*! YOU GOTTA MIX ACTION *WITH* YOUR FAITH IF YOU WANT TO CHANGE *YOUR* LIFE!

Yes, we are Christians by faith alone, but God is expecting us to get off our tooshies, *stop* blaming others, *stop* living in the past, and get up and do something! Jesus didn't sit around feeling sorry for Himself and neither should we! He was constantly on the move!

There is a woman in the Bible who "suffered with an issue of blood" (see Mark 5), she couldn't stop bleeding. Mark said that she had seen every doctor possible and spent all of her money trying to get this health issue fixed. But still "instead of getting better she grew worse" (Mark 5:26).

She was doing all she could—on her own. She had action, with no faith (I used to be *just* like that). Then one day she heard that Jesus was passing through town. She was absolutely *determined* to get next to this man who had been making crippled people walk and blind men see! She knew by *faith*, "If I could just touch his clothes, I will be healed" (Mark 5:28). WHAT AWESOME BELIEF!

But the problem was, Jesus was swarmed everywhere He went; a crowd followed all the time and it was nearly impossible to get near Him! BUT THAT WASN'T GOING STOP HER! Mark said, "A large crowd was pressed around Him…she came up behind Him and touched His cloak!"

SHE HAD SOME SERIOUS DETERMINATION! SHE HAD ACTION *AND* FAITH!

And look what happened after she touched Him! Jesus didn't even lay hands on her, or pray for her, NOPE! She zapped His power right from Him! "Immediately her bleeding stopped and she felt in her body that she was freed from her suffering!" (Mark 5:29).

THIS IS *CRAZY* TO ME! SHE "SKIMMED" A HEALING RIGHT OUTTA JESUS' POCKET! ROBBED HIM OF HIS SPARE CHANGE OF POWER!

When she did this, Jesus stood still…He paused…He looked around. I could only guess what He was thinking, *"Someone just touched me who believes in me so deeply, they stole a healing."* When He realized the power had gone *out* from him He turned around and scanned the crowd, "Who touched my clothes?" (Mark 5:30). The disciples were like, "What do you mean? There are hordes of people swarmed around you? It could have been anyone?"

But no, Jesus kept looking around. He knew that someone with *enormous* faith in Him had just dipped into His bucket of power without even asking Him first—someone had just combined their faith *with* action.

So the woman finally steps forward, falls at His feet, and admits it was her. And what does Jesus say? "Daughter, your faith has healed you. Go in peace and be freed from your suffering" (Mark 5:34).

YOUR *FAITH* HAS HEALED YOU! HER FAITH, COMBINED WITH THE FACT THAT SHE WAS *NOT* GOING TO GIVE UP ON CHANGING HER LIFE *THROUGH* JESUS! Oh my gosh, I could just *explode* right now!

She knew Jesus was coming through town and she got up! She didn't sit there feeling sorry for herself or talking about her problem! No! She had already done everything she possibly *could* do, and then she *went* to Jesus! She pressed through the people standing in her way, and she got her miracle as she combined action *with* her faith! She actually *did* something about her terrible situation by seeking Jesus out *as* her solution!

…Do you want to change *your* life? Friend, you can do this too. *You* can change your life! You can stop living by fear, by the flesh, or by unrenewed thinking. Just take your faith to Jesus and combine it with the *action* He keeps asking you to take. Then prepare yourself, because when you do this *everything* begins to change, in your mind.

**A prayer for you:** *Well good morning Lord! Wow, WHAT a beautiful* *morning it is! First off, I want to thank you for letting me live another day on your planet. I am grateful. Right now, I lift up all who are reading this, directly to you. For those who WANT to change their lives, help them. You don't force us to do anything, yet, you place opportunities in front of us all the time and then give us the grace and strength needed to act on them. We are ready to ACT! WE ARE READY FOR MORE! Teach us how to combine our faith and action, through you! Amen!*

# DAY 28

## HOW TO DESTROY PRIDE

*"But the tax collector stood at a distance. He would
not even look up to heaven, but beat his chest and
said, 'God, have mercy on me, a sinner.'"*

*LUKE 18:13*

What does it take to truly allow Christ to live through you? Just
what *is* the secret formula to becoming the best Christian you
possibly can be? "Best Christian?" you might ask.

Yes, just like an oak tree can be tossed into the river and become nasty
drift-wood, yet, another oak tree can become a beautiful, hand-crafted
desk—both are still oak trees—no matter what. Nothing can change that
fact. For Christians, since we have a supernatural DNA structure which
can't be changed because Christ will never die again (see Hebrews 7:25), it
is us who decides *how* our lives will turn out.

As a Christian, it doesn't matter if we become rich, poor, or in-between,
we are the decision makers of our own model. Through Christ, God has
freely given each of us the raw materials of spiritual perfection. However,
we are the architects who design our lives and then build it. God doesn't
do this for us. He is *with* us, but He doesn't *control* us.

This is why, as a child of God, we can have a nasty, non-fruitful life, or we can have an extremely loving, *orchard-size* fruitful life. But no matter what we decide to do or *not* to do, we are still children of God (see John 1:12, Ephesians 1:5, 1:13).

The gospel has nothing to do with our actions and attitudes ebbing and flowing, neither is it about our many accomplishments or lack thereof. Instead, it's about a promise between God and God, and us being the beneficiaries to that promise.

The author of Hebrews tells us "because God could not swear by anyone greater than Himself, He swore *by* Himself, and by these two unchangeable things (the Father and Son) we now have a hope which anchors our souls" (see Hebrews 6:16-20). The gospel is about their commitment to one another, it's not about our commitment to them.

As New Covenant believers, our only job is to say, "Thank you!" and then receive this gift by grace through faith (see Ephesians 2:8-9). Because of such good news, we are to wake up each day and say, "God, I'm available for you to use!" But even if we don't, we are still born of God because God's seed is now in us forever. Our spirits no longer even *have* the ability *to* sin (see 1 John 3:9). Our flesh? Yes. Our unrenewed mindsets? Yes. But not our spirits which is our true identity (see Galatians 2:20, Romans 8:19).

So when a person's life doesn't look "Christian" try to remember that they very well still could be. Just like we can't make ourselves unborn from our earthly father, no matter what our lives look like, we can't make ourselves unborn from our Spiritual Father either, no matter what our lives look like. We cannot be unborn. Our birth has already happened and it's irreversible!

We are privy to this heavenly birthright because of the Father's promise to Jesus at the Cross and our faith in that event as true for our sins! We've now been completely reconciled with God forever by being reborn through Jesus! (See Colossians 1:22, Romans 6:6-7). Therefore, in order to build up the best Christian life we can possibly have, we must make a decision of what we will do each day with one little word...*pride.*

Whatever we decide to do with pride on a moment-by-moment basis solidifies how our lives will be molded as heaven-ready people. Just because our spirits are perfect, that doesn't mean our flesh's choices are *or* our unrenewed mindsets are. The pride which comes from both the sin of the flesh and old mindsets—not from our spirit—will keep us drifting along the river as disregarded oak. Pride keeps us addicted, fearful, frustrated, codependent, selfish, uninterested, enraged, lazy, blameful, short-fused, out of control, jealous, legalistic, greedy, impatient, and self-righteous (among many other things which are not of the Spirit in you, see Galatians 5).

Pride screams, "I don't need to change my choices! I'm not doing anything wrong! Worry about yourself!" And we say these things as Christians while completely ignoring the Holy Spirit's guidance. "I'm not sinning!"— even though the Spirit has told us many times that we are. "But even if I *was* sinning, Jesus covers all my sins! So mind your own business, hypocrite!" Pride. Even the Jews who killed Jesus were so full of *religious* pride, they didn't realize what they were actually doing. Pride blinded them.

Pride destroys marriages, families, friendships, businesses, churches, and even countries. Pride will even dismantle the dreams that God has personally placed in our hearts all because we refuse to change our incorrect attitudes and actions. Pride says, "I'm never going to admit I'm wrong. Ever. I'm *not* budging," even though the Holy Spirit has told us a thousand times, "That's *not* you. This needs to change. That will never match up with your spiritual perfection no matter how many different angles you go at it."

Pride will even *kill* you (and others) if you take it too far. The heroin addict who just died from an overdose, they refused to admit they actually *were* addicted to heroin. The drunk businessman who just ran over the little girl, he threw fits all the time when he was called out on his drinking. The man who died after three heart attacks refused to admit he had an eating addiction, and now his family is left behind. The gangbanger who just got shot and killed *bathed* in pride over the loyalty he had to his gang. The stripper who got beat up and raped at the party, she would *not* listen to Grandma every time she said, "Baby, God has a better plan for your life."

The preacher whose church members' lives are falling apart because he refuses to preach on the bottomless grace of God, how we can be reconciled with Him, or anything about the unconditional love of Christ—but instead, he trains them with, "HOW BAD THE WORLD IS, HOW *WE* NEED TO TAKE IT BACK, AND HOW WE NEED TO MAKE THESE NASTY SINNERS REPENT!"—*that* is pride. Each and every Sunday, he instills severe pride deep into his patrons' minds by teaching them the very opposite of what God's character really is.

Pride is from the pits of hell. Pride chooses drugs, alcohol, sex, work, video-game binging and hobbies over its family. Pride would rather watch porn than have sex with its spouse. Pride beats *up* their spouses, and kids, and then blames *them* for the beatings.

Pride steals from their boss, and then blames the boss for it. Pride leaves their kids' dad for another man, while caring nothing about what that choice has just done to the well-being of their children. Pride gossips on social media. Pride *cheats* on social media. Pride appreciates nothing, while being handed everything. Pride refuses to learn and grow. Pride knows it all. Pride gives victory lessons. Pride judges how people look. Pride shows no mercy to those who make mistakes. Pride looks for the worst in others, while ignoring the best. Pride says, "End of conversation!" and then storms off. Pride is what got the most beautiful angel of all time, Satan, kicked out of heaven.

We must destroy pride! It's our choice! We do this by walking *out* God's Spirit *in* us! He's there, we just have to let Him come out! The Holy Spirit is not prideful! As you begin to allow Him to live through you more and more, what you'll soon see is that by walking out your perfect spiritual identity pride begins to organically fade away because that word doesn't describe you at all! You are not prideful! YOU'RE NOT! Begin to let Jesus live through you and you'll see that this is the truth! Let's goooooooooooooo!

**A prayer for you:** *God, I want to thank you for completely removing all pride from my spirit. Thank you so much. Right now, I lift up all who* *are reading this, directly to you. For those who may be struggling with an enormous pride issue, please, reveal it to them. In the name of Jesus, I rebuke any prideful spirit who has set up shop around them—not in them—but around them, make it go away! Help them, mold them, and teach them who they really are in Christ! In His name, amen.*

# DAY 29

## WHY DID GOD CREATE ME?

*"For we are God's masterpiece. He has
created us anew in Christ Jesus,
so we can do the good things
he planned for us long ago."*

EPHESIANS 2:10

One of my greatest joys is hearing the birds outside of my house each morning. The enthusiasm they have for every new sunrise makes my heart swell. I love my mornings. I usually get up between 5 and 5:30am, shuffle my way to the kitchen, let Harley and Charlie out the back door, and then make my pot of coffee. After it's brewed, I fill up a cup, and then head downstairs to my study. I call it a study, but it's really just a reading room.

In this room I have two big, plush leather seats, with an ottoman, along with a small fancy table in-between them that a lamp sets on. A bookshelf with all of my most favorite reads is on the opposite side of the room, and the walls are completely adorn with the words of Christ, the apostle Paul, as well as other famous Scriptures that even non-believers know.

But my most favorite part of this room is the centerpiece which hangs on its own wall with nothing else, an oversize painting of Jesus on the Cross with red words carefully brushed across His chest and arms from one nail to the other: "NO GREATER LOVE THAN THIS."

My friendly neighbor who is a great artist painted this masterpiece for me a couple years ago. It is absolutely magnificent.

So, each day, with coffee in hand, I tuck myself into this comfy chair, wrap the throw blanket around my lower torso, and open up my Bible. Although the Holy Spirit teaches me new things all day long, this time of the day my focus is solely on Him with no distractions, so it's as if He is *more* clear during my devotional time. And as I read, pray, and banter with my Creator, He supernaturally jump-starts my gift of writing, and off I go.

I can't describe *how* this happens—my love of writing through Christ—it just happens. Even with all of the adjectives stored up in my vocabulary, trying to explain what it *feels* like when my gift is activated each morning… well…it is out of this world—it's not "worldly." That's the best I got. It's not *of* this world when God says, "Matthew, write about this," and then stuff just starts to flow from my fingertips without any effort. When I'm done, sometimes I sit back and think, *"Where did this come from?"* It has *got* to be the Holy Spirit.

I love this time of day. The people who are sleeping in are missing out. I believe this dedicated, personal, one-on-one time with God has made me the man I am today. I don't know how I lived for so many years *without* using this time of day to build *up* my relationship with Him. Of course, I had to begin going to bed an hour earlier each night, but that last episode of Dateline or the 4th quarter of the game could wait. I needed my rest. I had an appointment with God Almighty first thing in the A.M.

Again, I want to stress that God is with us at *all* times of the day (because we are hidden *inside* Him, see Colossians 3:3), but when you dedicate a *portion* of your day to getting to know Him *better*, He rewards you with that very thing.

In the beginning of me doing this, Grace and Jennifer would call me an old man because I'd say, "Goodnight, I love you," and then head off to bed at 9pm. But I like my sleep, and I like to rise and shine when the birds do. Further, God has taught me it's imperative that I'm fully rested *physically* if I want to enjoy being fully rested in my mind.

But as I sit here, sometimes I'll be very still...I'll stop reading or writing, just look up, and sit quiet...I want to take in God's presence. The Bible says that we are to, "Be still and know that He is God" (see Psalm 46:10)...so I do that... ... ...just... ...silence. Nothing else...no worries about the ensuing day...no regrets over the previous one...no planning... no thoughts about *anything* except knowing that God is God.

As I sit here I'll soon say something to God, praising His greatness, like, "Wow. You are holding all of this together. How unsearchable is your power. Thank you for letting me be a part of this." All I have for Him at this moment is just...gratitude.

While making myself more aware of God's presence, I'll gaze out the windows of the double doors. The whole time I've been sitting here it has sounded as if the birds *outside* those doors have been enjoying a block party. They are just so darned excited about this new day! It's early May here in Missouri, so they are at their loudest, but in the winter, I don't get to hear them in the mornings. I guess it's too cold for their little bird feet, or they've headed south for warmer weather.

I can feel my soul expanding with God's love each time I hear this bird-celebration outside my house. I don't know what it is about them, but their loud social life is so awesome to me. To be honest with you, sometimes they are so loud that they become the background noise for my morning devotional, like music I'm intentionally playing in the room.

But what amazes me the most about these little feathered creatures is this: God knows about each and *every* one of them, and He loves them. Jesus said this in Matthew 10:29. God *created* these birds to *be* enthusiastic about the mornings He makes! Their songs are for Him!

Their songs are for...His *glory*.

And His glory is found in *my* enjoyment of His birds.

I am a part of God's glory, and so are you.

He loved us so much that He just *had* to create us! *You* were created *on* purpose and *for* a purpose! Just like these birds were made by God to sing, we too have individual God-given purposes as well! A purpose which is meant to bring glory to Him *and* us! (See John 17:22). A purpose which was personified perfectly *in* Jesus! And once you step into a relationship *with* your Creator *through* Christ, *you* will start to sing your very own song—a song that God would love to hear!

**A prayer for you:** *Heavenly Father, thank you—thank you for life! Thank you for creating me! So often we forget that just being here is a gift from you! Right now, I lift up all who are reading this, directly to you. I ask that you begin to reveal in their hearts just how special to you they truly are! I'm also asking for you to reveal to them WHAT exactly their song is, if they don't already know. Jesus is the music, but we provide the words! In His name I pray, amen.*

# DAY 30

## WHAT TO DO WHEN CHRISTIANS BAD-MOUTH YOU

*"Be kind and compassionate to one another, forgiving*
*each other, just as in Christ God forgave you"*

*EPHESIANS 4:32*

Let's face it, certain Christians talk bad about other Christians all the time. The ones who ignore the Holy Spirit's guidance on a very high level, the sin of the flesh can get a sick thrill from gossiping about other believers. They'll even candy-coat it by saying, "I just want you to know this so you can pray for them." But at other times, they don't even do that. They gossip blatantly. And on certain occasions, they're even quick to rip into a fellow Christian while having lunch after church.

For years, sadly, I participated in this incorrect type of Christianity. "Oh if you only knew *this* about them! Some Christian they are! I bet they aren't even saved!"

The devil works up a pretty good demonic lather in-between Christians who gossip horrendously.

*No* Christian should be talking bad about another Christian, even if what's being said is true. The Bible says, "love covers a multitude of sins," and if we *are* using our love to cover the sins of others we are "loving them

113

deeply" (see 1 Peter 4:8). But sometimes what Christians are so rudely gossiping about isn't even true—and at other times, it's even about you! When this happens and we get hurt, we have a decision to make:

1. Let it bother us, scramble trying to fix it, and then retaliate.
2. Decide to forgive, *beforehand*, and *think* of your accusers with love.

For most of my life I chose number one. I allowed myself to be bothered by something that I have absolutely no control over, gossip. As soon as I found out that a rumor was spreading about me, fear and anger would immediately grip my mind. What's really unfortunate is that a lot of times rumors begin through close loved ones, friends, church members or family members—even self-centered spouses who care very little about their vows.

*"Oh I'll show them! You do NOT mess with me!"* would be the first thing which popped into my unrenewed mind. Unbeknownst to me at the time, this was the power of sin and Satan using Christians *against* me. He wanted me to think of them with hate, and unfortunately the flesh gave him his way quite often. The good news is, now that I've grown in the knowledge of God's grace, I recognize this idiot's tricks as soon as he starts in on me—*even* when he's trying to use Christians against me. The battle, however, is spiritual, not physical. People are not my problem. The quicker I focus in on this truth, the quicker I can enjoy peace.

When I first began to allow the Holy Spirit to guide me, regularly, I can specifically remember an incident in which I was fuming over what another Christian had said about me. I shouted out to Jesus, "You just don't understand! Why would you let this happen to me?! I'm trying to listen to you and do the right things, but these people still hate me!"

In my heart, I heard, "Now you understand what I went through for you."

"...Okay...alright Jesus...you got me. Now I get it."

My friends, this is part of it. This is part of *growing* in Christ! When you begin to allow Jesus to live through you, you will be talked about terribly—by other Christians. Maybe they misunderstand you, maybe they are jealous, maybe you are stepping on their legalistic view of God and they are intimidated—whatever it may be, attacks are headed your way so be ready to forgive ahead of time.

If I could soften the blow for you it would be through this lesson I've learned: begin to understand that people's opinion of you is none of your business. This will take practice *through* the Spirit, and *through* being your true self. It's like Grandma used to say, "Matthew, just worry about yourself and don't worry about what others are saying. Instead, worry about your *own* reactions. That's all God expects of us anyway."

When we really break this down, people have every right in the world to bad-mouth you, but at the same time, you have every right in the world to react how the Holy Spirit wants you to react. We can't live our lives getting upset about what we can't control, if we do, then we won't be able to enjoy our God-given purposes. In turn, our lives will be terribly frustrating.

Friend, the devil is not excited about your faith in Jesus so he *will* break out the big guns from time to time. Begin to recognize that! Sure, there will be plenty of Christians who *are* following the Holy Spirit's lead, those who love you, and those who want to help and encourage you. But there will always be certain Christians who will *not* like you, no matter *what* you do—so don't worry about that!

The devil knows which people to use "the best" in order to get at you the best. He's been studying your life from conception and this whole time he's been trying to steal your joy, he's been trying to kill you, and he's *also* been trying to destroy all things good in your life (see John 10:10). So when he tempts someone to gossip about you, he's not always going to pick someone whose personal opinion you don't care anything about. Oh no, he tempts the people whom you *want* to like you the most.

Satan whispers into the minds of extremely close loved ones, relatives, co-workers, in-laws, pastors, teachers, coaches, neighbors—you name it. He doesn't *only* tempt Christians with hate and murder but also with gossip; and God sees all three—hate, murder, and gossip—the same (see Romans 1:29).

Friend, don't let gossip bother you! Honestly, who gives a crap about what they say?! Never place your value, identity, or joy into anything you can't control! If you *don't* do this, you will become a slave to the opinion of others! You will then live a life of anxiety, frustration, fear, and anger.

So choose to love, right now! Choose to forgive, right now! Before it even happens, make a decision *right now* to love and forgive other Christians before they hurt you! That way when it *does* happen you can react how Jesus reacted when He came under attack:

> *"When they hurled their insults at him, he did not retaliate;*
> *when he suffered, he made no threats. Instead, he entrusted*
> *himself to him who judges justly." (1 Peter 2:23)*

**A prayer for you:** *God, today I want to thank you for forgiveness and self control. I know that both of these characteristics of mine are fruit of the Spirit, so I thank you. Right now, I lift up all who are reading this, directly to you. Father, so many of these dear readers are dealing with gossip, strife, and lies which have been said about them. Please help them to begin to find their complete identity in what YOU say about them, and NOT in the opinion of others. Even if what's being said is true—on a fleshly level—help them to stay focused on your voice, your mercy, your love, and your grace! Keep reminding them of who they are in spirit! Lastly, help them to forgive their accusers ahead of time so they can enjoy peace. In the name of Jesus I pray, amen.*

# Month 2

*"You will seek me and find me when you
seek me with all your heart."*

JEREMIAH 29:13

*~God, hundreds of years before He gave us the opportunity
to have a new heart, through faith in the Cross*

# DAY 31

## WHY I DECIDED TO GET BACK IN CHURCH

*"Do you not know that your bodies are temples
of the Holy Spirit, who is in you, whom you have
received from God? You are not your own"*

1 CORINTHIANS 6:19

Let me tell you a secret that had I known all along, my bitterness toward church would have been nixed a long time ago: We are the Church. Us, all believers, all throughout the world as a whole, we form *the Church*. Church is not a building, but us.

So any time you read the word *church* in the Bible, rather than picture a bunch of holier-than-thou people huddled around together, trying to spray the world with cleaning fluid, *think* of the body of Christ. You, me, everyone—together. Don't think of a building, but think of us.

Friend, Jesus died to remove the need for a physical place to find God (see Matthew 27:51). Because of His sacrifice *we* are now the temples of God! You and I are individual, personal places where the Spirit of God actually lives and dwells! (See 1 Corinthians 6:19).

I didn't know that. I thought that if I didn't go *to* a church—an actual building—God wouldn't love me. In turn, I'd be a second-class Christian and He would rightly make my life miserable. Why was this? It was because of the false advertising from the religious Christians. By *religious Christian* I simply mean those who find their identity in what they do and don't do *for* God, rather than in what Christ has done *for* them.

Because of what they had taught me for so many years, I didn't understand that God loved me unconditionally even if I *never* stepped foot in a physical church building again. Further, sitting in a church *building* no more made me *know* God than me sitting in an emergency room made me know how to perform brain surgery.

There are many people who have been going to church for decades (some, even pastor churches) and they still have no clue about the never-ending love of Jesus. All they know is, "I go to church." They've created a self-righteous law called *Sunday Morning Church Attendance* rather than simply allow Christ to live through them seven days a week. Having your own parking spot at church and a worn out Bible means nothing if you still refuse to grow in the knowledge of God's grace.

However, church attendance is still very important as long as that church is showing people the bottomless love of Jesus. I wrote about this very subject in my first book, *True Purpose in Jesus Christ*. Here is an excerpt:

> *Next up, I'd like to address the excuse of, "I don't need to go to church to be a Christian." I used this one for years. And sure, we don't NEED to go to church to be a Christian, but that attitude in itself goes against Christ's. So instead of saying "I don't need church," let's turn it back around on ourselves. As I learned more about Christ WITHOUT church, I had no other option but to finally ask myself, "Why am I really NOT going to church?" My answer was this: because I don't like church people.*
>
> *According to the Holy Spirit in me, that's not okay. God counseled me away from this incorrect mindset, and I immediately knew I needed to get back into church—if not for any other reason than to fight the devil. "Fight the devil?" you might ask. Yes, he was heavily influencing my feelings towards self-righteous do-gooders. I seriously disliked how I FELT*

*when I got around the people who snubbed their noses at me. I was letting THAT have a negative effect on my life. And all it really was, was bitterness. Again, the Holy Spirit of Christ does not approve of that—and neither does my true self.*

*As a Christian, I'm supposed to love everyone. Yet I had somehow fallen into the pit of seriously disliking Christians AS a Christian. And what else is crazy, I developed an OVER-empathy for non-believers—especially those who got picked on by unloving Christians. Once again, this was NOT okay with God. I'm glad I can chuckle at it now, because that was really bad. To overcome this, I began to ask God, "Show me how to love religious people," and He has. This was one of my main reasonings for getting back in church.*

*Yes, we can pray at home (or anywhere), we can listen to Christian music and sing along WHILE we're alone. We can even study our Bibles and watch a grace-filled teacher on TV or online, but church attendance is still important because certain people AT that church might need our presence.*

*Hebrews 10:25 says we are "not to forsake the fellowship of one another"—and no, this is NOT a law telling Christians to GO TO CHURCH OR ELSE! After all, the first church BUILDING wasn't even established until approximately 200 years after Christ. Instead, this verse is saying our gatherings can be a time of wonderful encouragement. If you read the verse right before this one, it explains the context, "And let us consider how we may spur one another on toward love and good deeds" (Hebrews 10:24).*

*Furthermore, going to church also teaches us how to interact with each other as believers. Christian interaction is a very good thing! At church, we learn corporately how to act (and react) toward non-believers, new Christians, weaker Christians, and even mature Christians. Which, if Christ is the center of the church, will always be EQUALLY with truth and love.*

*Another neat thing you will experience by attending a Christ-filled church is that you get to see and FEEL what it's like to have the Holy*

*Spirit dwelling among so many people all at once! This cannot be described in words! It can only be felt in person and CANNOT be felt by yourself. No, we aren't "feeling chasers," but there is nothing wrong with feeling great feelings! The CORPORATE feeling of the Holy Spirit is amazing! And I believe this feeling is so important because it's a preview of what heaven will be like, which is ALL believers enjoying the presence of God, together, forever!*

**A prayer for you:** *Heavenly Father, I want to thank you for church buildings and gatherings. It is in these places that so many good things happen! Yes, I know that because we are fallible humans, and we run the churches, we can make mistakes. You knew this ahead of time, and that's why you have set up EVERY church based on YOUR grace! Right now, I ask that you help us to make the entire world the Church! We want to make it a place where your love and glory shines bright! Use us! Use our hands, feet, and mouths! Break down the four walls of the church buildings, as well as the walls in our minds, so that Jesus' name gets carried into the stratosphere! In YOUR name Jesus I pray, amen!*

# DAY 32

## HOW TO OVERCOME BEING A WEAK CHRISTIAN

*"But we are not of those who shrink back and are
destroyed, but those who have faith and are saved."*

HEBREWS 10:39

I have been a Christian for most my life, although for a majority of that time I lived as an extremely weak Christian. Sure, I believed in Jesus, but I mostly believed in Him because I didn't want to go to hell. Which, that *is* a very healthy fear. Hell is bad. So if you became a Christian for fire insurance, that's smart. However, it doesn't *end* there—not even close! That's only the beginning!

Jesus didn't die on the Cross and take away the punishment for our sin (which was hell) *just* so that we wouldn't be eternally separated from Him, there is *so* much more to it! He also died to *give* us an abundant life—*His* life! (See John 10:10, Colossians 2:10).

The very moment we believed Jesus saved us, something happened: *we* died too, and *we* were immediately resurrected *too*—spiritually! Once we believe He's forgiven us, *we* (our spirits) become crucified *with* Him, *we* get buried, and *we* get brought back to life *as* a brand new perfect spirit *while* still in these imperfect bodies! (See Romans 6:6, 2 Corinthians 5:17,

Colossians 1:22, Galatians 2:20, 3:2). This is not hyperbole, this is literally the gospel!

Understanding this fact will take you from being weak and defeated in your thinking, to being bold, courageous, and confident in your true spiritual identity: an actual reborn child of God who lives on planet earth! (See John 1:12, Ephesians 1:5, 2 Corinthians 5:20).

Now, there are some Christians out there who have made it their calling to *only* talk about being afraid of God. However, the Bible says once we are saved we never have to be afraid of God punishing us ever again (see 1 John 4:18).

But the fear-mongering Christians will ignore that. Their primary goal is to get others to walk on egg-shells around God (and them), *first* so they can manipulate and control you, and *second*, so that you don't "Trip up and fall back into hell!" They've twisted the good news of the gospel into *only* being good for them.

They are behavior focused rather than Christ centered. They are self-righteous, arrogant, and graceless. They have no clue about what Jesus has really done for us, all they truly care about is conservatism, counting, and coldness. They are fair-weather friends who grossly false advertise for the Holy Spirit with their unloving, legalistic lifestyle—and to make matters worse, they white-wash their disgusting treatment of others by calling it discernment.

THAT'S NOT ME. That's *not* my ministry. To be clear, for a time that *was* my actions and attitudes. But the Holy Spirit has cleaned up those parts of my unrenewed mindsets with gale-force winds. He's gotten out the broom and dust-cloth and gone to work on *all* parts of my mind that wants to lean toward conditional-grace, which is anti-gospel. I'm competitive, so this wasn't easy. But over time, He's taught me to stop looking at what all I'm doing, and instead, stay focused on what all Christ has done.

Let me also be clear about what people *should* be afraid of *if* they are non-believers: hell. Hell is real, and hell is bad. It is a horrendous place specifically reserved for those who reject Christ's forgiveness. So be sure you don't go there! *You* get to choose!

How do you *not* go there? God has made this very simple: *accept the free forgiveness of your sins through believing Jesus Christ is your Savior!* After that, your new life *in* Christ begins! By receiving His forgiveness *once* you instantly have nothing to fear *about* God, ever again! (See Hebrews 7:25, 10:10).

If you can't grasp this free gift of spiritual perfection then fear or hypocrisy will regularly ruin your life as a Christian. God doesn't want that! He loves you! He doesn't want you to be afraid, and He doesn't want you to be a nasty masquerader! SO STOP BEING AFRAID OF GOD! Remember, when God does decide to correct you it's always done out of a loving discipline (a word which was derived from *disciple*)—He never corrects you by punishing you because Jesus took away your punishment for good! (See John 3:17).

So today, my friends, know this: Be confident in your true spiritual identity, which is a heaven-ready heir to heaven! Never believe the lies of those who don't understand God's grace! Instead, ask God to teach you how to *treat* them with grace! It won't be easy, but it will be worth it because when you do this they will finally get to see Christ coming *through* someone with grace-filled, unconditional love! So be bold and begin to show the world the confidence of Christ! He lives in you!

**A prayer for you:** *Heavenly Father, thank you for confidence. Thank you for teaching me who I really am! Right now, I lift up all who are reading this, directly to you. For those who want to get to know you better, help them do just that. Lift them up! Teach them your grace! Teach them their value! Make them bold in knowing WHO they really are—a child of God! Amen.*

# DAY 33

## Are You Rooted in Love?

*"Be rooted and established in love."*

*See Epheisians 3:17*

For so many years I thought I knew what love was, but I had no clue. Like so many others, I believed love was simply a sentimental feeling—it's not. "Sentimental feelings" is just one small layer of love. Because I was so off base in my knowledge of real love, I thought that in order to love someone you had to do everything they asked you to do, and if someone loved *you*, they'd do the same. Christ's Spirit has taught me otherwise.

In Ephesians 3, Paul tells us we must be "rooted and established in love, and when we do we'll have power!" *"What does that even mean?"* you might think. Paul is teaching the Christians in Ephesus that when we are established in love, *rooted*, only then will we be able to "grasp how wide, long, high, and deep is the love of Christ" (Ephesians 3:18). The whole point of being rooted and established in love is to *grasp* the love of Jesus!

So real love is...drumroll please...the love of Christ! *This* is the nucleus of *all* real love!

Once I began to allow God to teach me this truth, my life as a Christian started to change dramatically, for the better. Over time, as I've let Him renew my mindset through His Spirit in me, I've grown to understand that real love truly *is* the love of Christ—no matter who I was applying it to, myself not withstanding.

So *as* we allow these heavenly roots to be established in our minds, we soon learn that love is not *completed* through a sentimental feeling, or through sex, or even through the feeling of butterflies-in-the-stomach. It is also not finalized in a parent/child love, brotherly love, or sisterly love—these are all simply *outward* layers of love, but *not* the actual roots.

This is why until the love of *Christ* is established in us, no other *layer* of love can possibly *be* completed—no matter how hard we try to force it or different angles we come at it. Our Creator has made it to where only Jesus can complete humanity's crackling foundation of love.

The great thing about God is He always gives us guidance—through His Spirit in us—on how to love others and ourselves. It's us who must pay attention. In 1 Corinthians 13 there's a list of characteristics of His love for us. So naturally, as we allow Him to live *through* us we will begin to grow this love in our lives from *His* roots (Jesus also touched on how this works in John 15:5). Eventually, many different flavors of His love is produced through us—not *from* us, but through us:

- Love is patient
- Love is kind
- Love is not jealous
- Love does not brag
- Love is not proud
- Love does not dishonor others
- Love is not self-seeking
- Love is not easily angered
- Love keeps no records of wrongs
- Love does not delight in evil
- Love rejoices with the truth
- Love always protects, trusts, hopes, and perseveres

These are the characteristics of God, and God lives *in* us! (See 1 Corinthians 6:19). "But Matt, you just don't understand what I'm going through!"...My friend, no, I don't...but God sure does. He'll get you to where you need to be—a place of peace and confidence—soon enough, as you allow Him to come *out* of you, little by little, day by day. God sees you, He sees your pain, and nothing goes unnoticed by Him. Give it time, trust, and truth—and allow His Spirit to comfort you as these roots grow deep and strong in your mind!

When we finally establish the love of Jesus Christ *into* our hearts, by believing in His forgiveness *once* (see Hebrews 10:10, Galatians 3:2)—we then become empowered from within to stand up against *any* unacceptable behavior. Being loving is not about becoming a human punching-bag, it's about exuding Christ. As He teaches us how to do this through the Holy Spirit, we begin to learn our value.

Once we begin to learn our value—a value so priceless Christ Himself died for us—we then stop putting up with the crap we've always put up with. But now, we do so in a truthful, respectful, *loving* way, because that's who we really are in our spirits. Loving others *will* require controlled confrontations over the things that must change. The stuff they are doing, causing, or contributing to—which is impacting your life negatively—*has* to go. And it has to go because you now know your worth to God.

When we finally get the gist of Christ's adoration for us (therefore learning our value) we stop reacting out of fear and frustration toward those who treat us poorly. We no longer allow their threats, aggressiveness, or silent treatments to dictate our joy or self-worth because we know that our joy and self-worth comes from *within* us. In turn, we begin to not give a rip about their intimidation or coldness because we know that ultimately, whatever they decide to do or not do, God has our back.

This becomes a new "fruit of the Spirit" growing *from* us which is called "self-control" (see Galatians 5:22, 23). Self-control strengthens our stance against people who try to use us or make us feel *less-than*, "If we don't do what they say! Now!" Eventually, we begin to grow deep, secure roots *in* our identity in Christ. In turn, we stop enabling them, and we stop bowing down out of fear or loneliness. Soon enough you'll see that God has taught you their tactics no longer *work* on you—AND YOU BECOME FREE!

As we *continue* the Holy Spirit also teaches us that sometimes the best form of love we can show is refusing to help someone who refuses to help themselves. He teaches us healthy boundaries! He teaches us what *our* responsibilities are, and what they are not. From time to time He will even lead us to take a step back and say, "I love you too much to be your crutch any longer, STAND UP!"

Remember, enabling is *not* a form of love. Enabling does *not* grow from your roots. Enabling is demonic. Enabling is the main ingredient to the formula of ruining the *other* person's life *whom* you are enabling. Enabling is also the main ingredient to ruining *your* life, to draining *your* joy, and to keep *you* painstakingly frustrated. STOP ACCEPTING UNACCEPTABLE BEHAVIOR AS NORMAL! This *is* possible! You will get this strength from your roots! (See Philippians 4:13).

So today, my friends, know this: The love of Christ will change your entire life! Let Him establish His roots in your heart, water them daily, and then watch them grow up and out of the soil of your soul, strong and tall!

**A prayer for you:** *God, I want to thank you for this day! I also want to thank you for your love! Right now, I lift up all who are reading this, directly to you. Help them begin to understand just how much love you have for them in Christ. If they don't already have a relationship with you, I'm asking you to form and mold a BEAUTIFUL relationship IN them, starting today! Begin to give them the desires of their hearts once they have you IN their hearts! Bury your roots of love deep inside them and make those roots grow up and out for all to see, admire, and find rest in its shade. Amen.*

# DAY 34

## STOP COMPARING YOURSELF TO OTHERS

*"Pay careful attention to your own work, for then you will get the satisfaction of a job well done, and you won't need to compare yourself to anyone else."*

GALATIANS 6:4

God has an individual plan for each and every one of us, and it's bigger than we can possibly imagine. The problem is, the devil wants us to be jealous of other people's God-given plans. He wants you to compare *your* gifts, *your* talents, and *your* abilities to everyone else's. God, on the other hand, doesn't want you to compare yourself to anyone. He made *you* to be *you*!

One of the enemy's main objectives is to try to get you to strive to be *exactly* like other people because he knows you'll never be able to achieve this feat! His goal is to force you into frustration and to steal your joy by *attempting* to get you focused on impossible tasks—stuff that God doesn't even expect you to do!

He wants us sidetracked, and so often we give this moron his way. Instead of us paying close attention to the wonderful plans God has for each of us *individually*, we *unknowingly* allow the devil and his idiots to place the idea of jealousy into our minds. Spiritually, he will say things like,

"You want what they have. You want to know what they know. You want to look how they look. You want to do what they do."

SO BE CAREFUL! Jealousy, when not noticed or overlooked, will knock you off the path of your *own* God-given purpose! Let me be clear about something first: God's *will* for your life is for you to believe in Jesus as your Savior (see John 3:16, 6:29). Once you do this, you inherit all of the raw materials you need to build up an awesome life in Christ! Not to be confused with God's will, our individual purposes can be *anything* which is built on top of Christ in us *combined with* our individual likes, talents, skills, preferences, gifts, and abilities. Your purpose will thrive when you are simply being yourself.

God doesn't expect you to do anything you weren't made to do, so you shouldn't expect yourself to do stuff you weren't made to do either. Therefore, when you find yourself comparing yourself to others—stop—pause, pray, proceed. Comparison is a big red flag the Holy Spirit throws up, so pay attention.

The best thing you can do at that point is begin to thank God for who *you* are! Thank Him for who He has made *you* to be! By doing this you are planting seeds of confidence in *yourself*, while appreciating God's gifts in *others*. Remember: *Christians are not in competition with each other*. The devil sure wants us to think we are, but God does not. Instead, we are all individual parts of One Body! (See 1 Corinthians 12:12). Your arm doesn't attack your eye, and your leg doesn't attack your nose—a body appreciates itself, takes care of itself, and works *together*.

This is why if we are not constantly thanking God for who He has made us to be as individuals, eventually we will secretly and subconsciously resent the people whom the flesh and our enemy wants us to be like. A foot will never be a hand! So that foot should focus on running and jumping rather than grabbing or carrying! That foot should be proud to get that hand in the position to where it *can* grab and carry! We work best *together*! The gospel is spread in greater ways *together*!

So we gotta stand up against incorrect mindsets! We gotta tell the enemy, "Nope! I'm not going there! I like who God has made *me* to be. I like who God has made *them* to be. He made us *both* for a great purpose and He loves us the same! I appreciate what *they* do, and I'm proud of what *I* do. We both have different assignments from God, and we are on the same team!"

This is where your confidence in who you are begins, which is understanding just how special *you* are to your Creator, and just how special everyone *else is* to Him as well. God didn't *have* to make us—but He did! The odds of us even *being* here are uncountable! And *you*, my friend, *you* are a one of a kind…a cherished rarity…if I could *just* get you to realize that, you'd see what I mean! You were not just randomly thrown into the mix of humanity—YOU WERE PLANNED BY GOD HIMSELF!

So today, my friends, know this: Be yourself! Stop trying to be like other people, and be *you*! Yes, it's good to have role models and mentors but at the end of the day God has a special plan and a special purpose individually picked out for you *in* Christ. You are an integral part of His Body! Nobody else can do what you do *quite* like you, so be you, you, you, you, YOOOOOOOOOOU! My goodness, we *need* you to *be* you! Did I say be you?

**A prayer for you:** *Heavenly Father I want to thank you for making me, me. For years, I didn't like myself, and I constantly compared myself to others. But you've taught me just how special I really am in Christ. After being beat down for years, verbally, I began to believe the lies of people who told me there wasn't anything special about me. Thank you for teaching me the truth! Right now, I lift up all who are reading this, directly to you. For those who may be trying to be someone other than themselves, help them. Begin to reveal in their hearts that you WANTED them to be exactly like they are in Christ! Make sure they know that they are NO surprise to you! Teach them how NEEDED they are to COMPLETE the Body of Christ! In His name I pray, amen.*

# DAY 35

## How Do I Grow Spiritual Fruit?

*"But the fruit of the Spirit is love, joy, peace, patience, kindness, goodness, faithfulness, gentleness and self-control. Against such things there is no law."*

GALATIANS 5:22-23

I f you have access to any place that grows fruits, go there. It could be an orchard, a vineyard or a garden, but go stand by those trees, vines, or plants. When you get there, I want you to get right up next to them, stand completely still...and listen... ... ...What do you hear them doing?... NOTHING! You don't hear them "doing" anything, but yet they are still growing fruit! This is how *we* grow spiritual fruit! We don't *do* anything except be ourselves *in* Christ! That's it!

You've never heard an apple tree straining to grow apples. The apples just grow simply and easily as the apple tree *is* itself. You've never stood in a garden and heard strawberry plants grunting and groaning trying to squeeeeeeeeze out some more strawberries—the strawberries just grow. You've never heard a tomato plant say, "I'm going to try real hard to do my best to produce delicious tomatoes! This time I'm committed! This time I'm giving it my very best effort!"

No, you've never heard that before. First off, because tomato plants don't have mouths, but even if they did, their tomatoes would *still* simply grow *as* the tomato plant *is* itself—not by its rededicated, hyped-up efforts from a garden pep rally.

You've never heard a vineyard worker walking by their grapevines yelling at the grapes, "Grow! You *better* grow! If you *don't* grow, then you should feel terribly ashamed of yourself!" No. Fruit growth doesn't happen through pressure or guilt. Instead, those grapes simply grow *as* they are connected to the vine!

This is the exact same way Christians produce spiritual fruit! We are connected to Jesus, so we don't have to do anything except depend on our source and relax! Christ Himself explains this supernatural epiphany in John 15:5:

> *"I am the vine; you are the branches. If you abide in me and I in you, you will bear much fruit; apart from me you can do nothing."*

For the fearful Christians—the ones who have been taught wrong—the first thing they will notice from this verse is *"If* you abide in me." Because of sitting under fear-mongering teachings, they'll think, *"I better do my best to abide!"* No! We don't *do* our best to abide! That is the wrong application for this word! Abide simply means *live*, and as Christians we *already* live in Christ! (See Philippians 1:21, Colossians 3:3, Romans 6:6, Galatians 2:20).

So if we break this verse down for Christians—for actual believers in Jesus—we have no choice *but* to abide in Christ forever because we've been born *of* Christ! (See 1 John 3:9, John 3:16, Ephesians 1:5). It's impossible to be unborn! This is why only non-believers don't abide in Him. So don't be afraid of this verse any longer, it is a comforting verse for us.

As we allow Christ to live through us while simply being the branches, we will organically—and without any effort at all—begin to produce some stuff called "fruit of the Spirit." Whose spirit? God's Spirit! The Holy Spirit! Paul calls Him the *Spirit of Christ*! (See Romans 8:9). This is the *who*

who lives inside you, who won't ever go away! (See Hebrews 13:5, John 10:28, 2 Timothy 2:13).

In Galatians 5:22 and 23, there is a list of the fruit of the Spirit—whom *we* are connected to—and this fruit grows naturally *from* us as we rest in God's grace (see Hebrews 4:11). Our only "job" as the branches is to wake up each day and say, "Hi God. I love you. I appreciate you. I'm available for you." In turn, you will begin to see this fruit falling off of you, left, right, and center:

1. Love
2. Joy
3. Peace
4. Patience
5. Kindness
6. Goodness
7. Faithfulness
8. Gentleness
9. Self-control

When I first read this list of spiritual fruit I was like, "Well crap. That's gonna be hard." But there is nothing *hard* about growing fruit of the Spirit, whatsoever. If growing this fruit begins to *seem* hard, *that* should be an indicator of us trying to *force* fruit to grow. Remember, we don't force anything, we abide. We simply *be* ourselves—branches.

As I've come to know the grace of Jesus on deeper levels, He has revealed to me that all I have to do each day, as a Christian, is be myself. As a result of me doing this, *all* of these fruits have grown in my life—in bunches! Have all of my unfair situations changed? No. Have certain difficult people changed? No. As a matter of fact, some of the situations and people have gotten worse. However, my spiritual fruit growth isn't contingent on situations and people changing, but instead, it's based on *me* allowing Jesus to live *through* me.

And make no mistake, these fruits are first and foremost for me to enjoy! Sure, other people benefit from our spiritual fruit—that is a very important reason to grow it! But God personally cultivates the soil of our souls for *us* to get the most out of our own fruit. Eventually these spiritual fruits will fall off of you everywhere you go, and around everyone you meet! But a "fruit-salad of the Spirit" is something *you* can always enjoy yourself!

**A prayer for you:** *Heavenly Father thank you for all you do, and thank you for another day of life! Thank you for teaching me how to rest in your grace! This lesson of learning to rest, while simply being myself, has grown SO much of your spiritual fruit in my life! THANK YOU! Right now, I lift up all who are reading this, directly to you. For those who desperately want change in their lives, but may be forcing it, help them to relax. Help them to be as the branch on an apple tree, growing its fruit effortlessly and easily. They can do it, THROUGH you! In Jesus' name I pray, amen.*

# DAY 36

## Is Going to Church Really Necessary?

*"Don't stop meeting together with other believers."*

SEE HEBREWS 10:25

"I don't need church to love God!" This was something I said for a very long time, and yeah, it *is* true, I *don't* need church to love God. But Jesus has taught me that *He* likes church, so I should too. He's also taught me that church is not so much for *Him*, as it is for *me*. And even when it's not for me, my presence there could be beneficial to someone else. We are a body of Christ, and body parts need one another to function at their highest levels.

For so many years I didn't think I needed church, even as a Christian. I thought church was a place specifically reserved for the "perfect Christians," you know, the ones who never made any mistakes? The people whom God loved more than me because they did everything just right? Those who loaded up on brownie points with our Creator through all of their Scripture memorization, mission trips, fried chicken dinner fundraisers, and youth group organization skills?

Oh my goodness, the sin of my flesh *loathed* these people! I wasn't privileged enough to grow up in a good church—or in *any* church for that matter—so I had no clue how to "be" like these people. I didn't understand them, and they didn't understand me. I'm no preacher's kid and my family life growing up was destroyed by adultery, divorce, addictions, and foster homes. As a boy, my siblings and I were split up like real estate, eventually being abused by employees *of* the State. It was very bad. No kid should ever have to deal with what we went through. The system is really messed up, and it wasn't fair.

So when it came to acting perfect and going to church, I fell short. My unrenewed mindset was not adjusted to this type of environment. It was like trying to enter a junk-yard dog into a Prettiest Poodle Contest—this was not natural to my old way of thinking. My spirit? Yes. But my mind had yet to learn the facts of my spiritual perfection. My *true* identity in Christ, I did not yet believe in full, because of bad teaching. So the parts of me which were really messed up (my thinking—which turned into my actions and attitudes) had no clue what to do *in* church or *with* church. I stuck out like a turd in a punchbowl.

Eventually, because I couldn't seem to live up to their cliquey standards, I resented those who went to church and disregarded them all together. However, I still felt a calling to *go* to church. It was strange. I now know it was Jesus *in* my spirit, but back then, I didn't know it was Him.

I constantly thought to myself, *"How am I supposed to go to church with people who make me NOT want to be a Christian?"* Truth be told, even if I didn't *want* to be a Christian, I still was, and nothing could ever change that—not even me (see 2 Timothy 2:13). Jesus knew this so He kept saying, "Matthew, get up and go to church." My reply was usually of the effect, "But I don't *like* these people! They make me feel like dirt!"

I would continue to put up a fight, "I do *not* want to go hang out with them, much less be *taught* by them!" Jesus replied, "Trust me. Just keep going. I'm trying to teach you how to handle this, but I need you *in* church."

Succumb to His relentlessness, I gave in, "Fine. I'll go."

As my relationship with Jesus grew deeper, He soon taught me that *He* loves everyone—even the legalistic people who have their theology off kilter by making a geographical location the end-all be-all. The whole reason

He was trying to get me to *keep* going to church with difficult people was to teach me how to show them grace!

This also resulted in Him revealing something else in my spirit: the people whom I *thought* were perfect in word and deed—or better than me—were not! Instead, Christ exposed the graceful truth that we are all exactly the same! We *all* have perfect spirits because of our faith in Him! HE REVEALED WE ARE EQUAL IN HIS EYES! (See Galatians 3:28, Colossians 3:11).

Christ continued to knock off the rough edges in my thinking as I continued to go to church. Even when the pastor's message didn't match up with my spirit, God Himself kept giving me lesson after lesson. Mainly, He was grooming me on how to *give* legalistic people grace— the very thing they withheld from me. At first, it felt as if I was being force-fed shards of glass, "*Ouch! Ouch! OUCH! I don't know if I can do this, but I will!*"

The reality was, I previously didn't like church because I had been hurt so badly by people *in* the church. So many of them tried to use the gospel to manipulate me and cause *fear* in me, that I didn't even want to shake their hands. *I* wanted to knock them upside their heads with a heavy frying-pan—*ahem*—my old, unrenewed thinking wanted to do this, of course, not *me*. That's not the behavior of a perfect, holy, blameless saint, a heaven-ready spirit (see Colossians 1:22, Romans 8:9).

And I'm not saying you need to make a law out of going to church by forcing yourself into a place where the unconditional love of Jesus is not present. No, not at all. *Leave* if that's how it is, and don't feel guilty or con-demned about it because you're not! (See Romans 8:1). What I *am* saying is, ask God to send you to the church you *should* be at. One that is grace-focused, Christ-loving, real, understanding, truthful, hopeful, empower-ing, and motivating. They *are* out there!

To find this place—either physically or online—simply pray and ask God to show you where it's at, and don't give up! You have 52 chances a year to find the right church!

And most of all, *while* you are searching, don't feel guilty *about* searching. Your identity is not in a building but in Christ! So be sure to enjoy your life in the process! The devil wants you to feel terrible about not being settled in a church, don't give that idiot his way! Tell him to shut up! Sometimes Jesus talked back to the devil, so occasionally we should too!

So today, my friends, know this: Is going to church *really* necessary? No. Anyone can go to church, even non-believers. *Being* the church is necessary. God's *grace* is necessary. Now, because *you* are the church and God's grace flows throughout *your* being—go to church! That place needs your grace and presence!

**A prayer for you:** *God, I want to thank you for making all of us the Church. What a great idea! Thank you for destroying the need to enter a physical building to be in your presence! Right now, I lift up all who are reading this, directly to you. So many of them have been hurt by people in church, today I speak healing and forgiveness over their minds and lives! Help them begin to understand we are all constantly growing in the knowledge of your grace! Teach them to GIVE your grace away to those who don't deserve it because that's exactly what grace is! In Jesus' name, amen.*

# DAY 37

## THE TRUTH ABOUT GOD'S LAWS

*"You have become obedient from the heart."*

*SEE ROMANS 6:17*

I f I told you to *not* think about a blue sports car, what would you think about? You'd be thinking about which shade of blue it is, as well as the model. You can't *not* think about something someone tells you to *not* think about. It's impossible.

The apostle Paul knew this, and for that very reason he was adamant about getting our minds *off* of laws and *on* to Jesus. He told the Romans, "Apart from the Law God's righteousness has been made known. The righteousness we now have comes through faith in Christ to <u>all who believe</u>" (see Romans 3:21-22).

*Apart* from the Law we are right with God, THIS IS FOR ALL WHO BELIEVE!

Now, for the person who finds their identity in their behavior, at first glance of this statement they will aggressively spout off, "That's a lie! Even the devil and his demons believe! Don't be deceived! There is more to it than *just* believing!" To that, I would say, "Have you ever tried decaffeinated coffee?" I'm kidding. I would *think* that, but wouldn't say it. Instead,

I'd reply, "Of course the devil and his demons believe. They know full well the truth of the gospel but they are already damned to hell. We aren't. It's too late for them, but *we* still have a chance to be saved."

The next rebuttal a grace-confused person will fire toward someone like me, is something that Jesus said, "I have not come to abolish the Law but to fulfill it" (see Matthew 5:17). My response would be a one-two counter:

1. **Yes, Jesus not only fulfilled the Law, but He did so by pointing out how much of a complete failure everyone is who *tries* to obey it**. Then, He upped the ante! He lifted up the bar of Law to its highest notch and said, "*Now* let's see how you do! If you want to live by the Law, here it is!": "Be perfect like God is perfect." "Sell everything." "Loan your money to everyone who asks to borrow." "If someone hits you in the face, turn and let them hit you on the other side of your face." "If any part of your body causes you to sin, amputate it." (See Matthew 5:29-30,39,42,48, 19:21). *That* is Law. So do we want Law or Him?

2. **Jesus completed the Law *in* Himself at the Cross**. Before the New Covenant was established through Christ, the annual Day of Atonement allowed the Jews to be forgiven of their sins through the blood of animals (see Leviticus 23:27, Hebrews 9:22). On this particular day, they would receive an entire *year* of forgiveness, none of this neurotic "daily" forgiveness stuff. By way of bloody animal sacrifices, their sins were "covered" for another year—never taken away, but covered, or *atoned* for. Jesus, on the other hand, was the *final* sacrifice for sin. This is why the author of Hebrews said, "If we deliberately keep on sinning after receiving the knowledge of the truth, there is no more sacrifice for sins left," as in, animal blood (see Hebrews 10:26). This verse, which is used a lot by the grace-confused Christians to create fear in *other* Christians, was written to the unbelieving Jews who kept trying to get forgiveness through animal blood *after* hearing the gospel. This verse is not applicable to Christians who sin (just imagine if that were true).

The Law *requires* the shedding of blood in order to get forgiveness (Hebrews 9:22). It does not require repeated *asking* or repeated *repenting* of incorrect attitudes and actions. BLOOD FORGIVES, NOTHING ELSE. This is why when Jesus shed *His* sinless blood, He fulfilled this law! Further, Jesus didn't simply "cover" our sins—like the animals—He banished them forever! Gone! Past, present, and *future* sins! (See 1 Peter 2:24, Hebrews 8:12, 10:10, John 1:29). This is one of the reasons why He yelled out, "IT IS FINISHED!" as He completed this law and *became* the final sacrifice for sin! (See John 19:30).

Paul reiterated this fact, that Jesus fulfilled the Law on the Cross:

> *"Christ has already accomplished the purpose for which*
> *the Law was given. As a result, all who believe in him*
> *are made right with God" (Romans 10:4).*

Friends, the Law never did anything for anyone *except* point out their need for a deep cleaning! Righteousness was never awarded to anyone who "obeyed" the Law! (See Romans 3:20). Rightness with God has *always* been based on faith, even *before* the Law was given! (See Romans 4:19-22).

On this side of the Cross we no longer have the option of having our sins covered up—even *if* we have faith in God alone (without Jesus). He *now* requires our sins to be removed *through* Jesus. So in order to tap into this New Covenant, faith in Christ's perfect blood is what God requires—not sin *covering*, but sin *removal*. This is the same God of the *Old* Covenant, but He has put the old agreement with humanity on the shelf marked "obsolete" and replaced it with a *New* Covenant! One that is much better! (see Hebrews 8:13).

The basis of the New Covenant is understanding that only Jesus has the ability to cleanse us, and He does this *once* (see Hebrews 10:10), not year after year, or day after day. And God, in His great love for us, has made access to spiritual perfection *through* Christ the most simple way possible:

*by grace through faith* (see Ephesians 2:8-9). Grace is simply getting something good you didn't earn, and it's also something you can't *work for* to keep or sustain. Paul spells this out:

> *"And if by grace, then it cannot be based on works; if it were, grace would no longer be grace" (Romans 11:6).*

Friend, righteousness with our Creator has always been based on faith alone. The Law was given so that faith alone would *increase*. Why would I say that? Because if *sin* increases through Law observance (see Romans 5:20), then faith *alone* increases too. This is because faith has *always* been what pleases God! (See Hebrews 11:6). So the Law was brought in so that we could please God even more *by* faith!

So what is faith? BELIEF! Once we *believe* in the event of Christ's sacrifice as true for our sin, we become sinless in our spirits too! Our old spirit dies *with* Christ, it gets buried with Him, and then it shoots up out of the grave, resurrected as well—even while still *in* these bodies! (See Romans 6:6, 2 Corinthians 5:17).

This happens by hearing the gospel with faith! (See Galatians 3:2). You might not have "felt" anything when this happened—or you might have (salvation isn't based on feelings, but a fact of faith)—but either way, your new spiritual birth is real and final! This is why Jesus told Nicodemus, "You must be born again" (see John 3:7). The Holy Spirit then moves *in* to us, makes His home in us, and He will never move out! (See John 14:23, 2 Timothy 2:13). No matter what the flesh does or doesn't do, or what our unrenewed mindsets *think*, God is staying inside us forever! That's the gospel! His promise to us!

As this relationship grows, He works together with us, constantly teaching us new things about Himself (see John 14:26, Philippians 2:13). He reveals in our hearts what He likes and dislikes, what He expects and doesn't expect (see 1 Corinthians 2:10). He teaches us His loving character (Galatians 5:22-23). And where is this all coming from? OUR *NEW* HEARTS! HEARTS THAT GOD CAN TRUST!

Paul wanted to make sure the Romans understood that their new hearts were *good* by telling them they can actually *trust* themselves (see Romans 6:17). We are *not* in a battle with ourselves! We have *good* selves! We are at battle with the power of sin—the force, not the verbs—our old, stinking thinking, and the enemy, but *not* ourselves! We can trust ourselves because God lives in our hearts! This is why we are no longer led by *any* law or commandment but instead by God's Spirit *in* us! We don't *need* them! We've got God! (See Romans 7:6).

"Yeah right Matt, you gotta have the WORD! How are we supposed to know what God expects from us without His WORD! And if you ain't got the King James Bible, then you ain't got the *real* Word!"

Well I wonder what the early Christians did before they ever had a Bible, not to mention 70% of them were illiterate. I also wonder how they ever made it through their day without access to the King James Version? *Who* could possibly make sure they understood God? Oh, I don't know... maybe His *Spirit*?!

Yes, we are fortunate to have the Bible, I *love* the Bible. Jesus was Jewish, so we are privileged to know the history of His bloodline *through* the Bible. All the Psalms and Proverbs, detailed stories of Christ's life, the "acts" of the apostles after He ascended, as well as the amazing Spirit-breathed New Testament epistles; we are very blessed to have so much information from God on paper, in a nice, tidy book.

However, the truth of the matter is when we try to make a law out of the Bible in itself, we *must* remember that the Bible wasn't even compiled until 400 years *after* Christ. And for the King James fanatics, *that* version wasn't written until 1200 years after that! This is why we must refocus on God *in* us, not simply words on some pages.

The Holy Spirit wants to teach us that He is the author *behind* the Bible! He is so much bigger than a book! Although the canonized Scriptures are infallible, it is *still* God's Spirit who ultimately counsels us into all wisdom and peace. So Christian, don't simply let a book guide you each day, let your *heart* guide you each day—your heart is good!

I'll address one last attack which I receive quite often, "Matt, you're a liar! Our hearts are wicked!" Friend, no, they're not. They *used* to be wicked before we believed, but now they are perfect just like God is perfect (see Colossians 1:22, Romans 6:6). The Prophet Ezekiel foresaw this amazing feat which God would perform for New Covenant believers, "I will give you a new heart and put a new spirit in you; I will remove from you your heart of stone and give you a heart of flesh" (Ezekiel 36:26).

Ezekiel knew that God would give us a *soft* heart by coming to live *in* our hearts. The writer of Hebrews builds on this same truth, "This is the covenant I will establish with the people of Israel after that time, I will put my laws in their minds and write them on their hearts. I will be their God, and they will be my people" (Hebrews 10:16).

God's *laws*, as in "what He wants and doesn't want"—NOT LAW—as in the Law of Moses, which was a total of 613 moral laws, dietary laws, wardrobe laws, ceremonial laws, and more. *God's laws* is what's written on our hearts—His very own desires! Everything He wants us to know He has personally placed *in* us from the very moment we first believed! Yes, we are growing in His knowledge day by day (see Philippians 1:6), but as *of* today, you really *do* want what God wants! This is how He can always trust us to make the right choices, which is through our perfect hearts! Hearts which are not bound by any law but have been set free in Christ! (See Galatians 5:1). Hearts which are indwelt by God Himself! So Christian, live from your heart! *Always* live from your heart! This is the only law God wants you to live by!

**A prayer for you:** *Heavenly Father, I want you to know how grateful I am for you. Sometimes I forget just how good you are to me! Thank you so much for making your home in my heart forever. Right now, I lift up all who are reading this, directly to you. For those who have been religiously abused with rules, commands, and laws, help them. Help them to grow in the confidence which is your grace. Help them to know you deeper and deeper each day as you guide them by your Spirit THROUGH their hearts. In Jesus' name I pray, amen.*

# DAY 38

## DEMONS ARE REAL

*"The thief (Satan) comes only to steal and kill
and destroy; I have come that they may have
life, and have it to the full." ~Jesus*

*JOHN 10:10*

Someone messaged me a while back, telling me how they were praying for me, which I always appreciate. They also said when they read their Bible they wake up in the morning with scratch marks across their body—scratch marks that look like actual *claw* marks.

Now, first of all, as a *Christian*, I want to be perfectly clear that neither the enemy nor his demons can touch you (see 1 John 5:18). The reason why they *can't* touch you is because *you* are possessed by Christ, literally and figuratively (see Galatians 2:20, Colossians 3:3, 1 Corinthians 6:19). He will never share your body with any demonic spirit. Can demons pester you? Can they hound you day and night? Absolutely. But *touch* you? No way.

So I was left with two situations in regard to the message I received:

1. This person is not a Christian, but might think that by reading the Bible they are.
2. This person *is* a Christian, but they are mistaken as to where or what these scratches are coming from.

Either way, I'm not the judge of this, only God is. Hindsight is 20/20, so I *should* have asked them, "Has there ever been a time in your life where you believed Jesus forgave you of your sins?" But I didn't. Instead, I suggested that they walk throughout their house and verbally bind any demonic force, telling them to *"Get out,* in the name of Jesus." Christ gives us this right! He says so in Luke 10:19:

*"I have given you authority…to overcome the power of the enemy."*

Although, yes, I should have asked them if they believed in Jesus from the get-go, what I said was still a good thing to say. But so often we *assume* that people are Christian, yet, they're really not. Instead of being a Christian, they simply know a bunch of Christian stuff—they could even be really nice people. But anyway.

I also recommended that if they had any open "spiritual windows" in their home, such as pornography, drugs, alcohol (if you're addicted to it), anything witchcraft, any music with words that glorify hate, greed, or immorality, any activity they do on a regular basis that goes against God's Spirit (see Galatians 5 )—*or* if they watch stuff on their TV and internet all the time, which is anti-gospel—get rid of it! Stop listening to it, stop doing it, and stop watching it.

I'm not saying shut yourself off from the world, I'm saying *pay attention.* We are holy, blameless, heaven-ready children of God (see Colossians 1:22, Ephesians 1:5), the enemy hates us even worse than non-believers. Therefore, he hits us *harder* with the things of this world in an attempt to shipwreck our faith. He can't destroy our faith, that would be impossible (see Hebrews 7:25, 2 Timothy 2:13). But he sure can get us stuck on a deserted island. Thankfully, even when we are *on* that island, Christ is there with us.

The apostle Peter said, "Stay alert! Watch out for your great enemy, the devil. He prowls around like a roaring lion, looking for someone to devour" (1 Peter 5:8). So all of the stuff *around* us which doesn't jive with our spiritual perfection *invites* spiritual forces that have no business being in our midst.

Certain things we allow in our lives, which are not of God, become a dinner-bell for packs of demonic wolves. They *love* the stuff that God *hates*. So when we are not conscious of these things, *we too* become just like a baby antelope with a broken leg on the Serengeti—making ourselves easy pickings to the dark part of the spiritual realm. For Christians, no demon can *enter* us—because Christ is there—but still, they can make our lives miserable if we allow it.

They can oppress us from the outside and use scare tactics and lies in our minds. This is why Paul said:

> *"Whatever is true, whatever is noble, whatever is right, whatever is pure, whatever is lovely, whatever is admirable—if anything is excellent or praiseworthy—think about such things" (see Philippians 4:8).*

So I didn't hear anything back from this person who messaged me about the scratches on their body, I thought no more about it. Then, not too long afterwards I received *another* message from them with actual *pictures* of this person's torso, and it was all clawed-up!

Again, knowing what I know now, I should have said, "Are you *sure* you've invited Jesus into your heart as your Savior?" The hairs on my neck stood up as I viewed the pictures. It literally looked as if someone *slowly* and meticulously scratched this person with long nails. They were "in a row" like fingers, and this happened while they were asleep!

Before I continue, let me make something perfectly clear: I'm not afraid of this by any stretch of the imagination, but when an event like this actually happens...it's *not* normal. It's not your everyday Christian experience! This is a moment when the spiritual world *physically* interacts with us! It's jarring!

Something like this smacks you in the face and says, "HEY! LOOK! GET OFF YOUR COUCH! THERE IS A BATTLE GOING ON! *PLEASE!* DO SOMETHING!"

All throughout the Bible demons have physical power over non-believers, so we can expect the same thing to happen today. In the book of Acts, Chapter 19, there is an account of some people calling on the name of Jesus to cast out a demon, but the demon fights back and says, "I know Jesus, and I know Paul, but I don't know who you are." The demon then leapt on them, overpowered them, and the Bible says they "fled out of the house naked and wounded"! (See Acts 19:13-16).

Obviously these weren't Christians but instead just religious people who never really *knew* Christ (see Matthew 7:22-23). I say that because Jesus dominated demons in the Bible! He would squint His eyes at them and say, "Shut up!" They *always* cowered at Him, and they *always* begged for mercy! (See Luke 10:19, Mark 1:23-25, 4:24, 5:12).

Are *you* a Christian? If you are, then guess what? Christ lives in you! Yep! If you've believed in Jesus for His forgiveness, and accepted it by grace through faith, He is now supernaturally infused *with* you! You and Him are one! (Ephesians 2:8-9, 1 Corinthians 6:17).

You have the same power of Christ *because* of your faith in Him! HOW AWESOME IS THAT?! The power of God in YOU?! THIS IS SPECTACULAR NEWS!!!

For the person who sent me the pictures of what this demon had done to them, they have a choice to make: STAND UP TO THE DARKNESS AND KEEP PUSHING FORWARD THROUGH CHRIST, or back down and shrink away in fear. But get this—this is gonna blow your mind: They said they had stopped reading their Bible because they got busy, but had *started* reading it again that very night. This is *when* the scratches on their stomach and sides came back!

This demon does *not* want them reading God's Word! DO YOU HEAR ME?! Demonic forces don't want *you* reading it either! They do *not* want you to know the truth of Christ's power within you! This is why we must fight back! No matter how weak we might *think* we are, a single flame coming from within us can start an entire wildfire for Christ! Don't cover up your flame any longer! Put it up *high* for all the world to see! Your flame is *Jesus*!

So today, my friends, know this: The forces of hell perk up when you begin to understand *who* you really are in Christ. Once you are *in* Him, they can no longer touch you. All they can do is shiver at the very thought of you. Remember, *they* are weak and *you* are strong! So look forward, scowl, and fight back!

**A prayer for you:** *Good morning Lord! Today, I want to thank you for my excellent health, my job, my home, my family, and for the life you've given me. I appreciate everything you've done! Right now, I lift up all who are reading this, directly to you. Help them begin to recognize when the enemy and his little doofuses are causing them problems. Your Word says the entire reason Jesus came to earth was to destroy the work of the devil, and we believe that! You've given us that very same power by making your home in us! WE ARE STRONG! WE ARE CONFIDENT! WE ARE WELL-ABLE TO FACE ANYONE OR ANYTHING— through Him! In Jesus' mighty name I pray, Amen.*

# DAY 39

## How to Combat Legalistic Christians

*"You who are trying to be justified by law have been
alienated from Christ; you have fallen away from grace."*

*See Galatians 5:4*

The short answer to the title of this devotional is: *with love.* As
Christians, we combat all things and all people in this world with
love—including those who are religiously overbearing and confused about
God's grace.

Compared to the early church, we Christians in the 21st century have
it pretty good. The first century Christians faced legalistic people on levels
unlike we've *never* seen before. But still, Peter, even in the midst of such
persecution advises the distressed original believers, "Always be prepared
to give an answer to everyone who asks you to give the reason for the hope
that you have. But do this with gentleness and respect" (see 1 Peter 3:15).

Remember, the legalistic Christians have simply been taught wrong.
So *we* must show them the authentic love of Jesus so that *they'll* want it
too. Do *not* attack them when they attack you. Please, learn from my mistakes, fighting fire with fire won't work. Don't take the bait, don't retaliate.
Instead, simply allow the Holy Spirit to guide you in your battles with

them. You'll know that you are letting Him lead you because you will display the fruit of the Spirit even in the midst of your most strenuous verbal circumstances (see Galatians 5:22-23).

I'm *not* saying we must overlook someone's hate and disrespect to the point of suffering severe turmoil. But what I *am* saying is to *think* of them with love. By having the Holy Spirit indwell us, we have the same mind as Christ (see 1 Corinthians 2:16). So even when we encounter those who twist the gospel into something it's not, we must allow God's Spirit *in* us to apply grace *to* them. This is not easy, especially when we've experienced traumatic furry in our lives from someone who claims to be representing Jesus. However, *through* Jesus, we can do this! (See Philippians 4:13).

When the Holy Spirit began to teach me this, that I can actually tap into *His* strength to *think* of legalists with love, it was as if the release valve on a boiling pressure-cooker in my soul had just been pressed. It was *such* a relief to finally understand that I don't have to be frustrated, bitter, or resentful toward those who think that Jesus' *legalistic* teachings are for Christians. For example, the Sermon on the Mount was *not* a "do your best" lesson for believers.

This particular sermon given by Jesus is a teaching that the conditional-grace Christians *assume* is meant for all believers in Christ. It's not—most of it anyway—when it's read in full context. The idea of, "Give it your best shot and God will grade you on a curve!" is not at all what Jesus was saying. This is why we must keep in mind that Jesus wasn't *always* preaching to believers. He also had a lot of hypocritical, self-righteous, religious people following Him around too. So His audiences needed to *also* hear the impossibility of trying to live by the old Jewish laws and commandments.

For the Jews who thought their wonderful behavior was creating them righteousness with God, Christ began to hammer nails into their self-made coffins of legalism. He wanted to be perfectly clear. Paul penned His message: *the Law kills and only Christ's Spirit can give life* (see 2 Corinthians 3:6).

So in Matthew, chapter five, what starts out as a sweet teaching for Christians, takes a *hard* left in verse 17. Jesus shifts His attention to the Law and the Prophets by pointing out how much of a failure the Jews are who *think* they are doing a swell job of following them. He lays them down in their pine boxes, puts the lid on, and begins to hammer away, one nail after the other. He then starts to throw dirt on *top* of their coffins by letting them know the real standards of the Law:

"If you set aside one *little* command, you will be the least in God's Kingdom."

"You've been taught not to murder, but I say, even if you are angry with someone, it's the same as killing them."

"If you do so much as call someone '*a fool*,' you are going to hell."

"If you are mad at your brother or sister, God doesn't even *want* your animal sacrifice."

"The Law says, 'Don't commit adultery,' but I say, even if you lust after someone, your *thinking* of sex with them is exactly the same."

"If your eye causes you to sin—pluck it out! If your hand makes you stumble—cut it off!"

"You're not allowed to divorce anyone unless they cheat on you, and if you do, then you will be branded as an adulterer for the rest of your life!"

"If someone punches you in the face, turn your cheek and let them punch you again!"

"If anyone wants *anything* from you, give it to them!"

"Do everything that everyone tells you to do without complaining!"

"Loan *all* of your money to *everyone* who asks! And you *better* not expect it to be paid back!"

*Nail* after *nail* after *nail*! As they heard this, the religious people had no other option except to do one of three things.

1. Continue their lives as hypocrites, ignoring the impossibility of living by the Law.
2. Try harder to do all of the new stuff Jesus just told them to do.

3. Realize that the days of living by the Law are over, and that faith in the Messiah is all that is left.

For the Jews who chose number one, they plotted against Jesus and eventually had Him killed. For number two, like today's Christians who think they are actually doing this stuff, they started to get mad at those who weren't "good like them." They began to cover up and hide their failures as they compared how obedient *they* were, to how obedient others were. And for number three, they found freedom in Christ.

For the people who chose wisely, they realized Jesus really *did* "come to give them rest for their souls" (see Matthew 11:28). They began to understand His yoke really *is* easy and His burden, light (see Matthew 11:29-30). These are the believers who stepped onto the narrow path of grace, walked through the gate of faith, and began to *enjoy* the lush pastures which *is* a loving relationship with Jesus (see Matthew 7:13-14, John 10:9).

But for me to understand these truths, the Holy Spirit began to teach me something which revolutionized my weak faith: *If any part of Jesus' teachings looked like legalism, it was, so that part does not apply to Christians.*

Another paramount fact which must be pointed out to the grace-confused person is this: *Are you Jewish?* If not, then you are already out of the loop in regard to following Jewish laws or commandments. You don't even have the *right* to be *able* to follow any of that stuff. You're a gentile, an outsider, you are disqualified. Only faith in Christ brings us *in* to God's Family—*not* old Jewish law observance (see Galatians 3:28, Ephesians 1:11).

This should narrow the field greatly. But let's just move forward and say they *are* Jewish. All we need to do is go to a book in the Bible which was exclusively written to Jews, *Hebrews*. So what was the Jews' main sin? What is nearly the *entire* book of Hebrews written about? What was the very thing the Jews *had* to change in order to be acceptable to God?... UNBELIEF IN CHRIST AS THE MESSIAH!

*This* is what they had to repent of—not repentance of incorrect attitudes and actions, but repentance of the *only* unforgivable sin: *rejecting God's*

*Spirit through faith in Jesus!* THEY HAD TO REPENT OF UNBELIEF! Only this can save!

The author of Hebrews, who is more than likely Paul, was a self-proclaimed "best Law-abiding Jew ever" (see Philippians 3). However, he builds his case from the beginning by telling the Jews how the Old Covenant is now obsolete because the *New* Covenant is so much better! This proves that even God's original chosen people to carry His Oracles *they too* must drop all laws and place their faith in Jesus! There is no other way!

But for a moment, let me digress even further into living the life of Law. Let's say you're actually allowed to follow the moral, ceremonial, dietary, and wardrobe laws—all 613 of them, not just 10—have at it. BUT—if you choose to live by the Law given to the people group of Israel by Moses, and you fail at just *one*, you are guilty of failing at *all* of them. Observing Mosaic Law is an all-or-nothing proposition. It's not a buffet line, picking what we like and leaving the rest. Paul tells the Christians in Galatia this very thing as they foolishly began to add Law in with the gospel:

> *For all who rely on the works of the law are under a curse, as it is written: "Cursed is everyone who does not <u>continue to do everything</u> written in the Book of the Law" (Galatians 3:10)*

James, the half-brother of Jesus, a person who didn't believe Jesus was the Messiah until after He rose from the dead, he said the same thing:

> *"For whoever keeps the whole law and yet stumbles at just one point is guilty of breaking all of it" (James 2:10)*

Further, if someone is bold enough to try to follow all 613 commands, and they fail at one of them, blood must be shed. God *only* forgives sin through blood—not through asking, and not through repenting until your repenter falls off. The writer of Hebrews makes this clear:

*"In fact, the Law requires that nearly everything be
cleansed with blood, and without the shedding of blood
there is no forgiveness" (Hebrews: 9:22).*

So the next time a Law-focused Christian goes to Red Lobster to have a nice meal, afterwards, they better hurry off to the closest livestock market and pick up a goat to kill. Jewish law says they're not allowed to eat shellfish, this is one of the 613 (see Leviticus 11). Now, they can either do *that*, or they can tap into the finished work of *Jesus'* blood which was shed at the Cross *for* them.

For the Christian who finds their identity in their behavior, they will fire back at me, "Oh Matt, you think you're such a smart guy, but you're not! That's just the *ceremonial* law, every *real* Christian already knows we don't have to slaughter animals any longer. So yeah, we *are* dead to ceremonial law. But we are *not* dead to the *moral* law! We need morals to be enforced by laws!"

Friend, the apostle Paul would disagree, as he struggled greatly with jealousy—a moral law (see Romans 7). So are we now cherry-picking moral laws too? NO WAY! Paul, in his battle with the sin of jealousy (one of the Ten Commandments) said that the only way to truly enjoy the life Jesus died to give us, is to realize we are not under *any* code which legislates behaviors and attitudes:

*"For the law always brings punishment on those who
try to obey it. The only way to avoid breaking the law
is to have no law to break!" (Romans 4:15)*

So today, my friends, know this: God doesn't need written laws or commandments to teach us *anything* any longer! He now teaches us everything *by* His Spirit! (See Romans 7:6). Jesus has given us *new* commandments to live by—commandments which are not burdensome! Commandments we don't need to *read* to know, or be *told* to know, but we know because God lives in our hearts! These new commandments are: *believe and love!* (See John 13:34-35, 1 John 5:3, Galatians

5:6). When we live by these commandments, we finally become free, and we *stay* free!

*"So Christ has truly set us free. Now make sure that you stay free, and don't get tied up again in slavery to the law" (Galatians 5:1).*

**A prayer for you:** *Good morning, Lord. Thank you for revealing the truth to me about your laws and commandments. Thank you for giving us new commandments which are much better! We have it so good on this side of the Cross! Right now, I lift up all who are reading this, directly to you. For those who have been lied to about what Christ has really done for them, begin to open up their minds to the truth. I rebuke any legalistic, religious spirit who pesters them regularly—and renew old mindsets today! Show them the proper way, which is Jesus—JUST JESUS! In His name I pray. Amen.*

# DAY 40

## WHY SHOULD I PRAY?

*"And pray in the Spirit on all occasions with*
*all kinds of prayers and requests."*

SEE EPHESIANS 6:18

Before I began to truly understand God's grace, I always felt obligated to pray. I had the incorrect mindset of, "I *have* to pray or God will be very upset with me." Because of terrible teaching, my prayer life was chained down with legalism as I had created time slots in which my prayer sessions *had* to fit into:

1. Before bed.
2. First thing in the morning.
3. Before every meal.

And if I forgot, I would feel extremely guilty and shameful. Ha! I can chuckle at this now because it's *so* stupid! My old unrenewed mindset about prayer had made a *law* out of praying! Also, I had made God out to be a terrible Father, as if He was either going to be furious with me or give me the silent treatment if I didn't pray!

Just *imagine* if I did that to my daughter! If Grace walked up to me and asked for something she needed or wanted, and I immediately barked at her, "NO WAY! You ain't getting *nothing* from me until I see you've come to talk to me a minimum of five times a day! Until then, you are out of luck! Get out of here!" Then I turned around and ignored her.

You'd think I'd lost my mind! This is called *mental* abuse! Grace-confused Christians *teach* mental abuse and it's not okay! God does *not* mentally abuse us! What a wacko idea of "I'm not taking care of my daughter unless she talks to me regularly." Friend, God is not like that either. We must stop making laws out of simply talking to Dad.

Jesus poked at the religious people of His day for legislating their prayers (see Matthew 6:5-8). If you look at how Christ prayed, He just, *prayed*. He talked to His Father. There was no forcefulness in His prayers *unless* He was trying to set up the self-righteous people by teaching them how legalistic prayers will leave them far *from* God (see Matthew 6:9-14).

Sometimes Jesus prayed in front of people and sometimes He didn't. He never stopped to think, *"Should I pray?"* No, He just prayed. Sometimes He even went off in private to pray alone (see Luke 5:16). For me, once I began to understand Christ's example of prayer, the cogs started to turn in my mind toward grace. But first, I had to unlearn the lies of, "I'll be *more* holy if I pray more," or "God will love me more if I pray *better*," or "God will show me more *favor* due to my scheduled prayer life."

In *regard* to my so-called prayer life, it was so jacked up, sometimes I'd pop up out of bed in the middle of the night, having panic attacks because I forgot to pray. *"God forgive me!"* Then I'd say my prayers, *"Whew…almost ticked off God there. Glad I remembered. Thank you God for reminding me."*

What I didn't know was that it wasn't *God* who was reminding me to freak out and pray. It wasn't *God* who was trying to legislate our relationship through forceful, repeated begging. It was my unrenewed *stinking thinking*—my mindset. I WAS TAUGHT WRONG. TERRIBLE EXAMPLES WERE SET FOR ME THROUGH LEGALISTIC PEOPLE, AS WELL AS THROUGH WELL-*MEANING* CHRISTIANS WHO WERE TAUGHT WRONG TOO.

I was also taught the lie that God won't even *hear* my prayers because, "You got sin in your life, boy!" as if He sticks His fingers in His ears, saying, "La la la la laaaaaaaaaaa," ignoring the sacrifice Jesus made because *I* still make mistakes. This was coming from the same people who taught me that God will only bless me with money if I give at least ten *percent* of my money to them.

To top it off, they'd say, "Oh, but that's just the tithe, you're simply giving *back* to God what God has loaned to you. Your tithe doesn't even impress God! If you *really* want to be blessed financially, you'll give *above* the tithe, with an offering! Only then will God open up the floodgates of heaven and pour out a blessing in which you can't handle!" GARBAGE!

Again, imagine if I said to Grace, "Now baby, I'm going to give you this twenty dollars for the movies, but you need to give me ten percent of this money *back*, or I'm not giving you dinner tomorrow." MENTAL ABUSE! These were the same hypocrites who said God will only bless my life if I pray *harder*! No wonder my prayer life sucked!

The truth is, there is no wrong *way* to pray or wrong *time* to pray. Once we begin to understand God's unconditional love for us we even start to realize He isn't so much paying attention to our *words* or length of prayers, as He is listening to our hearts. "What is it my child *really* needs from me?" This is how God thinks of you as you pray, which is in a *loving* way.

The Holy Spirit was trying to teach me this but it would have been easier for Him to lasso a cheetah. Yes, I know He's God, He can do anything, but because of hearing sermons where the preacher had no self-control as he legislated—not only prayer—but tithing and church attendance, I was *trained* to freak out about such stuff. There is a lot to unlearn as Christians.

The truth about the gospel is that there is no law in any New Testament epistle which states a Christian must pray a certain amount of time each day, or tithe, or attend *any* actual building—only when the gospel is twisted are laws created.

As a result of today's Christians mixing in the Old Covenant with the New Covenant, modern-day church laws have grown in our congregations like ugly warts. In the first century, the Galatian Christians tried to do this very same thing and Paul called them fools (see Galatians 3:3). So what makes us any different?

Because of legislating prayer in my own mind, the Holy Spirit kept trying to say, "Hey, Matthew, relax. Just talk to me." But no! Off my mind would race into the wrong direction *again* with lighting speed! "Prayer can't be that easy! Bye!" To that, He'd reply, "But it is. Come back. Sit down. Let's have a conversation."

My prayer thoughts were *so* warped, He was working overtime in order to make things simple. "Matt, it's *okay* you've not prayed today. I'm still here. I love you. I'm not staying with you based on your amazing prayers, but because I *live* here now. Also, try to remember that when you pray, you don't have to keep giving me the same exact list each time. Just talk to me. I'm here for you."

Friend, when you pray all you're doing is having a one-on-one conversation with your Creator. It's not a trade-off system, a check-list or a duty, it's just talking to Dad. No matter what you say or don't say, or how often you say it, He will always be your Dad, He will always be available to talk, and He will always do what's best for you *and* humanity as a whole.

Soon enough, as my mindset began to transform, I started to realize the reward I was getting from praying was simply growing in trust with God. As the years went by, I figured out that even if He decides to *not* give me what I'm asking Him for, I can rest assured that I'm better off *not* getting it at that particular time, or ever. But no matter what, I still trust Him.

By growing in the knowledge of God's grace, He helped me whittle down my long, pitiful prayers, to mostly sporadic thoughts and short sentences directed at Him all throughout my day. You know, how we mostly talk to *people*—which is quickly and simply?

Yes, of course, sometimes we sit down at a meal or have a cup of coffee with someone for longer conversations, but most of our *human* communications are based on quick chats or low amounts of sentences. This is the same type of relationship God longs to have with *you*—a normal one, not a religious one.

God has no interest in a relationship with us based on fear, guilt, or obligation. After all, no *good* relationship is constructed on such a terrible foundation. Instead, God's desire is to have an alliance with you which is based on love and respect—both *Him* for you, and *you* for Him.

This teaches us that we don't have to continually spout off fancy prayers or get loud and out of control. His Spirit also teaches us that we don't need to use a middle-man in a wooden room, with a little window between us. Further, our geographical and physical positions are of no importance, *and* we don't have to use language and accents from the 1600s. All we gotta do, is talk. *Just* talk.

Honestly, and this is going to sound strange, sometimes you don't even have to say or *think* words because God hears even the *unspoken* words of your heart (see Jeremiah 17:10). He knows everything about you *deeper* than even you know it. And on the days where it feels as if you don't know *what* to pray or *how* to pray it, the Holy Spirit will actually step in and pray *for* you (see Romans 8:26)—so there is never any pressure on you *to* pray.

God just wants to have a continual "back and forth" with you through His Holy Spirit from sun up to sun down. The Bible says, "Pray without ceasing" (1 Thessalonians 5:17), this simply means to have an *attitude* of prayer all day long.

So today, my friends, do this: Pray. Talk to Dad. Present your requests to Him. Run things by Him before making decisions or saying something. Tell Him what you want. Tell Him what you need. Ask Him for advice. Ask Him for wisdom. Thank Him *all* the time in *all* situations. *Listen* to Him when He tries to guide you into peace and confidence. Eventually, as you continue your life talking to Him, you will get to a point where you don't even notice your own prayers. Your relationship with God will be like breathing.

**A prayer for you:** *Heavenly Father, thank you for the ability to be able to talk to you. What a good God that you would invite us into an actual relationship! Right now, I lift up all who are reading this, directly to you.*

*Touch their souls today and begin to teach them just how much you love them. Teach them that prayer is meant to be a good thing, a relaxing thing, a comforting thing. Continue to guide us all day long as we talk to you. We love you. Amen.*

# DAY 41

## LOVE MY ENEMIES? NO WAY!

*"Love your enemies, do good to those who hate you, bless those who curse you, pray for those who mistreat you." ~Jesus*

LUKE 6:27, 28

L ove my enemies?
Do good to those who hate me?
Bless those who curse me?
Pray for those who mistreat me?
ARE YOU SERIOUS?!

These are some of the most difficult things to do, not just as a Christian, but as a human being. These two verses, Luke 6:27 and 28, spoken by Christ Himself, go against the very grain of our spirits—*if* our spirits are not one with Christ. In context, Jesus is preaching this to the hypocritical religious people who believed they had *all* they would ever need—without Him.

In Luke 6, Jesus begins with some very encouraging words for those who believed in Him. Then, all of the sudden, He starts to pick apart the lives of the Jews who did *not* believe in Him. With a fury of verbal jabs, He boxes the legalists into a corner—those who *thought* that because they were following sacred Jewish laws, they had no use for Him as the Messiah. Many of them were extremely successful financially, while basking *arrogantly* as commandment-following public figures. In turn, they hated Jesus because He was exposing them for the impostors they truly were.

Right before He tells them to love their enemies, do good to those who hate them, bless those who curse them, and pray for the people who mistreat them, He lays out just *how* far off-base they are with their lifestyles and nasty hearts. These men and women refused to put their grace-hating mindsets away and simply believe in Him. In turn, He scoffed at their artificial righteousness:

> *"But woe to you who are rich,*
> *for you have already received your comfort.*
> *Woe to you who are well fed now,*
> *for you will go hungry.*
> *Woe to you who laugh now,*
> *for you will mourn and weep.*
> *Woe to you when everyone speaks well of you,*
> *for that is how their ancestors treated the false prophets"*
> *(Luke 6:24-26).*

Just like today's legalistic Christians, the Jews who looked to religion rather than to faith in Christ, these were some of the most decrepit people on the planet. Jesus makes this perfectly clear as He continues to tear them apart for the next 23 verses. Even though their lives *appeared* to be great, He made sure they knew how messed up they really were.

But for us, *for those who believe*, what does He say about us? Jesus makes an amazing claim! He said we will do even greater things than Him! (See John 14:12). How is this possible? It's *possible* because we have His Spirit *in* us—ALL OF US! He's no longer the only human to have God's Spirit indwell His body! We now have Him too! Jesus' Spirit literally lives inside *of every single Christian!* (See Romans 8:9). His Spirit—the Holy Spirit— is *everywhere* in *everyone* who believes! This is the "how" we can do even greater things than He did! This is the hope of glory for all of humanity! GOD IN US! (See Colossians 1:27).

God in us is who teaches us how to love our enemies, and one of the greatest things He wants for all of us, is peace. These same harsh verses, which were spoken to the faithless people who criticized Jesus, *we too* can tap into them when we forget *who* we really are inside.

When we need to refocus on Jesus we can look at these impossible, legalistic verses, and say, "You know what? I'm *not* like this. This stuff does *not* describe me. You're right Holy Spirit!" So by reaffirming our identity in Christ, *peace* comes back to us. Therefore, when we forget who we are— holy, blameless, co-heirs with Christ—all we need to do is look at a dirty mirror. Christ *in* us then says, "Wipe that off so you can see your face."

As Christians, we don't live by any written rules, laws, or commands (see Romans 3:21-22, 7:8), plainly stated, we don't *have* to do anything. Instead, on this side of the Cross, we *want* to do things, and we *want* to not do things. We live from a want to, not a have to. As heaven-ready be-ings, we have desires written on our hearts because the very *fabric* of our hearts is woven together in a supernatural mesh with God's own Holy Spirit (Colossians 3:3, 1 Corinthians 6:19).

So the results of us being *in* God, and God being *in* us, causes us to find delight in doing things His Spirit is guiding us *to* do—and His Spirit always wants you to be at peace with everyone, as far as it concerns you (see Romans 12:18, Hebrews 12:14). I repeat: *as far as it concerns you.*

These are the key words to remember in regard to having peaceful relationships with those who try to cause us harm. For me, because of the cobweb and dust-filled parts of my unrenewed codependent thinking— which I've abandoned—at first, this was hard to learn. However, over time, the Holy Spirit has led me to a sweet-spot of recovery by teaching me how I *can* "be at peace with others as far as it concerns me." He wants to do the same for you!

By simply learning how to say, "No, that's not going to work for me"—among many other boundary-defining expressions—He has helped change the landscape of my self-pity-soaked life for the better, by leading me into peace. This peace came from my confidence, my confidence came from understanding my value, and understanding my value came from knowing Jesus loves me so much He died for me.

Heaven will be a very peaceful place! Once we shed these fleshy-shells and enter into eternity, we will never have to worry about *any* enemy—that's because we won't have any enemies in heaven! But for now, we can enjoy a heavenly peace while still in these bodies, this happens through the guidance of the Holy Spirit!

So today, my friends, do this: *Listen* to God, just…listen…begin to tap into the Person inside of you and allow Him to teach you how to love your enemies, make no mistake, He will! You've got all of the graceful strength you'll ever need, right inside of you, right now! Peace awaits you!

**A prayer for you:** *God, thank you for your Spirit in me. It hasn't been easy, but by allowing my mindset to be transformed by your guidance, I HAVE found your peace. I thank you. Right now, I lift up all who are reading this, directly to you. For those who have shouted at you, "NO! IT'S JUST NOT FAIR!" please begin to teach them how to trust you. You ARE fair. Help them to understand that IN their weakness they'll find strength! Especially when you are teaching them how to love their enemies! Guide them today, protect them today, and help them to understand your grace on the deepest level possible. In Jesus' name I pray, amen.*

# DAY 42

Learn Your True Identity to
Grow Delicious Fruit

*"In the same way, the gospel is bearing fruit and growing
throughout the whole world—just as it has been doing among
you since the day you heard it and truly understood God's grace."*

SEE COLOSSIANS 1:6

Have you ever heard someone say, "You're not acting very Christian."?
Unfortunately, this is a *very* incorrect mindset that a lot of people
have. The word *Christian* is not a verb whatsoever. It's not something we
can do better or worse than others. *Being Christian* is not what you do at
all, instead, it's what you are! *Christian* is a noun! You *are* Christian—or
you aren't. There is no middle ground.

Just like an apple is an apple, you can't make it *not* an apple—no matter what you do to it, where it goes, or what your personal opinion is *of*
that apple. That apple will stay an apple for the length of its lifespan.
The genetic makeup of that piece of fruit will always be "apple"—it's
unchangeable.

Same with you when you became a Christian. From the moment you
first believed that Christ forgave you completely, your genetic spiritual

makeup was altered for eternity (see Romans 6:6, Galatians 2:20). So no matter what someone else might think you should or shouldn't be doing, in order for you to "stay" a Christian or to be a "better" Christian, that doesn't matter. Their opinion means bupkis in regard to who you really are inside.

Even *you* can't change your own heaven-ready spirit (see 2 Timothy 2:13, Ephesians 4:30). Your spirit has been born *again* so it can't be unborn or reborn *ever* again. It's over. You are now complete in Christ. This is why you should never talk bad about yourself or say things like, "I suck at being a Christian!"—that's a lie. You don't have the ability to suck at being a Christian, just like an apple doesn't have the ability to suck at being an apple. Even if the apple falls to the ground and gets nasty, it's still an apple. Its DNA cannot be changed—same with you.

Once you accept Christ's forgiveness, your old spirit dies off and you get a new one which is intertwined with God's own spirit (see 2 Corinthians 5:17, Colossians 3:3). Your spirit didn't simply get shined up with a bunch of religious cleaning fluid—it was killed *with* Christ, buried, and it rose again instantly, in the supernatural realm. Christians have brand new *perfect* spirits, not patched-up spirits, or spirits that are *becoming* perfect (see Colossians 1:22, Galatians 2:20, Hebrews 10:10).

This is the exact reason why sin never feels good permanently. It's because your sinless spirit-man (or spirit-woman), the real you—won't agree with it. No matter how many different angles you try to finagle sin into your life, your spirit will never allow it by saying, "Sure, that's fine." It is absolutely impossible for sin to mix with your spirit because your spirit is perfect like God—I'M TALKING ABOUT YOU!

You might have noticed this inner battle going on from the time you were saved as a kid, like I have. Or, you might have just recently become a believer so now sin sticks out like a big, fat, swollen thumb. Either way, *all* Christians have *new* desires to live a sinless life. We don't always pull it off, but the desire will be there forever. On the other hand, unbelievers couldn't possibly care less about sin, but that's not you! You hate it because you are *already* a part of God's Holy Family!

The facts are this: from the very *instant* you believed what you heard about Jesus, you received God's life into your body (see Ephesians 2:8-9, Galatians 3:5). You are no longer the same spiritual person you once were, your spirit is completely different!

Sure, your flesh is the same—as in, it's dying. But your flesh, soul, and spirit are now blameless exactly as they are! (See 1 Thessalonians 5:23). What you do and think isn't, but all of *you* is. As a Christian, your perfect spirit begins to reshape your mind by listening to the Holy Spirit who is interwoven with *your* spirit like wicker in a wicker chair.

Each day, rather than obey our old way of thinking, we listen to the loving guidance of God's Spirit. Our flesh does not guide us, our spirit does. What is our flesh? It is but an earth-suit for our spirits. Our spirits are not made up of matter, so they need something physical to indwell in order to be a part of this physical universe. Our flesh is temporary and soon to be discarded and remade. Once our spirits have left our flesh, our current bodies are of no more value or use.

When we don't set our minds on things above we can be influenced by the power of sin, which is a force everywhere on planet earth like gravity (see Romans 7:8, Genesis 4:8). Sin can even influence our brains, creating sinful thoughts. When we act on those thoughts we bring sin to life. The power of sin coming to life through our flesh can be called *the* flesh, but *the* flesh is not *our* flesh. *The* flesh isn't our physical bodies, but the parasite of sin expressing itself. The flesh likes what it sees and it wants it now! But we no longer walk by the flesh! We walk by God's Spirit within us! We are holy, blameless, blemish-free sons and daughters of God! (See 1 Thessalonians 5:23, Galatians 5:16,24-25, Romans 7:6, 8:19, Colossians 1:22).

So by realizing our true spiritual identity, we can then start to grow good fruit in our lives! And no, God did not call us to be fruit inspectors, but instead, branches. Fruit growth happens without effort as we live our lives as spiritually perfect people because it is Christ who's producing the fruit *through* us. We are forever connected to Jesus and because of this divine union we've become branches who produce *delicious* spiritual fruit!

(See John 15:5). This fruit we grow cannot be legislated and can only be grown organically. Here is what your fruit should look like:

*"But the fruit of the Spirit is love, joy, peace, patience, kindness, goodness, faithfulness, gentleness and self-control. Against such things there is no law" (Galatians 5:22-23).*

I want to point out two things from this amazing passage:

1. Each characterization of spiritual fruit is not only descriptive but it is also active. Therefore, Christian fruit growth is something that we *do*—it is a verb. It is action! *Christians* are not verbs, but our fruit is!
2. The second sentence makes clear that *growing* spiritual fruit can never be forced, it can only happen as we simply *be ourselves*. You can't file a lawsuit against a tree to force it to grow fruit. Same with us. A Christian's natural spiritual fruit production only happens in a restful, non-legislated state of mind.

So today, my friends, do this: Grow delicious fruit by being yourself! "But Matt, I still—" NOPE! Be yourself. "But what about—" NOPE! Be... yourself. As you live out *who* you really are, you'll soon see these struggles fade away. You'll never have to struggle to grow spiritual fruit, by being yourself.

**A prayer for you:** *Dad, today I want to thank you for teaching me who I really am on the inside. Understanding my identity in Christ has helped me grow so much spiritual fruit. I honestly don't know what to do with all of it! Right now, I lift up all who are reading this, directly to you. For the Christians who have been lied to about their real identity, help them to refocus on their perfect spirits. Begin to empower them to grow tons of delicious fruit! Fruit which will feed the hungry people of this entire world! Amen.*

# DAY 43

## How to Hate Sin as a Christian

*"For it is by grace you have been saved, through faith—and this is not from yourselves, it is the gift of God"*

*Ephesians 2:8*

G od hated sin so much that Jesus had to be killed. Because of sin, the only human being who was born of God's own loin and *not* from a human male, was ridiculed, beaten, and then slowly tortured until He died—GOD'S ONLY BEGOTTEN SON. Begotten, as in, "to bring a child into existence by means of reproduction."

Yes, as Christians, we too are children of God, but through adoption (see Ephesians 1:5). Christ however, was not brought to life through spiritual adoption or by human sperm, but by God's supernatural sperm (see John 3:16, 1 John 3:9). Yes, God borrowed Mary's womb, but He still used His own seed.

I know it's weird to go this route, but my point is, Jesus was literally our Creator's *own* flesh. So God's own flesh, His Son, *had* to die because of sin, and Jesus literally *became* sin on the Cross (see 2 Corinthians 5:21). By me laying out the importance of Jesus' life, as well as the seriousness of sin, I'm hoping this puts things in proper perspective as to *how* serious God is about sin *removal*.

Thankfully, God's wrath over sin was completely satisfied at the Cross (see Romans 5:9). Because of that event, now, all who place their faith in Jesus instantaneously become reconciled with the Father's sin-debt ledger. Because Jesus never sinned, yet He took on *our* sin in His own flesh, we've become holy, blameless, and blemish-free too! (See Colossians 1:22).

Why did Jesus' flesh have to be sacrificed and not our own or someone else's? Because it is our *flesh* which must suffer *for* our sins—with death. Our spirit is already dead, it was born this way (see Romans 5:12). Paul explains this to the Romans, "For the wages of sin is death" (see Romans 6:23). So this should teach us that Christ didn't deserve to die, because He never sinned. This *also* means that as a result of Jesus taking on the wages of sin *for* us—death—*we* receive a gift from God of eternal life! Paul hammers this home as he finishes up his sentence, "but the gift of God is eternal life in Christ Jesus our Lord" (see Romans 6:23).

So let me be perfectly clear about something before I talk about how to hate sin as a Christian: GOD'S WRATH OVER SIN IS SATISFIED. IT WAS FINISHED AT THE CROSS. HE'S NOT MAD AT US ANY LONGER. JESUS' BODY BROUGHT IN A NEW COVENANT.

Yes, it is the *same* God, but a *new* Covenant (see Hebrews 8:13). His focus is now on Christ! He wants all men and all women to come to re-pentance of unbelief in His Son! (See 2 Peter 3:9). With that being said, we need to shift our focus off of sin and *on* to Christ as well! We need to begin to understand that it is the goodness of God which will lead people to Jesus—not hounding them over sin! (See Romans 2:4).

"Matt, this is *so* deceptive! STOP LYING! You're just giving people a license to sin! You're saying, 'Sin is just fine, go right ahead'!"

My friend, no, I am *not* saying that. I *hate* sin. I hate *my* sin. I hate what sin does to people's lives as well as the lives of those around them. But let's go ahead and state the obvious: *nobody needs a license to sin.* You, me, non-believers and believers the like, we are all sinning just fine without a license.

"Yeah, but for us *real* Christians—those of us who are *true* men and women of God—He only counts *willing* sins against us! I'll start praying for you harder because you need it the most! There is a special place in hell for liars like you who love to tickle ears!"

Well I gotta say, that theology crumbles pretty fast. First off, whose ears are really being tickled? The people who are being told that Jesus has done everything for them, or the people who are being told how wonderful they are because of their great behavior? And not only will I *not* be going to hell—because Jesus will never die again (see Hebrews 7:25)—but I'm *already* supernaturally seated with Christ in heavenly places (see Ephesians 2:6).

But let's back up, the idea of sins not counting against us because they are not "willing" sins, that's not true either. There is no such thing as a non-willing sin. Even if we are desensitized in our minds to a particular sin—because we choose to do that sin so often—that sin is *still* a willing sin. It is impossible to accidentally sin.

But let's digress even *further* into such two-time talking. Let's say we actually *do* have the ability to sin *un*-willingly. Is God not going to pay attention to that sin because *we've* ignored it? No. Sin is sin. Period. We can stick our heads in the sand all we want or try to belittle our sin with a bunch of amazing religious works and church attendance, but at the end of the day a turd is still a turd, and a sin is still a sin. There is no need to try to spray perfume on it or polish it.

Further, there are not different *levels* of sin to God. On earth, sure, there are different consequences for sin—different *results* which come *from* different sins. But to God, all sin is the same. For this very reason, Peter tells us that Jesus died once for *all* sin:

> *"For Christ also suffered once for sins, the righteous for the unrighteous, to bring you to God. He was put to death in the body but made alive in the Spirit" (1 Peter 3:18).*

How could Jesus have died once for all sin if we weren't even alive *to* sin when He was crucified? Simple. God is not bound by time, *we* are. We are made of matter, He's not. Only *matter* is bound by time, and God is *spirit.* Spirit is eternal. He has no beginning and no end. The very notion of "time" was created for us *by* God!

So when Jesus, who was God "in matter form" died, God, in His infiniteness looked down the physical timeline of humanity and forgave *every* sin of *every* believer. The author of Hebrews attempted to teach the Jews this very same thing, that Christ forgave *and* sanctified every person *instantly* who would place their faith in Him:

> *"And by that will we <u>have been sanctified</u>*
> *through the offering of the body of Jesus Christ <u>once</u>*
> *<u>for all</u>" (Hebrews 10:10)*

Key words: *have been sanctified*, and *once for all*! The word *sanctified* means *holy.* Both words simply mean *set apart.* Who are we set apart from? The non-holy, non-sanctified unbelievers—spiritually. Obviously we are still walking around on planet earth, but in the supernatural realm, we've already been seated with Jesus in heaven, as I mentioned above (see Ephesians 2:6).

How is this possible? It's *only* possible by having our sins removed forever, and that's exactly what Jesus has done! He *removed* our sins! Unlike the blood of animals which *covered* sins for 365 days at a time, Jesus *removed* them from us forever from the very moment we first believed! He has taken them away! He hasn't covered them, but banished them! John the Baptist's legalistic ministry was put aside the very moment he saw Jesus. Why? Because John knew that Jesus would solve the world's sin *covering* problem forever:

> *The next day he saw Jesus coming toward him, and said,*
> *"Behold, the Lamb of God, who <u>takes away</u> the sin*
> *of the world! (John 1:29)*

Do you see that? Jesus takes *away* the sin of the world! Let's jump back over to Hebrews for a moment and read how its author builds on this fact of sin removal. He re-quotes the Prophet Isaiah who foresaw what the Messiah would actually do:

> *"For I will forgive their wickedness and will remember*
> *their sins no more" (Hebrews 8:12).*

I can already hear a behavior-focused person yell at me, "What a load of crap, Matt! Every God-fearing Christian knows that we have to confess our sins to be forgiven! And you are lying about us being sanctified! None of us are fully sanctified until we get to heaven!"

Friend, confession has never forgiven anyone. The verse which the grace-confused people take out of context so often in order to get a confession-based theology is 1 John 1:9. "If we confess our sins, he is faithful and just and will forgive us our sins and purify us from all unrighteousness." The apostle John was not speaking to Christians when he wrote this part of his letter, *this* was written to the Gnostics.

The Gnostics were a group of people who thought they had *never* sinned, as in, the very *word* "sin" was not a real thing. John was saying, "Hey guys, guess what, as humans we actually *do* sin. Sin is the stuff that our Creator does not approve of. Simply confess this as true—that you *do* have sin—place your faith in Jesus as your sin-forgiver and your spirits will instantly be sin-free."

As for confession, there is not a single verse in any New Testament epistle, written to Christians, which states, "Confess your sin to be forgiven" or "Ask for forgiveness." This is because confessing and asking never forgave anyone. The Jewish apostles knew that only *blood* could forgive people, not words:

> *"In fact, the Law requires that nearly everything be cleansed*
> *with blood, and <u>without the shedding of blood</u>*
> *there is no forgiveness" (Hebrews 9:22)*

Why do you think Jesus had to shed *His* blood? Are we starting to get this? And I want to back up and talk about sanctification for a moment. We are fully sanctified, right now, as Christians—our identity is (see Hebrews 10:10, 1 Cor 6:11). Our actions and attitudes are *being* sanctified over the course of our lifetime, but we are not our actions and attitudes.

Do we have unrenewed mindsets? Yes. Are we constantly learning and growing in the knowledge of God's grace? Yes. Are we being transformed by the renewing of our minds? YES! But our *thoughts* are *not* us! We are spiritually perfect children of God! (See Galatians 5:16, Romans 12:2, 7:6).

So today, my friends, know this: Notice how I didn't talk about how to hate sin as a Christian? Instead of doing that, I focused on Jesus? I just proved to you that Christ alone should be our focus! So please stop worrying about hating sin! We don't have to do that! That's not our job! Our job is to relax in God's grace and simply be a branch (see John 15:5). Our job is to love God and love people. Our job is to let Christ live through us! Sure, this will be hard to do at first, especially when we've been taught to hate the sin of the world, but through Christ we can do anything! (See Philippians 4:13).

**A prayer for you:** *Heavenly Father, thank you Jesus' blood sacrifice at the Cross! Thank you for loving me enough to send Him here to make me spiritually perfect. What a gift! Right now, I lift up all who are reading this, directly to you. For those who may not feel like their sins are completely forgiven, ease their minds today. Help them to understand that they ARE forgiven IN FULL from the very moment they believed they were! When we sin, please help us to turn from it and realize that SIN will never match up with our spiritual perfection. Empower us with your grace as we walk by your Holy Spirit and not by the flesh. Renew our minds by teaching us how to focus on loving others rather than hating their sin—and help us to do the same for ourselves! In Christ's name I pray, amen.*

# DAY 44

## DOES JESUS' LIGHT SHINE THROUGH YOU?

*"The eye is the lamp of the body. If your eyes are good, your whole body will be full of light. But if your eyes are bad your whole body will be full of darkness. If then the light within you is darkness, how great is that darkness!"*
*~Jesus*

MATTHEW 6:22-23

I used to be a Christian who watched and listened to just about everything. I wasn't going to be known as one of those stiff, prude, religious people—NO WAY! Nobody likes those people anyway, except for *other* religious people. And then all they do is get together to compare their levels of legalism to one another. Count me out.

So because of my refusal to filter out the stuff which I regularly watched and listened to—as well as my blatant stonewalling to think twice about the places I frequented—I always felt as if something wasn't quite right. I couldn't quite put my thumb on it, but there was an uneasiness in my soul.

The opening verse of this devotional explains this uneasiness perfectly. Now, in context, He's explaining the identity of Mosaic legalists, but we can still glean from it for today's point. When I was living *against* my identity, Jesus still dwelled in my spirit; but because I was constantly allowing my body to watch things juxtaposed to us, and I frequented places which were not beneficial, a conflict was happening in my mind.

Jesus tells us why we have that "wrong" feeling, it's because we're allowing darkness into our minds. Even when it seems as if we're not doing anything *too* bad or *too* harmful, He still calls it darkness. If we have darkness in our minds, we should want Him to remove it! The good news is He will by renewing our minds! (See Romans 12:2). Even better news, He still loves us unconditionally as our minds are being changed.

With God, it's not, "Do whatever, I've got your back." No, it's, "Please listen to me. I love you and I know what's best for you. I want my light to be reflected by you." This is why it matters so much that we observe very closely *what* we regularly watch, *what* consistently entertains us, and *where* we spend a lot of time. It's very important for the good health of our thoughts!

It's vital to be on the lookout for "what and who" we constantly listen to—or read—because we're always subconsciously filling up our minds. We're consistently—and most of the time, unknowingly—training ourselves on how to react to people, unfair situations, success, disappointments, as well as how we see the entire world around us.

This is why we must *choose* to see the world how Christ sees it! Even though He lives in us as believers, we can still muffle Him. How? By filling up our heads with bad stuff instead of good stuff! By ignoring His loving guidance which is trying to pull us *away* from bad stuff!

Friend, not only do we have to pay attention to what and who we are paying attention to, but we must *also* pay attention to the environments in which we place ourselves on a regular basis. Keeping our mind strong requires us to observe our surroundings and make good choices. And no, I'm not just talking about bars, nightclubs, and parties, I'm talking about attending unloving, graceless, dead works churches. Mostly non-viewable sin is dominant in such places, but sin is still the same. So we must remember it goes both ways.

There are lots of saved people who go to bars every single day, and there are lots of unsaved people who go to church each time the doors are opened. The grace-confused, church-obsessed people don't get a free pass here, and neither do those who need their minds renewed from bar-hopping, drug addictions, and improper sexual practices.

For this reason, any place we go, we must ask ourselves, "Am I impacting this environment in a positive way for Jesus?" or "Am I allowing this environment to cover up the light of Christ in me?" We have to be environmentally-conscious as Christ-possessed people. Everything we do and every place we go, it's imperative to be led by the Holy Spirit!

So today, my friends, know this: Jesus said, "You are the light of the world!" (See Matthew 5:14). Again, in context, He was speaking to the Jews, but on *this* side of the Cross, Christ lives in you and re-flects Himself *through* you! So it's our honor to shine! Shine, shine, *shine* baby! Darkness has no power over light! All darkness really is, is the absence of light! So be yourself today! Let's goooooooooo!

**A prayer for you:** *Good morning, Lord! What an absolutely gorgeous morning you've given me! The cardinals are outside my window here, they are so bright-red and beautiful, thank you for them! And thank you for the light of Christ in me! Right now, I lift up all who are read-ing this, directly to you. I pray that you begin to help them discern what they should and shouldn't be watching or listening to. Protect them from darkness! I also pray that you give them wisdom about the places they frequent—where to go and where not to go. Help them understand* *you're not looking to make any law out of this, but instead, you simply want them to be guided by your Holy Spirit in all of their decisions. We love you. Amen.*

# DAY 45

## JESUS LOVES USING MESSED UP PEOPLE!

*"For it is God who works in you to will and to
act in order to fulfill his good purpose."*

*PHILIPPIANS 2:13*

D o you ever feel like you're not good enough to be a Christian—let alone do any good works for God—because of your track record? Let me tell you a secret: *the Bible was written by a bunch of messed up people.*

From David, to Solomon, to Peter, to Paul—the bad stuff these saints did who wrote the Bible could fill up a long list! Let's take for example, the apostle Paul. He wrote most of the New Testament, however, Paul never met Jesus in person during His short ministry on earth.

After Jesus ascended? Yes. Paul had an explosive confrontation with Christ *in the flesh* on the road to Damascus (see Acts 9). But before that? No. Paul was not even one of Jesus' original disciples. Actually, he is the only apostle to write letters which were included in the canonization of the Bible who *didn't* sit under Jesus' teaching. The very word *apostle* means "a person who saw Jesus in the flesh and was taught by Him," but Paul didn't learn anything from Christ until Jesus' body had already disappeared into the clouds (see Mark 16:19, Luke 24:51, Acts 1:9).

Before his encounter with Christ, Paul was a persecutor of the early church! He was an Old Testament, Law-abiding legalist in the fullest! He said so himself! (See Philippians 3:4-6). Paul didn't go to the places Jesus went as He taught the masses. Paul didn't see Christ walking the country-side, healing people. He wasn't even a witness to a *single* miracle Christ performed; and he wasn't there when Jesus died or rose from the dead. Instead, he was probably in the crowd of legalistic Jews who yelled out, "Crucify Him!" as Jesus stood on trial!

Paul was a messed up, Christian-hating Jew! As a matter of fact, he oversaw *with delight* the very first believer being killed for their faith, Stephen, as he was stoned to death (see Acts 7). The same man who wrote most of the famous Bible verses you and I quote all the time to help build *up* our faith, he tore *down* as many believers as he possibly could! He went from city to city, persecuting Christians on a grand scale, and throwing them in prison. So what happened? *He crossed the path of Jesus.*

Paul, whose name was originally *Saul*—before he became a Christian—had a severe disdain and disrespect for Christ. But that didn't stop Jesus from calling him to the Light Side! Jesus *still* had a wonderful plan and a purpose for his life! Christ had a way for Paul to find real joy, real peace, real confidence, and real love! None of that religious stuff, but a *real* rela-tionship with God!

In Acts 9, when Paul was on his way to Damascus to terrorize more Christians, Jesus personally stopped him! To make a long story short, Paul finally came to know Jesus for who He really is. Afterwards, his entire life was never the same as he went from persecutor to promotor.

Paul went from hating Jesus the *worst*, to respecting Him the *most*—just as if he was an actual disciple! What's so neat to me is that Jesus *specially* reached out to a bounty-hunter of Christians and said, "This man is my chosen instrument to carry my name" (see Acts 9:15).

After He did, the newest apostle went on to establish tons of roots for the gospel—that might be the biggest understatement I've written in a while. Paul did more work for God than perhaps any other apostle—ever! Jesus is calling *you* to do the same!

No matter what you've done or where you're at in life, Jesus wants to use you to help fulfill His good purpose! (See Philippians 2:13). What is His good purpose? To bring spiritually dead people to life! To stock the halls of heaven with souls! To *teach* people just how completely forgiven they really are! To establish a joy, peace, and confidence in the lives of the lost! Christ wants to live *through* you! Yes, I'm talking to you!

So today, my friends, know this: God is not upset, worried, or mad about your checkered past—just look at Paul. I'm sure you aren't running around killing Christians, but even if you are, Paul is proof that God still has a plan for your life. God is not only *not* upset about your past, but He wants to *use* your past *for* your purpose! I look back at how jacked up so many different parts of my life was, and then I see what God has done *with* those parts of my past—and I'm proud I went through it! You'll never know how to help others unless you've gone through what they are *currently* going through! So if you don't know Him yet, if He isn't living inside your body by grace through faith—STOP!...Stop running from Jesus!... Just stand still, and turn around...He's *right* there...saying, "C'mon. Let's go do some wonderful, eternal things, together."

**A prayer for you:** *God, today I want to thank you for never giving up on me. Although my spirit was saved, my unrenewed mindsets fought you like a madman. Out of all those times I thought I was alone because of my terrible behavior, I wasn't. You were still there with me, inside me. Thank you for never leaving me. Right now, I lift up all who are reading this, directly to you. For those who don't know you and haven't yet accepted your free gift of spiritual perfection, help them. Like you did for Paul, do whatever it takes to get their attention, and let them know it's you. Paul was such a messed up person, but you still loved him and reached out to him. I know you're doing the same for people right now. Give them a new purpose, in Christ. Give them a new life, in Christ. I know you will! We love you! Amen.*

# DAY 46

## WHAT SHOULD I DO WITH MY BAD THOUGHTS?

*"Finally, brothers and sisters, whatever is true, whatever
is noble, whatever is right, whatever is pure, whatever
is lovely, whatever is admirable—if anything is excellent
or praiseworthy—think about such things."*

PHILIPPIANS 4:8

We don't have to believe everything we think—or worse, we don't have to become a victim of our own thoughts. For years, I allowed myself to be swept away mentally by thoughts of dread, fear, insecurity, and anxiety. Eventually, depression and suicide gripped my thought life on unprecedented levels. *"Where is this coming from? Why am I thinking this?"*

Bad thoughts bombarded me day and night. Soon enough, I started to believe that just because I was *thinking* horrible thoughts, I *had* to act on them and accept them as the truth. How wrong was I?!

Friend, you can't always control what you think, but you *can* always control how you *respond* to every single thought. And you might say, "But Matt you just don't understand! I have no self-control for how I respond to anyone or anything, much less for how I respond to my thoughts!"

Well, do you believe that Jesus is your Savior? If so, you actually *do* have self-control for how you respond to everyone and everything. Paul tells the Christians in Galatia that they can control themselves *because* of Christ living in them (see Galatians 5:22-23). Not because of their amazing efforts, but because of His Holy Spirit! So if Jesus is the same yesterday, today, and forever, then you *too* can control yourself because that very same Spirit lives in you today! (See Hebrews 13:8).

As I've gotten to know God's grace deeper and deeper, He has taught me that I don't have to believe everything that enters my mind when it comes to bad thoughts—especially if those thoughts go against His truth and love for me. Grandma used to say, "Baby, just because the crows fly over your head that doesn't mean you have to let them make a nest in your hair." I didn't understand it at the time, but she was saying, "No, you *can't* always help what you think, but you *can* always help what you allow to permanently stay in your mind."

How do we do this? How do we protect ourselves from thoughts we know aren't true? First of all, we have to stop trying to sheriff our thoughts. Thoughts have free reign in our souls, we can't control them coming and going—so give up on that right away.

Because of sin being a parasite in our flesh (see Romans 7:8-11,17-20, Genesis 4:7), as well as the spiritual realm constantly attacking our thought life (see Ephesians 6:10-19), we have to stop trying to force ourselves to *stop* thinking certain thoughts! Stop trying to stop thoughts! We don't have the ability to legislate brainwaves, sin, *or* the spiritual realm!

So let them glide through, and let them glide out. When a bad thought enters your mind and tells you, "I'm here to cause trouble." our response should be, "I know you are, come on through. Don't let the door hit you in the butt."

Random thoughts will happen all the time—so what. Those thoughts in themselves don't define you in any way. And remember, *sinful* thoughts have absolutely nothing to do with your spiritual perfection. They are just that, a sinful thought. It is when we *grab* a sinful thought and say, "Here, have a seat. Hang out for a while. Can I get you a cold drink?" that things begin to go south. Hosting, feeding, and then acting on any wrong thought is what gets us in trouble and causes us pain—but *not* the thought by itself. It is just a thought.

Just yesterday, I walked into my closet to put my shoes on to go running and I had the most God-awful thought about someone. Immediately, I was like, "Nope! I know where that's coming from! I'm not going there." Had this been four or five years ago, I would have easily jumped on that train and taken a ride through a very dark tunnel. But instead, I immediately disagreed with it and let it pass.

I didn't stand there and concentrate on *not* thinking about that thought anymore—that's impossible. We *will* think about whatever we are thinking about, period. But as we allow Christ to lead us *by* His Spirit in us, He is the one who helps filter our thoughts. So as a result, that bad thought passed as I sat down on the bed and put my shoes on. I haven't even thought about that thought again until just now. See what I mean?

We have to stop being a slave to our thoughts! We must begin to realize that thoughts are like vapors—they are random, small (yes, small, you'll see), mostly unnoticeable, and you can't catch them. So simply *let* bad thoughts happen, *try* to notice them—so that you can correct them—and then move along. There is nothing wrong with a thought *per se*, but there *is* something wrong with *agreeing with* and *acting on* every thought you have. So relax! Your thoughts don't dictate your life! You do! Allow God's Spirit in you to sift *through* your thoughts, rather than believing all of them!

The second thing you must do is something you've probably read in my writings many times. As a matter of fact, this is the title of the final chapter in my first book, *True Purpose in Jesus Christ*, and that is, FIGHT BACK! Notice I didn't say "Stop the thoughts from coming!"? Remember, we can't do that, but we sure can fight the thoughts that try to stay!

When a thought hits you and tries to set up shop "in your hair" by attempting to make you feel sad, mad, depressed, anxious, fearful, not good enough, lacking, unloved, unwanted, unattractive, unappreciated—*anything* that you *know* Jesus does not agree with, you *have* to speak up against it! Don't just sit there and take it as the truth, fight back!

You can do this out loud or to yourself, but you must begin to practice overcoming wrong thoughts with God's truth. When you have a bad thought, ask yourself, "What does God say about this thought?" When you do this, little by little, those thoughts begin to lose their power. In turn, you will stop reacting to your bad thoughts how Satan wants you to, which is fearfully or sinfully. There is another way! God's way! (See John 14:6).

The Bible says we are to "take every thought captive and make it obedient to Christ" (see 2 Corinthians 10:5). This means when a thought pops into your head that does not match up with what the Holy Spirit says about you—or your situation—YOU GOTTA KILL IT! You gotta *kill* that thought! Don't be passive! FIGHT!

*Thought* after *thought* after *thought*—FIGHT! KILL! FIGHT! KILL! GET YOUR MIND IN ORDER BY FIGHTING BACK! Don't *agree* with the bad thoughts—agree with God! Practice this on a moment by moment basis! Soon enough, the devil will become perplexed because this is where he does his greatest work—*in our minds.*

When you begin to not just put *on* the full armor of God—but also become offensive—your enemy *and* sin doesn't stand a chance! We're like, "BOOM BABY! BRING IT! WE GOT THIS! CHRIST *IN* US HAS GOT THIS *WITH* US!" I want you to get excited about this! You can have a great time fighting back!

You and Jesus are a team! It's not all of Him and none of you! NO! That's garbage! It's both of you together! So don't just stand there and take the pounding, *fight back with Christ*! I heard a terrible teaching the other day where someone was claiming, "You've made Jesus your Savior but not your Lord!" HOGWASH! It's impossible for Him to be your Savior and *not* your Lord! You and Him are one! What a stupid idea! What a stupid *thought*!

Now…I'm not going to lie to you, at first, fighting back will be a severe conflict of epic proportions. You'll notice *every* fight, over *every* thought, and sometimes you'll get knocked down. Friend, that's okay. Jesus will always be right there next to you with His hand out, saying, "Get up. I'm here. Let's go."

The great news is eventually you won't notice the battles very often. You'll exude strength, boldness, and confidence—because that's who you really are in your spirit. God's protection around your mind will become like a mighty fortress. Sure, some vapors might slip in now and again, but overall, *you* have the mind of Christ, and *you* are stable and fortified!

So today, my friends, know this: Relax and fight back. Yeah, relax and fight back. This is the paradox of living the Christian life which is most enjoyable. When you find yourself in a state of rest, you will find yourself in a state of power. Only God's grace can enable you to discover this sweet spot. Once you find it, and a bad thought enters your mind for a moment, it will see you, and scurry out quickly. It wants no part of you. *Nothing* stands a chance against God Almighty, with you, inside you.

**A prayer for you:** *Heavenly Father, thank you for teaching me how to win the battles in my mind, which is through your truth. You are so good to me! Right now, I lift up all who are reading this, directly to you. For those who have been losing the battle in their minds for a long time now, strengthen them. Help them to begin to discern the truth from lies. Give them a new confidence in knowing you are with them no matter what they think. Teach them how to relax, and teach them how to fight. In Jesus' name, amen.*

# DAY 47

## THE TRUTH ABOUT GOD'S LOVE

*"There is no fear in love, but perfect love casts out fear. For fear has to do with punishment, and whoever fears has not been perfected in love."*

### 1 JOHN 4:18

How often do you feel like God doesn't love you, or that He's furious with you? For years, I saw God as a big cruel ogre who was constantly waiting for me to mess up *just* so He could punish me. And as soon as I *did* mess up, I would scramble around trying to do a bunch of religious stuff to make up for my failures.

I was petrified of God, even as a Christian. I didn't understand the truth about His love. This is not okay. The reason I thought this way was because of the teaching from people who didn't know God very well—if at all. Instead, all they knew was church, conservatism, hating sin, and behavior-improvement programs for "bad" people.

Due to the non-gospel teaching of God's love being conditional, I always felt as if everything bad happening in my life was God rightly punishing me for my poor choices. Either that, or He was putting the hammer down because I missed too much church—or because I didn't have enough good works. "God hates backsliders! You gotta be quick to repent! If you don't repent *daily*, and if you don't get to work for God, then you'll get exactly what you deserve!"

I constantly thought God was "getting me back," I was *so* afraid of Him. Eventually, I wouldn't even ask God for help when I needed it, *"It's no use. I'm such a terrible Christian. I don't even deserve God's help."* The anti-compassionate people had taught me, "You better get that sin out of your life or God will never even *hear* your prayers!" Sadly, I believed them for far too long.

It's no wonder why so many people hate Christians, it's because of the complete misrepresentation of God's love by people claiming to *be* Christians.

Soon enough, my level of *The Fear of God* had peaked. Fear then turned into anger, and anger morphed into rebellion. Finally, I said, "The heck with it (only I didn't say *heck*). I can't be good like these people keep saying I have to be, and God keeps punishing me anyway, so I'm just going to do whatever I want."

Little did I know, I actually wanted what *God* wanted because He lived inside me! Even if my flesh and mind rebelled against legalistic people—rightfully so—my *spirit* would always stay holy and blameless! My *spirit* would always have the same desires as God—and even better, God's *loving* opinion of me would remain the same for eternity because I was His child! (See 2 Timothy 2:13, Colossians 1:22, Romans 6:6, John 1:12, Ephesians 1:5).

Looking back, I could see that it was the Holy Spirit rebelling against such garbage, not just me. I had to unlearn a lot of untrue stuff about God. This wasn't easy. In the beginning, He was teaching me who He really was by comforting me in my darkest hours, but I was still so petrified of Him I believed I already had one foot dangling into hell.

Because of the religious abuse I endured, certain parts of my unre-newed mindsets were still very afraid of God *and* hell. But *He* didn't want me to be afraid of either! The truth is, God has no desire for us to enter into a relationship with Him through fear. So if you did, He doesn't want you to stay there. He wants you free from all fear.

God's aspiration for us is to be confident as His cherished children! The Bible says, "Do not throw away your confidence; it will be richly rewarded" (Hebrews 10:35). The number one reason why we *can* be confident is because we won't be judged guilty for any sin we ever commit. Past, present, and even future sins are already forgiven. Jesus tells us this in John 3:17 and 18:

> *"For God did not send his Son into the world to condemn the world,*
> *but to save the world through him. Whoever believes in him is not*
> *condemned, but whoever does not believe stands condemned already*
> *because they have not believed in the name of God's one and only Son."*

The writer of Hebrews doubles-up on our once-for-all forgiveness:

> *"And by that will (God's will, the New Covenant), we <u>have</u>*
> *<u>been</u> made holy through the sacrifice of the body of Jesus Christ*
> *<u>once for all</u>" (Hebrews 10:10, note added).*

"Have been," as in *past tense*; and "once for all," as in *once for all*! This is the foundational reason why we *shouldn't* be afraid of God! Because we are holy and forgiven forever *through* Jesus' body, we have nothing to be afraid of!

The word *fear* is what comes to mind when we know we will be punished for something. For Christians, when it comes to being punished for sin, *we* won't be punished! Therefore, we have nothing to be afraid of when it comes to our Creator! The apostle John tells us this in 1 John 4:18. He also says that God's love for us is perfect, and if we are afraid of God then we really don't understand His love!

Old Betty Blue-Hair will be quick to correct me by saying, "Matt, do yourself a favor and study God's Word harder! You're telling people they can just sin away with no consequences whatsoever!"

To that, I'd reply, "Yes. That is exactly what I'm saying, you old goat." I'm kidding! I wouldn't say that last part! But yes, there are no *heavenly* consequences for any Christian's sins, ever. Earthly consequences? Yes, absolutely, but not heavenly. Jesus has already forgiven all of our sins so there are no consequences left to be had. Christ didn't say, "I'll forgive you of all your sins unless you sin too much!" No, He said:

> *"Very truly I tell you, whoever hears my word and believes*
> *him who sent me has eternal life and will not be judged*
> *but has crossed over from death to life" (John 5:24).*

However, the person who is focused on their wonderful behavior will say, "Liar! All Christians will be judged for their sins, and *you* will be judged the worst for telling people they won't be judged!"

To that, I'd say, "Calm down, Sparky. I'm sorry you didn't get your Christmas bonus to pay for the pool, but you don't have to have a come-apart." I'm kidding! I wouldn't say that! That's from *National Lampoon's Christmas Vacation* for those of you who didn't get the joke.

But seriously, the Bible says *no* Christian will be judged for their sins because Jesus was already judged for them—and the punishment was death (see 1 Peter 2:24, 3:18, 2 Corinthians 5:21). The Prophet Isaiah foresaw what Messiah would do by *absorbing* our sins, 700 years before His birth:

> *"But he was pierced for our transgressions, he was crushed*
> *for our iniquities; the punishment that brought us peace was*
> *on him, and by his wounds we are healed" (Isaiah 53:5)*

By *His* wounds *our* spirits are healed. Healed of what? Sin! Still, this won't be enough biblical proof for most grace-confused Christians. They will rebuttal this amazing verse with a taken-out-of-context verse, 2 Corinthians 5:10:

194

*"For we must all appear before the judgment seat of Christ, so that each of us may receive what is due us for the things done while in the body, whether good or bad."*

The key words here are "whether good or bad." I agree that all of humanity will stand before Christ in judgment, each person after they die, but we Christians don't have anything *bad* to be judged for. What are bad things? SIN! And what has Jesus done with our sin? He has taken them away! (See John 1:29, 1 John 3:5).

So yes, Christians will give an account on the Day of Judgment, but only for the *good* they have done—not for anything bad. Even better, Jesus said if we do so much as give a cup of water in His name, we will be rewarded (see Mark 9:41). So us *Christians* should be excited about being judged! But let's be clear, simply *knowing* Christ is our true reward! We don't do stuff on earth in hopes of *getting* stuff in heaven! We do what we do because Jesus already lives in us!

Yet, the frustrated Christian *still* won't be happy with my answers. After all, they've worked way too hard for God and someone like me isn't going to come along and take away all their gold stars, without a fight. "So Matt, you're saying that no matter *how* much you sin, God will never leave you? What a lie! You gotta *prove* yourself to God in order to *keep* His love!"

Friend, Jesus said, "I'm with you always, even until the end of time" (see Matthew 28:20). He didn't say, "I'm with you *sometimes* and when you are not doing religious stuff, nope. You are all alone."

Johnny McAngry will bark back, "You mean to tell me that we can do whatever we want and Jesus won't send us to hell *or* leave us?! You're crazy!".

Buddy, I hear you. This makes no sense. The truth is, we want what God wants. It seems like a crazy idea, but the gospel doesn't make any sense at all, *especially* if you think about it.

Here, this might help you understand: If my wife told me, "Matt, I love you so much, I'll never leave you no matter what you do. Because of my love, you are allowed to do whatever you want, whenever you want. You can even have as many affairs as you please, and I'll still be here for you. My love and commitment to you will *always* remain the same."

Seems ludicrous doesn't it? But what do you think my response would be? Do you think I would *want* to go sleep around, knowing without a doubt, that Jennifer would never leave me and her love would stay the same? If I knew that I could go blow all of our money, get drunk all the time, beat up her and Grace—but yet, she'd never show me resentment or hard feelings? What a cray-cray idea!

But this is how God sees *us* because of our faith in Jesus! (See Romans 5:1). He has taken our *heavenly* punishment *away* by Christ being killed on the Cross! (See Colossians 1:22). So no matter how many poor choices we make in these bodies, our salvation is secure because of Jesus' death and resurrection! (See Hebrews 7:25).

Also, I would have to be a selfish fool to cheat on such a person or actually look *forward* to causing them pain—and I'm not! *No* Christian is like that—at their core—because of the Holy Spirit giving them a *new* spirit! (See Romans 6:6, Galatians 2:20, 2 Corinthians 5:17). Our *want to* is in the proper place *because of* God's unconditional love *and* because of our new hearts—our new spirits! This is why God never has to use guilt or anger to motivate us into a closer relationship—only people do that. Instead, He uses agape love, *loving* discipline, and never-ending commitment!

Next, I want to address the issue of using "the fear of hell" as a means to get people to come to know Christ. Yes, hell is a real place, but why would you want to establish such a fearful foundation in a relationship with God? No good relationship has ever been built on fear, only bad ones!

Let's just say for a moment that hell is not real—which it is—but for now, let's say it doesn't even exist. When we die, if we are not in Christ, instead of going to hell, we are annihilated. Again, not the truth, but for my point, let's just think about that for a minute.

Even if there wasn't a hell wouldn't you still want people to know Jesus? Yes! Yes, you would! This is why our focus as Christ's ambassadors must be on knowing Jesus rather than being petrified of a very bad place. It's all about our focus! Our focus should be on relationship!

I've tried my best to teach my daughter to be confident in not being afraid of God. Some people teach their kids the opposite, and that's why they rebel. They don't want anything to do with a mean God—that, or they become uber-religious and nobody can stand being around them. I don't want Grace to be either. I want her to live her life until she's 102 years old from a place of peace with God. I want her to always feel secure in her relationship with God. I try my best to let her know the more mistakes she makes, the deeper God's love for her goes. Because I'm teaching her the truth of the gospel, at 12 years old she already knows that she never has to worry about going to hell no matter how many times she messes up or how many times she misses church. She is confident in God's love, and this is how it should be!

My goal is to make sure Grace knows that God's love is unconditional, from start to finish. So on the day she hears the false teaching of fear tactics, she will immediately fight back with, "That's a lie, and I know it. God is for me, He is not against me. I don't have to be afraid."

Friends, God is *not* unloving, He is *not* graceless, He is *not* a fair-weather friend or a controlling, vengeful, hateful, *manipulating* God! The people who teach this stuff might be, but God is nothing like that at all. So who is He? Believe it or not, God is not so much a *who* as He is a *what*! God is love! (See 1 John 4:8) He *is* love! Love is not just a characteristic of His but it's *what* He is!

Nothing can separate you from God's love! Not even your sin! (See Romans 8:37-39). God did this for you for free, through Jesus dying on the Cross! That's how much He loves you! How amazing!

So today, my friends, know this: You can't be bad enough to lose God's love, and you can't be good enough to maintain it. He loves you no matter what. Now, because of this good news of the gospel, aren't you confident? Don't you *feel* loved? Doesn't this love make you *want* to love Him back? I know it sure does me! So join me! Join me in showing the world what confidence in a loving God looks like! Don't be afraid any longer! You are loved!

**A prayer for you:** *Heavenly Father, thank you for showing me how much you love me through Jesus. Because you gave Him to us, you not only saved us, but you showed us what you are really like in person— LOVING! Right now, I lift up all who are reading this, directly to you. For those who don't understand just how much you love them, and for those who have been taught to fear you, touch their lives today. Teach them about your unconditional love! Begin to build up a CONFIDENCE in them THROUGH your love! In Jesus' name I pray, amen.*

# DAY 48

## HOW TO THINK, FEEL, AND ACT LIKE GOD

*"Have the same mindset of Christ Jesus."*

*SEE PHILIPPIANS 2:5*

The short answer to the title of this devotional is: *be yourself.* That is, if you are a Christian. For too many years, I was led by my unrenewed mindsets rather than being led by the real me—my perfect spirit. The problem with doing this is old stinking thinking doesn't match up with God *in* me *or* me. Like strands of thread in a single piece of fabric, God and I have been one since I believed in Jesus as a young boy. So me—a perfect, heaven-ready spirit—and God, we always want the same thing! However, parts of my mindsets which are not yet spiritually mature want the very opposite of what God and I want (see Romans 7:5-6, 8:9, 12:2, Galatians 5:13-25, 1 Corinthians 13:11).

Our minds are trained to think *whatever* we train them to think. Also, our bodies have the parasite of sin in them because we live on planet earth. Thankfully *we* rule over *it*, not the other way around (see Romans 6 & 7, Galatians 5). Our spirit is God and us together as one—yet separate—like a vine and a branch (see John 15:5, Colossians 3:3, 1 Corinthians 6:17,19). This is why the false teaching of "All of God and none of me" is incorrect. The correct version of the gospel is "All of God and all of me together!" You got a new "me"—a new spirit—from the very moment you first heard the gospel with faith! (See Romans 6:6, Galatians 3:2). Living by our spirit is now the correct way to live and train our minds. Paul tried to explain this to the Christians in Rome when he said:

*"Be transformed by the renewing of your mind."*
*(See Romans 12:2)*

Let me be clear about what your soul is. It is your mind, free will, and emotions. Your soul is holy and blameless just like your spirit and body (see 1 Thessalonians 5:23). Your spirit isn't changing, but your thinking is maturing.

Let me also be clear about your flesh, your body. There's nothing wrong with your flesh, God *likes* your flesh. It was His idea! It is but a tool for your spirit! It's a costume made up of matter for your non-matter, supernatural self, to be in on this earth. You are hitching a ride in your flesh for 70, 80, or 100 years. Although there's nothing bad about your flesh, it has a parasite in it called *sin* which we inherited from Adam (see Romans 5:12, 7:17-20). When we walk by that parasite's desires, we are walking by *the* flesh—not our body. But as you walk by your true spiritual identity rather than by the flesh, you will be putting to death sin each day! (See Romans 6:12).

God wants us to *choose* to think, feel, and act like Him. This happens when Christians simply *be* themselves! All we gotta do is wake up each day and say, "Good morning, God. I sure do love you. Help me to be who you've already made me to be, in my spirit. Help me to walk this out! I'm ready! I'm available! Let's go!"

God knows that if we do this—just be ourselves—we can fulfill our *individual* purposes for being new creations in Christ, as well as our *corporate* purposes—with other people! (See 2 Corinthian 5:17, Romans 11:29, Hebrews 10:24-25).

However, there is a big problem that constantly tries to pop up in our lives! This problem is what caused Adam to eat the fruit, David to sleep with Bathsheba, and Judas to betray Jesus. This problem comes from the sin in our flesh and from the areas of our decrepit mindsets.

Some people never overcome it—both Christians and non-believers the like: *pride*.

As Christians, pride prevents us from being ourselves. It puts a halt to fully living out and enjoying *who* God has created us to be! Pride does *not* come from our spirits! The Christian spirit is pride-free! We are on the same level as God because of our faith in Jesus—and God is not prideful! (See Romans 5:1, Galatians 5:22-23, 1 Corinthians 13:4-8).

Pride keeps us from thinking, feeling, and acting like…Jesus. "But Matt, I can't help what I think or feel!" Okay, I'll give you that, I understand what you are saying. But as a believer you *can* control how you act. Self-control is a fruit of the Spirit that grows in our lives when we are walking *by* the Spirit (see Galatians 5:22-23). The seed of self-control is in you because God's Spirit is in you!

So if you will water that seed and let it grow, you *can* begin to control how you outwardly express your true character. Soon enough, your thoughts and feelings will catch up a lot more often!

Your Christ-like actions—which is simply spiritual fruit growth—are not contingent on your feelings *or* thoughts. Godly feelings and thoughts gradually sprout up and out *with* your fruit as you walk out your true identity: *God's child* (see Galatians 3:26). For proof of this, just look to the Cross. How did Jesus feel as He carried that thing up the hill? What was He thinking? We don't know, but we saw His *actions*.

He overrode His physical flesh's desires—which was *not* to be tortured and killed. Therefore, His self-controlled thoughts of not running away, but pushing *through*, not only overrode His flesh but also His feelings! There is no way He felt like doing what He did! The agony in His mind and emotions poured out in the Garden of Gethsemane! (See Luke 22:39-44). However, His choices produced a harvest of free salvation for all who would believe! How did this happen? With self-controlled *action*! We can do the same because His Spirit lives in us! (See Romans 8:9, Philippians 4:13).

Paul advises the Romans to "be transformed by the renewing of your minds" (see Romans 12:2). This is a process! This takes time! The key word in this verse is "renewing." Renewing means *gradually*. So having our lives transformed by the renewing of our minds is a process that will not end until we die or Jesus comes back. Paul tells the Christians in Philippi not to become discouraged during this process:

*"And I am sure of this, that he who began a good work*
*in you will carry it on to completion until the day*
*Jesus Christ returns" (See Philippians 1:6)*

So today, my friends, know this: You won't be complete in thought, feelings, *or* actions until you shed this earthly shell! Therefore, be easy on yourself, *be* yourself, and enjoy each day of God's love, mercy, and grace!

**A prayer for you:** *God, today I want to thank you for the passion and enthusiasm you've placed in my spirit. I know it's you who is spurring me on, so thank you! Right now, I lift up all who are reading this, directly to you. For those who have accepted Christ as their Savior, but don't know who they really are in their spirits—reveal their true identity! Once they understand that they are spiritually perfect like you, only then will their thoughts, feelings, and actions begin to match up organically! I ask these things in Christ's awesome name. Amen.*

# DAY 49

## WHAT I'VE LEARNED AFTER TWO YEARS OF SOBRIETY

*"Do not conform to the pattern of this world, but
be transformed by the renewing of your mind. Then
you will be able to test and approve what God's
will is—his good, pleasing and perfect will."*

*ROMANS 12:2*

\* **W**ritten *May 8th, 2016, the second anniversary of my sobriety.*

"BE TRANSFORMED BY THE RENEWING OF YOUR MIND..."

"BE TRANSFORMED..."

"RENEW, MY, MIND..."

This Bible verse, Romans 12:2, had become a chant for me. I wanted *so* badly for my life to change—I wanted to be transformed! Over the course of my 30+ years, I had chased everything I *thought* would make me happy and content. I achieved all of it, *all* of it.

A family.

A thriving business.

A custom-built home, with a pool.

Nice vehicles and fun trips.

A beautiful wife.

Fun hobbies.

A "spotless" reputation as a super-nice guy.

I had an envious life but that didn't matter because I still hadn't found what I was searching for. Even after years of hard work, dedication, and reaching all of these goals, my life was pointless and empty.

Why? Because I hadn't yet allowed God to begin renewing my mind. I believe He blessed me in nearly every single way I wanted Him to *just* to teach me this: "Matthew, none of this stuff will fulfill you, you'll see. You need to know me on a much deeper level. I'm in you, and I'm not going anywhere, but *only* knowing me more intimately will give you what you're looking for."

But I didn't want to hear it! Or so I thought. Rather than allow God to start changing my thinking *through* me humbling myself—I decided to numb my mind with alcohol. Of course, my drinking always started out innocently, "WOO-WHO! Let's drink!" I never woke up shaking uncontrollably at two in the morning, reaching out for a fifth of vodka like those *bad* drunks. Oh no, not me! "I'm not like them, look at my life! I'm doing big things!" My selfish arrogance, which is simply denial, was ruining my life as well as the lives of those around me.

The fact of the matter was that after I "enjoyed" myself of an evening, drinking *way* too much—yet again—the torment I felt all night long as I tried to sleep, was that of a nightmare. I can remember having severe heart palpitations, gut-wrenching nausea, night terrors, and dry-mouth so terrible I'd stumble my way to the bathroom several times during the night just to stick my mouth under the faucet and chug.

"But I'm no drunk! BACK OFF! Who do you think you are?! I'm *having* myself some beers! Look at yourself!" I was acting so stupid. My mind hadn't yet been *renewed*.

Soon enough, I got over my denial and I was ready for change. I just didn't know how. I *wanted* it, but I had no skill set to even be *able* to recover.

To make matters worse, I was extremely embarrassed to admit to others that I had a terrible drinking problem (this is a trick of the devil to keep us addicted, by the way—it's called *pride*).

To compound my failing recovery efforts, I had learned to become a closet-drinker. Even though I had the desire to quit, this new way of drinking gave me easy access to continue to drink and *hide* my binging. Sure, I'd get crap-face drunk with you if I knew you drank too much like me, but if you were a *proper* drinker, I'd drink before we met up, while we were together, and then after—and *you* would have no clue I drank before and after. Because of drinking so much, so often, my tolerance level was that of an Irish pub owner. I could be 15 drinks in, and you'd think I only had 4.

One of my main problems was that I refused to give up my fake reputation! I was the cool, successful alarm guy, who loves God and talks about Jesus all the time—my Facebook account proved it. Yet, I'd have some beers with you at the end of the day, or at your barbecue, knowing full well that I had no business drinking a single drop. I had succumbed to *admitting* that I needed to stop, but my ego wouldn't let me, neither would my social life or my stinking thinking. So I had a conversation with God:

"How am I supposed to stop drinking completely? I don't know how. Plus, what will people think?"

He replied, "I'll give you the tools to stop, *if* you'll get to know me better. And who cares what people think."

"I do!"

"No. WHO. CARES. WHAT. PEOPLE. THINK. This is not a question, but a fact."

He was trying to help me understand that I had become a slave to the opinion of *people*. He was trying to kick-start my mind renewal, but I was still resistant! He wanted to take our relationship to the next level so He asked me, "Do you want to hang on to your frustrating life? Or do you want me to *use* your frustrating life for great things? Pick one. I'm not letting you have both."

"Fine. Take it. Use me."

WHOOOOOOOSH!!!!...I was done. That was it. The tide had turned.

This is the beautiful part! This is the part where I got set free from incorrect thinking! The part where I no longer cared about *anything* except for what God wanted from me! This is the part of my life where I knew I would feel extremely uncomfortable, but I was ready for it!

May 8th, 2014, the day I decided to stop taking advantage of God's grace and begin to live out my spiritual perfection. The day the devil was like, "Oh…crap. Send in reinforcements."

So here we are! OVER TWO YEARS OF SOBRIETY! It just so happens that this particular year, my sobriety date falls on Mother's Day. I love my mom! I honor my mom. I've *forgiven* my mom. Forgiven her for what? For the poor choices she made when I was a kid—when *she* was deep in her own addictions.

Because of the terrible things she did as a young mother in the 80s and 90s, my upbringing was that of a child's life from an episode of *Intervention*—unfair, horrendous, abusive, and very sad. The word *heartbreaking* comes to mind, as every child deserves to feel secure and loved. Because of Mom's selfish decisions, I didn't get that. So as a grown man, I had a choice to make:

1. Choose to be bitter, unforgiving, and hate her—which does not match up with my true spiritual identity.
2. Choose to forgive her completely, once and for all, like Jesus did *me*. This choice matches up with my spirit, where God resides, just right.

Of course I chose number two! Who the heck am I to hold grudges?! Not only do grudges *not* mesh at all with who I really am—but grudges are not fair! The same God who made me, made Mom—and He made her first, just so that He could have the ingredients to make me! So this years' sobriety celebration is also a day of honor, love, and respect for my mom. I hope she understands that she is completely forgiven.

My friend, I learned these amazing truths from God only after I got sober. There is so much freedom that comes from allowing God's Spirit to renew your mind! If I had continued to drink and ignore the Holy Spirit each day, I'd still be in a miserable place of unforgiveness, stress, and torment. God wants better for us.

The Spirit of Jesus has also taught me that forgiveness is instant and free—but *trust* is not instant *or* free. Trust is something which must be earned over time. He has taught me the difference between unconditional forgiveness *and* trust. I am grateful.

Over the course of the past two years, I've learned from Him that the only way I could ever overcome *any* level of bitterness and resentment is to *give away* unconditional forgiveness, just like a Christmas present. No strings attached. "Here, I forgive you, take this." So now, I've got my mind made up to forgive people even before they hurt me.

To get to this healthy mental state, God has educated me on what *boundaries* are. Boundaries are very important for our own mental, physical, and spiritual well-being. When we establish boundaries, we hammer stakes into the ground around us, creating protective barriers. These are not walls, these are fences, so people can come and go as we allow them to—key word: *allow*.

These boundaries are for our own protection and they teach us to say, "This is as far as you go. Stop." "That is not okay, it needs to change immediately." "NO. That is *your* responsibility." "Sure, come on in." "No. That won't work for me." "Go, get out. That is not healthy." "Your actions are impacting my life negatively. Change it, now. That is no longer allowed here."

By learning how to establish healthy boundaries, God has taught me that I don't have to put up with any crap from *anyone* any longer, period. *And* I don't have to drink to cover *up* my feelings about being mistreated or taken advantage of. I MATTER. MY FEELINGS MATTER. MY NEEDS MATTER. MY WELL-BEING MATTERS. These are boundaries.

In order to be able to establish boundaries you must understand your value to God. My mind renewal has brought to the skyline just *how* important I am to God! The grace-confused people want you to turn into a door-mat, overlooking the severe mistreatment of others. Churches are rampant with this type of boundary-crossing abuse, as manipulating folk twist the gospel for their own personal gain.

Jesus, however, wants you to live *out* who you really are in your spirit! Who are you?! You are a confident, loving, respectful person, who holds your chin up high and protects yourself from harm! You are an infinitely loved child of God who deserves to be cherished! YES! YOU REALLY ARE!

I didn't know these truths when I was depending on drinking to make me feel happy, important, and confident. Instead, I was blind to *all* of the devil's tactics...I hadn't yet allowed my mind to be renewed...those days are over.

So today, my friends, know this: God has an amazing plan for your life! This plan is knowing Jesus deeply! This plan is full of heartbreak, tears, and humility—but it's also full of love, grace, and peace! Step into this plan today! It's a really nice life, with Jesus!

**A prayer for you:** *Well hello Heavenly Father! My goodness, look what we've done! Over two years without any booze in me! Thank you for giving me such strength! On my own, I could not do this. You and I both know I tried to quit for years, but all along, you didn't want me to quit—you wanted me to BEGIN! You wanted me to begin living OUT my real life with you! I know that if I had died back then I would have gone to heaven, but you had so much more for me to do here. Thank you for empowering me to talk about my former addictions and my past life with such shame-free courage!*

*Right now, I lift up all who are reading this directly to you, who want the same. For those who are afraid to take that step—or have tried a thousand times and failed—let them know I was just like them! STRENGTHEN THEM THROUGH THEIR WEAKNESS! STRENGTHEN THEM THROUGH HUMBLENESS! Teach them that you show unlimited grace to the humble, and that ALL of their strength comes directly from Jesus! Give them a glance of what the sober life is like—just how amazing it is! And please let them know you love them JUST as they are, RIGHT NOW, today, no matter what addiction they are struggling with. But most of all, show them that you have a great plan for their life, with them only having one addiction…YOU. Amen.*

# DAY 50

## GOD WANTS YOU TO USE WHAT YOU'VE GOT

*"The kingdom of heaven is like a mustard seed, which*
*a man took and planted in his field. Though it is*
*the smallest of all seeds, yet when it grows, it is the*
*largest of garden plants and becomes a tree, so that*
*the birds come and perch in its branches." ~Jesus*

*MATTHEW 13:31-32*

Do you ever feel like what you do for God doesn't matter? You might think to yourself, stuff like, *"Why even try? It's not enough, it's too small. I'm not doing any of this right."*

Or maybe you've had an unloving person convince you that you have no business telling others about Jesus because you are still struggling with a particular sin pattern yourself. Newsflash for them: *that* is sin—discouraging weak-minded Christians.

Or maybe a loved one has verbally abused you so badly, for so long, that the devil has used their harsh words *perfectly* when it comes to convincing you you're not good enough to help build God's Kingdom.

ALL OF THESE ARE LIES! We must begin to recognize that! If we don't, we will be like James and Paul said, "waves of the sea, tossed back and forth" (James 1:6, Ephesians 4:14).

HERE IS THE TRUTH ABOUT YOU: "God *chose* the foolish things of the world to shame the wise; God *chose* the weak things of the world to shame the strong" (1 Corinthians 1:27, emphasis added).

He chose us! And He chose us as we are! Jesus decided to use fishermen not Pharisees! The religious folk have earned *nothing*—they only think they have! These people heap mud on the Cross by degrading Christians who aren't self-righteous! They can't *stand* the fact that God loves us all the same, and that our faith alone makes us just as righteous as Christ Himself! (See John 1:12, Romans 2:11, 8:17, 2 Corinthian 5:20).

But still, they ignore these biblical truths and only have conditional love—which is no love at all. They have "church people love" and "church people grace." They say, "Come to Jesus and be completely forgiven." Then the next week, "Backslider! There is no hotter place in hell than for the likes of you!" To top that off, they find their identity in how much they supposedly "know," how "little" they sin, and how amazing their "level" repentance is.

One thing they've not repented of, is a nasty heart. Christ can have nothing to do with a nasty heart. This is why He must give us a new one! (See Ezekiel 36:26, Hebrews 8:10, Romans 6:6).

My friend, don't let these people knock you off your God-given path in life. All that stuff they do and don't do, it might have an *appearance* of goodness, but God doesn't care about how stuff looks on the outside—He is focused on our hearts (see Matthew 23:27, 1 Samuel 16:7). These are the people whom Jesus will say to, "Depart from me, I never knew you," after they plead to Him, saying, "Lord, we did all these things in your name!" But He will repeat, "I NEVER KNEW YOU!" (See Matthew 7:22-23).

As Christians, we are supposed to find our identity in our spiritual perfection—not in a bunch of religious works. *He* is our foundation, not the stuff we do, and not our lack of sinning. The fruit we grow in our lives comes *from* Christ *through* us (see John 15:5), it's not just us! It is God Himself who is working *in* us to will and act according to *His* good purpose (see Philippians 2:13).

He's invited us to join Him—not take over—and when we forget about this truth, everything we do and don't do becomes...*dead religious works.* We have to refocus! We are finite—*created*! He is God—*Creator*!

So while we are in these temporary bodies, we must simply *use* what He's given us—no matter the size, and no matter what the religious people say about what we have to give. Friend, nothing is too big for God, and nothing is too small either. When this fleshy shell wears out, your eternal spirit will go on to live *with* God, and you'll get to see the amazing results of your labor in heaven! (See Matthew 25:14-29). All of the love, respect, and organic effort that you put out *for* Christ, He'll show you what you've done—eternally! OH, WHAT A DAY!

Listen, I know what it's like to have self-doubt, I know what it's like to have a religious leader ask you to leave his church. I also know what it's like to have someone you love very much, tell you that nobody cares about what you have to say about Jesus. I KNOW HOW YOU FEEL! I KNOW HOW IT FEELS TO FEEL SMALL!

...And you know what? Jesus likes small stuff. He said that with faith the size of a mustard seed—EXTREMELY SMALL—we can tell a tree to be uprooted, and then be replanted somewhere else (see Luke 17:6). I now know that God has allowed all of this heartbreaking stuff to happen in *my* life in order to teach me how to handle discouragement as He approves—which is by simply being my spiritually perfect self. By doing this, I've learned that I don't want to retaliate how the devil wants me to, and when I do, he wins a battle.

Our job, as people literally possessed by Christ, is to overcome evil with good, and hate with love (see 1 Corinthians 6:19, Romans 12:21). Our job is to stand up to those who refuse to speak the truth of Christ *with* love (see Ephesians 4:15)—*and* to actually love them too despite their blinding legalism. That used to be hard for me, now it's not. I can honestly say that I genuinely care for these grace-confused people. But I'll speak to them just the same as I'll speak to someone who is caught up in heavy chains of addiction: "You need to know Christ deeper. His graceful truth will set you free."

God is a just God *and* a loving Father. He's paying close attention to everything happening in our lives on a much deeper level than even we are. And even better, He's using *all* of it—good times, heartbreaking times, mundane times—to strengthen us! He's using the hate-filled, arrogant people, as well as the unfair situations, to give us the opportunities to react according to our spiritual perfection. He simply wants to see some effort on our part with...*what we've got.*

All God wants is what you *currently* have—nothing more, nothing less. What you currently have might seem really small. I know exactly what that feels like. I've been there. You want to move forward, but you don't think it's enough. My friend, it's enough. *Use it.*

Or maybe you feel so defeated right now that all you can give Him are tears. That's okay. Give them to Him. He wants them. He will use those tears for good. He will use those tears for your purpose. He will use those tears to water the seeds that He's planted in your heart. Just hand Him over what you've got, and then, watch it grow!

**A prayer for you:** *Good morning, Lord! For so many years, I thought that what I had to give to you wasn't enough. Thank you for teaching me how wrong I was! Right now, I lift up all who are reading this, directly to you. So many of them have been beat down by religion, self-doubt, and unloving people—some are even close to ending it all. Please let them know you are patient and kind, not pushy and mean. Comfort them and give them confidence! Send new people into their lives! Remove the people you want gone! Give them the courage to hand over to you what they CURRENTLY have, right now, today! Amen!*

# DAY 51

JESUS, A HOMETOWN HERO? YEAH RIGHT.

*"Coming to his hometown, he began teaching the people
in their synagogue, and they were amazed. 'Where did
this man get this wisdom and these miraculous powers?'
they asked. 'Isn't this the carpenter's son?... Where then
did this man get all these things?' And they took offense
at him. But Jesus said to them, 'A prophet is not without
honor except in his own town and in his own home.'"*

SEE MATTHEW 13:54-57

To the Jews who believed Christ was the Messiah, Jesus was an absolute rock star. Everywhere He went, hordes of people swarmed
Him. One time, a lady with a lifelong issue of bleeding heard He was
coming through town and went to see Him. Because of the enormous
crowd, she couldn't even get close enough to touch Him without forcing
her way through (see Mark 5, she was healed by the way, just by touching
His clothes!).

Everywhere Jesus went, He had to find a way to get the crowd to relax,
back up a little, and give Him some space. Why was this? Was it because everyone knew who He was? No, not all of them did. For many of them, they

crowded Jesus because of what He had been *doing* for people—performing miracles! They wanted their miracle too! Jesus obliged them more often than not, but like Grandma promising an ice cream after church, they had to listen to His messages along with getting the reward.

However, there was an area of the Middle East where the people did *not* like Jesus—even though they knew about the things He had been doing and the stuff He was teaching—they resented Him. Where was this place? *His hometown.*

The jealous, bitter, and self-centered people who knew Jesus as He grew up, they said, "Isn't this Mary and Joseph's son? How did He get so much power? Why are people paying so much attention to Him?" (See Matthew 13). The Bible says they "took offense" (Matthew 13:57), they *took* offense. Notice that Jesus didn't *offer* offense to be taken. No, instead they snatched it up!

Really, this is the only way you can take offense from others. Even when someone is trying to hand it out to you *to* take, it's still your choice. You don't *have* to take it, you can let them keep it for themselves. This is why you've never heard someone say, "You really gave me some offense!" No, not ever. But you *do* hear, "I really take offense to that!" all the time. *We* take it. Why not start letting others hang on to their own offense? It's not even yours.

Friend, it's always our own personal choice to act oversensitive, sour, suspicious, contentious, or unforgiving. Again, *we* choose that. *I* chose that for years—and I was loaded up with truckloads of excuses and blame as to why. Nobody controls our attitudes, ever. This is the one thing in our lives that we always have a grip on and no person or circumstance can forcefully adjust. Some people have the best circumstances in the world, but yet their attitudes are atrocious. For others, they can have the *worst* circumstances you could possibly imagine, but their attitudes are delightful and pleasant. *We* choose.

So for the hometown folk with the poor attitudes toward Jesus, notice they *think* they know Him so much better than the people who just now got to know Him—but they don't. They don't know Jesus at all, and they never have. Instead, their hearts are black and cold concerning this new wave of goodness sweeping the area! "Oh, but I know Him!" they say. No sir, no ma'am, you do not.

Which brings me to today, you and me, modern-day Christians whom Christ's Spirit personally indwells. There are many people from our past who do not like us as we currently are. Their life would be so much easier if we continued on acting recklessly and making choices which go against our spiritual perfection. For so long, they enjoyed using *our* mistakes as an excuse to make mistakes themselves. That, or they used our struggles to beat us over the head with how amazingly behaved *they* are. Let's talk about that.

When you decide to fully live out your spiritual identity—a heaven-ready child of God who doesn't even *want* to sin—there will be two groups of people against you. The devil's plan is to make your situation even more sticky by influencing those from your hometown or area you are from. So be ready:

1. **Religious Christians**. When I say *religious Christians*, I'm not trying to disrespect anyone (disrespect does not match up with who I am in my spirit). Instead, I'm trying to call out a disgusting condition that has overtaken our churches. A *members only group* who shuts out the world from their clique. They vindictively meddle in everyone's lives, condemn others, have hierarchies, try to instill fear, and they judge people on a level that is hellish (Christian or not). They make the good news of the gospel only good for themselves. They are fair-weather friends who will kick you out of their circle if you don't conform to their style.
2. **Non-Christians, or grace-abusing Christians. (I'll get to this group in just a minute).**

First up, let's discuss the religious Christians, the people who are supposedly representing Jesus for the world to see and want through *their* lives. They claim to be Christians—however, they express no love for anyone unless they do exactly what they say. They are grace-confused and loooooooooooove when you are having problems because then they can tell you how to fix them. "Look, be like me. Here's what you need to do. You are getting what you deserve because you are not living like I am."

When you were living a life contradictory to your perfect spirit, the religious Christians judged the heck out of you—it was one of their favorite pastimes. Now that you're being authentic, they're still doing it. This is where they're incorrectly finding identity and getting kicks—*being ubercritical*—which is influenced demonically, it's sinful, and is coming from unrenewed parts of their thinking *if* they truly are children of God. Please understand this and don't let them pull you down.

Before you decided to begin showing Jesus that you actually *do* love Him, you may or may not have felt condemned by these people (I sure did). But when you finally came to understand what Paul said, "there is now no condemnation for those who are in Christ" (Romans 8:1), you got hip to their game. You see right through them now because you *know* that you are *not* condemned—no matter what they say.

You're no longer a little "church-people soldier," getting in line for them to approve of you. You're not worried if they pass you up after service without saying, "Hi, how are you?" because you're no longer a slave to religious people's bad attitudes. This is a really good thing!

Instead of being a minion you are now a leader! The hometown religious Christians see your good deeds, they see your life-change, and that *still* isn't good enough for them—NOTHING IS. "Fix this." "Stop that." "You're doing it wrong." "The Lord told me to tell you," blah, blah, blah. Oh, and if you don't shape up?! Forget it! "You're not really a Christian." Garbage. Demonic garbage. Pay it no mind.

When we encounter such legalism the flesh wants us to say, "Let me tell you where you can stuff those lies," but don't do it. Let it go. At the end of the day, they think they know you but they don't—so what. All they truly know is religion and barking at lost people, "You need to go to church or you're going to hell!" Don't take the bait, don't retaliate. Move along.

The second group from your hometown area who won't fully understand you is the non-Christians—the people you sinned with for so long. And I should say, this group isn't always non-Christians. Sometimes they are actual believers who know God but ignore Him all day long. They muffle the Holy Spirit, take advantage of His grace, and shout things like, "Don't judge me!" This was me for a very long period of my life.

What this group doesn't understand is, yes, we *are* saved by grace through faith, but our dumb choices and ignoring of the Holy Spirit's counseling will cause us—and those around us—tons of heartache and pain. Not only that, we will live a powerless life as a weak-minded Christian! Jesus has a better way! That way is living *out* who we really are in spirit. Paul explains this to the Philippians:

> *"Therefore, my beloved, as you have always obeyed, so now, not only as in my presence but much more in my absence, WORK OUT your own salvation with fear and trembling" (Philippians 2:12, my emphasis added).*

Work *out*, as in, "Get what is inside of you *out* of you!" Notice that Paul didn't say, "work *for* your own salvation," but instead, "work out". Paul also said to do this with "fear and trembling," as in, "Awe and respect for a great Creator!" This doesn't mean we are to be petrified and shaky of our loving Dad. After all, perfect love casts out *all* fear, and God's love for us is perfect in Christ! (See 1 John 4:18).

"Fear and trembling" means we are to realize we have God Almighty inside of us! And when we work Him *out* of us—like squeezing toothpaste out of a never-ending tube—we will be able to do things our minds can't comprehend! (See Ephesians 3:20). The religious Christians have been taking Philippians 2:12 out of context for centuries in order to create fear in the minds of believers. Their goal is to manipulate us by trying to get us to believe God is constantly mad at us. That is not okay, and it's a big fat lie.

Like the Christians in Philippi from 2,000 years ago, Paul wants us to realize we have everything we need on the inside of us right now! It's simply our responsibility to let it out! It's our responsibility to let *Him* out!

The people from your past, they don't care that you're actually allowing this to happen! Instead, they see the life you now live, and say:

"Give it time, they'll be right back to where they were."

"Isn't this the same person who used to curse people out on Facebook and then take drunken selfies?"

"Ha! I know them! All they used to do is brag on how hot their wife is, and show off their cars! Fake!"

"Who does this person think they are? They ain't fooling me!"

"Isn't that the same woman who cheated on her husband and almost left him? I remember her commenting on the same guy's photos on social media after she cheated. What a phony, posting Bible verses and checking-in at church."

THESE PEOPLE WILL TRY TO RIP OUT YOUR HEART AND DESTROY YOUR REPUTATION. So what. Let them try. You don't even *own* your reputation any longer, it belongs to Jesus! Overlook it and have your mind made up to forgive them even before they hurt you. Be sure to pray that God blesses them. Don't get frustrated, or worse, scramble around trying to defend yourself...*let it go. Who cares.* God is paying close attention to your reactions, so react like the real you. You *are* a loving person (see 1 Corinthians 13:4-8, Galatians 5:22-23). So love those who hate you.

Yes, I know it feels like a punch in the stomach, but that pain will pass and God will strengthen you through your self-control. You are growing. Pain happens during growth. *As* you grow, by simply being yourself, you will have peace, comfort, confidence, and a sound mind—even when the world is crashing in all around you. God is remolding your image to match up with your spirit...let Him. Don't fight it.

So today, my friends, know this: If Jesus got severely disrespected by people in His hometown, then we should feel honored when the same thing happens to us! The Bible says, "God withholds no good thing from those who walk upright!" (See Psalm 84:11). So keep doing what you know your spirit wants you to do! Pray for the religious Christians with genuine love and respect. They are just as lost as non-believers, in their mindsets, if they don't understand the real grace of Christ. And for those other people whom you used to run amuck with? Show them what a new creation in Christ really looks like! You may be the only Bible they ever read, so make them *want* Jesus—not hate Him. Show them grace, truth, and love—equally. Show them your real self! They need you more than you'll ever know!

**A prayer for you:** *Heavenly Father, you are such a good Dad. Even when we are learning how to walk in our true spiritual identity, you keep us safe. Even when people attack us or gossip terribly about us, you keep us secure in Christ. Thank you. Right now, I lift up all who are reading this, directly to you. For those who WANT this life in Christ, give it to them. Maybe they've mistakenly acted legalistic, maybe they've abused your grace, or maybe they WANT to believe this very moment—HELP THEM! Help them to listen as you speak to their hearts, not just right now, but all day long. Guide them in the right direction! I know you'll do it, because you love us. In Christ's name I pray, amen.*

# DAY 52

## WHY DID JESUS WALK ON WATER?

*"But when they saw him walking on the lake, they thought*
*he was a ghost. They cried out, because they all saw him*
*and were terrified. Immediately he spoke to them and said,*
*'Take courage! It is I. Don't be afraid.' Then he climbed*
*into the boat with them, and the wind died down."*

MARK 6:49-50

The short answer to the title of today's devotional is: *Because He needed to get to the other side of the lake!* HA! No, but seriously, Jesus had to get out to a boat in the middle of a lake, which was full of disciples, so He walked on water to accomplish this feat.

He and his closest followers had just fed over 5,000 people. I say *over* 5,000, because the Bible says "5,000 men," it doesn't say women and children (see Mark 6:44). So with my hypothetical theory, by the time you add up wives, widows, and kids—Jesus had just filled up the bellies of over 10,000 people!

For those who don't know the story, Jesus miraculously multiplied a few loaves of bread and fish which fed a very large crowd—*and* there were leftovers! He didn't just provide what they needed, but also, what they *wanted*, which was more than enough!

But that's just what Jesus does, He shows off! All of His miracles were performed for *our* benefit, not His. He already knew who He was. He did what He did because He wanted the people following Him around to believe that He was the Son of God. The only way to do that was to perform some godly tricks, also known as, *miracles*.

This is why He performed *every* miracle—so we would believe Him! If it weren't for the miracles, we could easily chalk Him up as one of the craziest people who ever lived. Performing miracles is what makes Him God in the flesh! He even told the legalistic Jews who were trying to stone Him, "If you don't believe what I'm saying, at least believe me based on my miracles" (see John 10:31-39).

So when Jesus and His 12 disciples had just fed all of these people, He went up on the side of a mountain for some one-on-one devotional time with the Father. While He was there, the disciples took off in the boat to get to the other side of the lake without Him. When Jesus looked out onto the water, He saw that it was very windy, a storm had blown in. The waves were going crazy, and the rowing of the disciples was not helping! So what does Jesus do? The Water-Walker just strolls on out toward them, right into the storm! No big deal.

As they see Him coming, they freak out and say, "It's a ghost!" but Jesus just gets closer, and closer, and then finally, He calms them down. "It's just me, relax. Don't be afraid." Now, in the book of Mark, his account doesn't record Peter getting out of the boat (Mark 6:47-51). Neither does John's writing of this event (John 6:15-21). But Matthew tells us about Peter getting *out* of the boat, and walking on water!

Peter is just a regular person, like you and me! But yet, he walked on water like the Son of God! Why?! How?!...Because his focus was on Jesus. His eyes were set on the power of Christ—*not* on the waves. Jesus had just trekked 3.5 miles on H2O (see John 6:19), and I'm guessing He is a power-walker because He got out there fast. Maybe He just kinda *glided*...I'm not sure, but I'm going to ask Him one day.

So with this huge storm happening all around them, and Jesus standing out on the lake, Peter says, "If it's you, tell me to come out on the water" (Matthew 14:28). So Jesus does just that! Imagine it! Getting to walk on water!

The Bible says Peter "walked on water and came towards Jesus" (Matthew 14:29)...Wow...I wonder how that felt! Here he is, in the middle of a huge storm, *in a little dingy*, and Jesus Himself says, "Come out onto the water with me. It's safe. I'm here."

That's just mind-blowing to me! And it shows me the heart of Christ! He is not afraid! And He tells *us* to not be afraid! Even when life is crashing and smashing all around us, when we are in the middle of the storm and nothing seems to make sense, Jesus says, "I'm with you." That is amazing! That is comforting! THAT'S MY JESUS!

Friend, even when we think we're going to drown because we're obeying Christ as He calls us out onto the water, He *still* says, "Come with me into the storm, deeper. I'm here. I won't let it hurt you. Don't be afraid."

So many of us don't even want to get out of the boat! So many of us *Christians* want Jesus to hurry up and get into the boat with us, in our safe little spot! But *He* is saying, "No, walk out on the water *with* me. I won't let you sink."

This is what we gotta do! We can no longer be afraid of what will happen to us when we stand up to the storms in our lives! We can no longer be afraid when the devil uses people to discourage us! All we gotta do is continue to *look* forward with our eyes fixed on Christ...He is *right* there... wind, waves...and all.

And He is smiling warmly, gesturing with His hand stretched out, saying, "Come."

Peter had that focus, briefly. He started to walk on the water but got afraid and began to sink. He cried out, "Lord, save me!" (Matthew 14:30)... and, Jesus did. He reached down into the water, lifted him up and said, "You of little faith, why did you doubt?" (Matthew 14:31). Then they climbed into the boat where the storm died down. Baffled, all of the disciples' eyes were wide open and fixed on Jesus, absolutely *astonished* at what they had just witnessed!

And there's Jesus, sitting there. I believe He was grinning from ear to ear. I can almost hear Him saying with eyebrows raised, "See?..." as the disciples stared in awe, worshiping Him, *knowing* that a fact was now clear. They had actual evidence which would cause them to alter their entire lives: "Truly you are the Son of God" (Matthew 14:33).

> **A prayer for you:** *Good morning Lord! Thank you for yet another day on your planet! What an honor it is that you've chosen me to be alive today! Right now, I lift up all who are reading this, directly to you. I ask that you help them to understand just how big you are. Help them to understand you created the very notion—the idea—of gravity. It was your thoughts which made the very law of it! Therefore, you are not bound by any law of nature, because you are nature's Creator! I know this is why, and how, Jesus walked on water, as you've revealed this to me through your Spirit. You created the very laws of nature which are necessary for this planet to float and spin—and for it to be at just the right distance from the sun to give us light and warmth! Help these dear readers to not doubt your greatness! Help them to realize you created all of this, for us—so that we could have a place to live out our lives. But even more, you created our lives so that we could join you in a loving relationship forever, starting now. In Jesus' name I pray, amen.*

# DAY 53

## WHAT MAKES JESUS MAD?

*"And he said to them: 'You have a fine way of setting aside the commands of God in order to observe your own tradition!'" ~Jesus*

MARK 7:9

There's not many places in the Bible when Jesus yells at people, but in Mark 7:9, this was one of them. Why was He so riled up? *Because of religious hypocrites.* Jesus snapped at the Pharisees more often than our modern-day, legalistic-minded Christians want to talk about. The reason for this is because they share many of the same characteristics.

Like so many of today's confused Christians who chop up the grace of God, the Pharisees loved to look down on and correct "sinners." They literally strutted around town showing off how much more "holy" they were, and how they were in so much "better standing" with God because of what they did and didn't do (see Luke 11:43, 20:46, Mark 12:38). Jesus had enough of these vultures one day, so He put them in their place. And don't forget, Jesus had a ministry for *two* groups of people:

1. The lost/rebellious, or non-religiously educated (Gentiles).
2. The self-righteous religious people who *thought* they knew God, but did not. All they really knew were rules, laws, and old customs (non-believing Jews).

Jesus came to shake things up for both groups! Not just for the people who were blatantly sinning, but for those who thought they weren't! Why? Because He wanted people's hearts to change toward Him, both the lost and the religious!

So one day He flew off the handle at these legalists who followed Him around, looking to criticize His every move (know anyone like that?). As He and the disciples sat down for a meal, they didn't wash their hands before eating, therefore *breaking* a law of the Jews (see Exodus 30:17-21, Leviticus 15). The hyper-critical Pharisees were quick to point that out.

Jesus then barked at them, "Isaiah was right when he prophesied about you hypocrites; as it is written: 'These people honor me with their lips, but their hearts are far from me. They worship me in vain; their teachings are but rules taught by men'" (Mark 7:6-7).

After He continued going off about how pretentious they were, He finished up with, "Thus you nullify the word of God by your tradition that you have handed down. And you do many things like that" (Mark 7:13).

My friend, Jesus is *not* focused on your style, but instead, your substance! He cares about the inside of you! Does His Spirit live there?! He's not looking for you to change cosmetically or as aesthetically, but spiritually! He likes your style! He simply wants you to mash it together with Him!

Jesus is longing for you to come to know Him *so* deeply, that you would be willing to buck tradition—not truth, but tradition—in order to reach more people for Him and change even *more* lives! And how do we change lives? We change lives by helping others change their hearts; and we help others change their hearts by first allowing God to change our *own* hearts into a new one! (See Romans 6:6, Ezekiel 36:26, Hebrews 8:11, Romans 7:6, 8:9, Galatians 2:20, 2 Corinthians 5:17, Colossians 1:22, Hebrews 10:10).

After that one-time event happens, His Spirit in you *teaches* you how to plant good seeds of love in others. Plant, not force into the soil of their souls. We don't have that ability, especially if we're acting self-righteous, judgmental, or condemning. Try to also remember, once those seeds are planted *you* can't make them grow, only God can! And even still, that person has to *choose* to allow this to happen. Sure, God will continue to nudge their hearts, but He'll never go against a person's free will. He loves us too much.

So today, my friends, do this: Be yourself. As a Christian, you are *not* self-righteous, you are *not* aggressive, and you are *not* legalistic. No! You are kind, truthful, and full of grace! Simply keep planting seeds, keep standing up to legalistic behavior *peacefully*, and keep reaching out to the lost—but more than anything, do all of this with love! Be confident because Jesus is never mad at you!

**A prayer for you:** *Lord, I want to thank you for opening up my mind to your truth. Before I came to know you deeper, I didn't understand that Jesus corrected the uber-religious people in the Bible for their non-belief and self-righteousness. Thank you for that revelation. Right now, I lift up all who are reading this, directly to you. I pray you open up their minds to who you really are, as well as to who THEY really are! Help them come to know your bottomless grace, through the Spirit of Christ! In His name, amen.*

# DAY 54

## WHEN GOD WINKS AT YOU

*"The Pharisees came and began to question Jesus. To test him, they asked him for a sign from heaven. He sighed deeply and said, 'Why does this generation ask for a miraculous sign? I tell you the truth, no sign will be given to it.'"*

MARK 8:11-12

Do you keep asking God for a sign? For so long, I lived my life this way, a way which was counterintuitive to the comment made by Jesus above. I'd pray immature prayers like, "God if you'll just *show me* what it is you want me to do, *then* I'll do it! Show me!" Other days I'd pray things like, "Lord, give me a sign, so I'll know."

Jesus makes it clear that God doesn't work this way. The Bible says we are to "walk by faith" (see 2 Corinthians 5:7). Christ wants us to believe "as a little child" (see Matthew 18:3). He wants us to stop asking *what* we should be doing, and just do SOMETHING, just do ANYTHING! He wants us to stop asking for confirmations and signs!

However, sometimes God *does* give us signs, but they come randomly—when we least expect them. They happen when we feel like idiots, doing things His way, blindly, repeatedly, through complete trust in Him.

And when He does give us a sign, I call them "God Winks." Like, God is winking at us as a loving father would while looking down at his child. I heard it called this from the name of a book, *God Winks*, which I never read, but that title stuck in my head.

One time, I had a God Wink, a blatant sign from God. It was a very difficult time in my life, I had driven an hour away to church on a Tuesday; this is easy to do on Sunday mornings or Saturday evenings, but not during the work week. Why was it so important I go on that particular day? Because that was the only day I could get baptized.

Everyone else had someone there supporting them and celebrating this wonderful event, but I was all alone. "You're going to be tired for work tomorrow, this is stupid," was a thought the devil tried to creep into my head, but I kept speaking against him. "No it's not. I'm having a good time. I'm glad I'm here. I want to show Jesus how much I love Him by getting baptized. I want to celebrate my spiritual birth! I've never done that before!"

So there I was, standing in line, ready to step up the ladder to get into the water; and although I had nobody there who cared for me, I was *still* full of joy because of what was about to happen: my public display of my already *inward* change for Christ—not to earn anything—but like a wedding, to show my affection for Jesus and to make an outward spectacle of it!

The building was packed. 300+ people were getting baptized that night. On top of that, everyone's loved ones, friends, and family were there snapping pictures.

So the line was very long. While waiting and hearing people's names announced before they got dunked, the crowd then roaring in approvals, I opened up Facebook on my phone—and here it is, my God Wink:

The very first thing I saw was a picture of Jesus being baptized by John the Baptist! Above the picture were spoken words *about* Jesus: "He will baptize you with the Holy Spirit and fire!" (See Luke 3:16). I immediately took a screenshot! It's still on my phone to this day!

Oh my gosh I thought I was gonna start sprinting through the church! *What* a God Wink! A sign from God telling me He was paying very close attention to my life! I was *not* alone, at all!

Now, let me be clear about something. I was already *spiritually* baptized into Christ by grace through faith—which is all that is required to be saved (see Romans 6:6, Ephesians 2:8-9). My spirit had been killed off, buried, and resurrected *with* Christ since the time I first believed as a boy. Water doesn't save, only faith does. Peter makes that clear, as does Paul. (1 Peter 3:21, 1 Corinthians 1:17).

Water baptism is a celebration of your spiritual birthday! Unless you first believed that day, it is *not* your actual day of spiritual birth, and it does not *cause* your spiritual birth. You can put swimming trunks on a monkey and dip him in water, saying, "I baptize you in the name of the Father, Son, and Holy Spirit!" but that won't give him a new *perfect* spirit—or a spirit at all. We must stop making a law out of water baptism. Many people stay in bondage because they think it didn't "work" the first time, but there was nothing to *be* worked! You celebrated! That's all you did! Going down into a liquid and then back up didn't *achieve* anything!

However, I cannot describe to you how I felt on that drive home…that warm September night, windows down, smile on my face, and a feeling of complete contentment.

Since then, I can't say God has flagrantly given me other signs, maybe He has but I've not noticed. Honestly, I don't need them. I believed *before* I got any sign. So if I never see another wink by God, I'll keep doing exactly what I'm doing each and every day, which is being my spiritually perfect, unconditionally loved, child of God, self! Will you join me in walking by such faith? It's a good life!

**A prayer for you:** *God, I want to thank you for the little things you do. I now understand that life in itself is a wink from you! You winked at the world in person when you sent Jesus here! Thank you! Right now, I lift up all who are reading this, directly to you. I ask that you touch their soul on a deep level. Help them to come to know you personally, through the life of Christ. In the meantime, if you want to give them a sign or a wink, do that too. We love you. Amen.*

# DAY 55

## WEAKNESS IS YOUR GREATEST STRENGTH

*"My grace is sufficient for you, for my power is made perfect in weakness." ~God*

*SEE 2 CORINTHIANS 12:9*

What is perhaps the greatest characteristic you can develop as a Christian? *Weakness.* I believe hordes of more people would come to know Jesus Christ if they thought they didn't have to become weak. However, weakness is how you enter into the deepest levels of God's grace! Weakness is how you become the most strong! It's a strange paradox which God has set up!

The Bible says, "God's power is made *perfect* in our weakness" (see 2 Corinthians 12:9, my emphasis added). So what does that even mean? How can God's power be made perfect in *our* weakness? To the human mind, that makes no sense.

First off, don't confuse weakness with sin or passivity. When Paul wrote this verse, he wasn't saying we should sin more to get stronger, or to sit on our hands while chanting, "Grace...grace...grace..." No. He was saying when we begin to make choices based on the leading of God's Spirit in us—even to the point of it making us *seem* weak—then, in *that* weakness, we are strong!

Your entire life will change for the better when you begin to do this! Yes, in the beginning it requires severe humility on your part. This is because you're no longer doing things according to the flesh or unrenewed mindsets. However, humility is Christianity 101! The entry level course! *This* is the very beginning! Humbling yourself to God's guidance and saying, "Yes. You are correct. My perfect spirit was not created to make these choices. Help me" (see James 4:6).

Friend, until we finally say, "Jesus, you're right, I'm wrong. I need your wisdom." nothing will change. But afterwards, TRUE STRENGTH DEVELOPS! It's amazing how this works! I know it seems counterproductive to become weak, but God knows what He's doing! This new weakness creates confidence, and this confidence is coming from Christ *in* you germinating *out* of you! He's molding you on the *outside* with what you already have on the *inside*—PERFECTION! (See Hebrews 10:14, Philippians 2:12, Colossians 1:22).

So when we stop reacting to difficult people and unfair circumstances based on how we feel, and instead, we react according to what the Holy Spirit in us approves of, a brand new strength comes from within us! You'll see!

You will be amazed at how your relationships begin to change when you stop reacting how you always have—that is, before you knew God had made your spirit holy forever, once and for all time (see Hebrews 10:10). When someone does you wrong and the flesh and stinking thinking want you to react in a manner that is not you (see Galatians 5:16-18)—but instead, you override *both* with your true perfect spirit, God will be sure to take care of you, that relationship, *and* your circumstances. This results in you being able to rest in confidence and peace—anxiety free—even in your most strenuous situations.

Honestly, as Christians, without living by our perfect spiritual identity, when people treat us unfairly or when difficult seasons arise, we will react in one of two ways—or both at the same time:

1. Fearfully.
2. Sinfully.

God doesn't want you to react with either because *neither* describes you! God wants you to react in the proper way, which is by being yourself (see 2 Peter 1:5-9). As we choose to do this in the midst of our turmoil, we will originally produce love, joy, peace, patience, kindness, forgiveness, gentleness, and self-control...self...control, as well as many other good things which are inside of us as Christ-possessed people (see Galatians 5:22-23, 1 Corinthians 13:4-8, 6:19, Colossians 3:3).

The Holy Spirit will always speak to our hearts and guide us. It's up to us to make the flesh become weak for Him. We accomplish this feat—gracefully—by walking *by* His Spirit, rather than by the flesh.

Paul said, "That is why, for Christ's sake, I delight in weaknesses, in insults, in hardships, in persecutions, in difficulties. *For when I am weak, then I am strong*" (2 Corinthians 12:10, my emphasis added). FOR WHEN I AM WEAK, THEN I AM STRONG! C'mon somebody! This is good stuff!

Paul even went on to say, "I have made a *fool* of myself" (see 2 Corinthians 12:11, my emphasis added)—and ain't that the truth? Isn't that how we feel in the beginning of doing this? In being *ourselves* and letting Christ live through us to the point of weakness? We *feel* foolish—BUT THAT'S OKAY! WHO CARES?! GOD DOESN'T SEE YOU AS A FOOL! HE SEES YOU AS STRONG! (See 1 Corinthians 1:27).

When you are doing your very best to live Him out—even when every fiber of the flesh says to do the opposite—YOU ARE STROOOOONG! YOU. ARE. STRONG!

You are showing God that you love and respect Him by being who He created you to be as a new creation in Christ! (See 2 Corinthians 5:17). And you are doing this *with* your actions...*with* your weaknesses. You're not just talking about it, you are *being* about it! This is a good thing, a *very* good thing! (See James 1:22, 1 John 3:18). You are acting like your perfect spiritual self! As we *continue* to do this, God takes care of the results. We *trust* Him, we *rest* in His grace, we just gotta *be* ourselves. How simple.

So today, my friends, know this: You are the most strong when you are the most weak. When the wind is blowing hard, all around you, and you feel like you're going to break; when you beeeeeeend like a tree in a hurricane because *life* is trying to blow you over—know that you will never break! Why? Because your roots are firmly planted in Christ—*who is your strength!* (See Philippians 4:13).

**A prayer for you:** *Father, thank you for your strength, thank you for Jesus. Thank you for making me, and thank you for another day! You are such a good Father! I also want to thank you for my good health, for my job, my home, and every blessing you've given me that I don't even recognize. THANK YOU! Right now, I lift up all who are reading this, directly to you. For those who want to become strong in the strength of Jesus, yet, the devil keeps fighting them, help them! Renew their minds and teach them that true strength can only be found in Christ! Amen.*

# DAY 56

## HOW TO HANDLE BEING LIED ABOUT

*"When they hurled their insults at him, he did not
retaliate; when he suffered, he made no threats. Instead,
he entrusted himself to him who judges justly."*

### 1 PETER 2:23

N obody likes to be lied about, it doesn't feel good—and with the invention of social media, it's easy to post or tweet a lie, and then have others read it as if it's the truth. Some people even go on to *like* it, comment on it, or share the fake news, therefore compounding the lies. The individuals who choose to use their social media this way are acting in a very immature and vindictive manner.

I'm a grown man and even I have experienced the negativity caused by online fabrications. I can't imagine what today's kids in school feel like when an ugly rumor gets started in cyberspace.

Heck, back in the 1990s when I was in school, if you wanted to tell a lie about someone to get a scandal started, you had to actually tell a person face-to-face, call them, or pass them a note, *then* the rumor-mill began to churn.

Now, people with poor decision-making skills can simply get on their phone, tablet, or computer to easily stir up a hornet's nest. When I think about our younger generation, my heart goes out to them. What a tough way to live out what is a very trying time anyway—transitioning from a child into an adult. It's no wonder teenage suicide is so high.

So what should we do about this? What actions should we take when someone lies about us?

"LET'S GET 'EM BACK! AIN'T NOBODY GONNA TALK ABOUT ME LIKE THAT!"

For years, *that's* how I handled such problems. Because my mind hadn't yet been renewed by God's Spirit in me, my knee-jerk response was to scramble, defend myself, and retaliate. But now I recognize where every lie comes from: *the devil and his crew.* They are the inspiration behind all falsities. Jesus said that Satan is "the father of lies" and that there is "no truth in him" (see John 8:44).

"So Matt, are you saying that every time someone lies, they are possessed by the devil?"

No, that's not what I'm saying, and let me back up a step here. Yes, they *can* be possessed by a demonic force if they are not a Christian. However, if someone *is* a Christian, it's impossible for any demon to touch them (see 1 John 5:18). Sure, demons can pester and influence us, but they can't touch *or* possess us. Christians are literally possessed by the Spirit of God and He will never share your body with an evil spirit in any way. Even *you* had to die and get a new perfect spirit before He joined you (see John 10:28, Romans 6:6, Galatians 2:20, 1 Corinthians 6:19, Colossians 3:3).

Whether a hounding demonic presence *around us* is strong or weak *that* is up to us. Demons hang out with us based on what we allow into our lives, minds, and homes on a regular basis (see Ephesians 4:27). They know if you are a Christian so they want to make your life as miserable as you *let* them. We open up supernatural "windows" for spiritual forces to join us and our loved ones *through* the things we expose ourselves to consistently. But more than likely, the person who is lying is *not* possessed. Possibly? Yes. Likely? No.

Friends, the devil influences us in our minds. Please be aware that a spiritual battle is happening at all times of the day and night and *we* are in the middle of it (see Ephesians 6:10-17). Is every lie coming from a demon? No. We, as humans, have unrenewed thinking (see Romans 12:2, Philippians 4:8). We can choose to think on lies based on our free will, along with the influence of the enemy. However, if we are choosing to walk by our perfect spiritual identity, we *won't* lie. To do this more often than not, we must allow our spirit—which is enmeshed with God—to train our mind rather than demons from hell. This is the graceful goal we restfully strive to achieve each day.

With the combination of old stinking thinking, as well as demonic forces lying to us every chance they get, we can soon begin to *act* on those lies. To combat this, we must begin to recognize lies and start to sort them out based on the truth of God's Spirit in us. If we don't, eventually we will begin to believe lies *as* the truth. It's all uphill from there.

Jesus said the devil has only three main goals for his existence: *kill, steal, destroy* (see John 10:10). You can apply one or all three of these to anything good in your life and if there is suffering the devil is in the midst of it. To top it off, our enemy and his imbeciles know how to bait us the best, they've been studying us since Adam and Eve. Therefore, they can cause us even *more* trouble through temptations.

HOWEVER! In the very same breath of telling us Satan's M.O., Jesus said, "but *I* have come so that you may have *life* and have it *abundantly!*" (See John 10:10, my emphasis added). Another version says, "I have come so that you may enjoy your life and have it to the fullest!" And *another* version of the Bible says, "My purpose is to give them a rich and satisfying life."

*A rich and satisfying life!* That's good! That's what we all want! How do we allow Jesus to give us this gift of a rich and satisfying life? I can tell you that it's *not* through defending yourself against the lies of others. Instead, it's *through* Jesus. Jesus said that He is "the way, the truth, and the life" (John 14:6). Let's break that down so we can have this rich and satisfying life He's talking about:

1. ***The way***. The way to what? To heaven! The way to a peaceful, confident, abundant life! When we do things *His* way, we *get* what He wants to give us! When we *don't* do things His way, we can expect to deal with problems. Not because He is punishing us, but because problems naturally grow in our lives when we make poor choices that go against our perfect spirits.

2. ***The truth***. Jesus didn't simply say that His *words* are the truth, but that *He* is the truth! How amazing is that?! As Christians, we have a God *in us* who *is* truth! So when we begin to speak His graceful words over our lives, the lies of the devil stand no chance. This truth builds confidence in us and it also purges our minds of un-renewed thoughts. The world needs truth. We *have* truth. Truth is good!

3. ***The life***. We've all heard the saying, "Aaaaaahhh, this is the life." It is a phrase most people say as they sip on a piña colada on the beach, or while relaxing on a Sunday afternoon. Jesus wants you to have days like that every single day! He wants you to enjoy your life in times of testing, times of trials, times of rebuilding, and even in the mundane times of our regular lives: *eat, sleep, work, repeat*. He came to give us *the* life because that's what He is—THE LIFE!

This wonderful life happens through trusting Him. It happens through acting and reacting how we should as heaven-ready people—*even* when someone lies about you. Without Christ's Spirit leading us, when someone tells a tall tale about us, the sin of the flesh will react and our mind will think, "Sick 'em!" There is no peace in that, we weren't made for that, and the devil wins in even greater ways when we *choose* that.

As a Christ-indwelled person, rather than go against your true identity and fire back, you should pray that the person lying about you would come to know God's grace. My friend, I know it hurts when people lie about you but you're going to be fine. God uses this stuff for a good *future* purpose (see Romans 8:28). You simply have to give it time and let Him work it out. You are His child and He loves you. Go to Him for comfort, don't go to an addiction or anything else, or, any*one* else. *He* is your strength! Tell Him, "This hurts very badly, but I trust you." He will be quick to respond with, "Everything will be okay, eventually. You'll see."

Try to remember that God wants to use *all* of your painful situations to strengthen you! None of your tears and sorrow gets wasted! He is preparing you for greater things! The devil, on the other hand, wants you to respond to the lies of others in a manner which will destroy your life, steal your joy, and keep you frustrated. So be sure to choose wisely when responding—that is, if you even respond at all. You don't *have* to respond.

Speaking of choosing wisely, here is a short prayer that I believe will help you when situations like this arise: "God, please give me the wisdom to be able to handle this like I should." Why pray for wisdom? Because God will actually give you wisdom at your asking! The Bible says, "If you lack wisdom, you should ask God for it, and He will give it to you generously, without finding fault" (see James 1:5).

So pray! Pray for wisdom to be developed in your life! The seeds are already in you! Remember, you are strong, you are confident, and you are full of peace! By God's Spirit being in you, He has given you all of these things! Wisdom is inside of you too! Ask God to help it come *out* of you—and grow big and strong! As you do, soon enough, the lies of others won't bother you at all, because you *know* the Truth!

**A prayer for you:** *God, I want to thank you for another day alive. What a gift it is to have yet another chance to impact this world for you. Right now, I lift up all who are reading this, directly to you. So many of them have believed the lies about themselves, and they shouldn't. Lots of these dear readers have been horrifically lied about, slandered, and unfairly treated by others. I know you've seen it! I know you are just! I know* *you are sovereign! I pray right now that you strengthen them in their inner-being! Reveal to them that you are using those lies for good! Let them know that what the enemy tries to use for our harm, you use for wonderful things! We are grateful. We love you. In Jesus' name I pray, amen.*

# Day 57

## How Can I Believe in Jesus?

*"He said to him, 'If they do not listen to Moses and the Prophets, they will not be convinced even if someone rises from the dead.'"*

*Luke 16:31*

What does it take to believe in Jesus? The answer to that question lies within the question itself, your belief. The way you believe Jesus is real—that He is who He said He is—is the same way you would believe Harry Potter is real, or that Allah is real, or that evolution is real: *belief.*

We are allowed to believe whatever we want, this is called *free will.* Free will is the greatest ability God has given mankind. It allows us to *be* like Him. It allows us to be able to make our own choices! And one of the many choices we get to make throughout our short lifetime is *what* we will believe in.

We *will* believe in something, even if it's nothing. Believing in nothing is still faith in nothing. Why can't we *not* believe in something? Because humans have a belief system built in to us by God Himself. Just like He gave our physical bodies the longing to drink water, eat food, and breathe air, He gave our *spiritual* bodies desires which must be quenched as well.

For this reason, the Bible says, "God has placed eternity in the heart of every man" (see Ecclesiastes 3:11).

Our spirits are restless until we establish a belief system, *even* if we establish *nothing* as our god. This is why an atheist feels satisfied with giving up on a particular deity—incorrectly satisfied mind you—but still, my point is that this part of our spiritual DNA *refuses* to stay quiet.

Some people even choose to rely on the fairy tale of "Mother Nature" as an actual deity. We simply *cannot* get away from looking up at the sky and wondering where everything came from. God made us this way on purpose. Thoughts about our origin and eternity is what sets us apart from all of God's other creations. *"Where did I come from?" "Where will I go when I die?"* These are thoughts an everlasting being thinks. *You* are an everlasting spirit who *has* a body.

Sometimes, as everlasting spirits, we'll even attempt to meet our spiritual needs with a physical distraction. A particular hobby, an activity, money, sex, an addiction, a person, place, or thing—we can even be distracted by focusing on ourselves in an unhealthy way. Not that there's anything wrong with ourselves as Christians; and not that any of these things are in competition with God, He's God. But such can divert our attention away from who He truly is, as well as who *we* truly are. So we must keep things well-balanced because even good things *can* be distracting.

Being distracted is usually an involuntary effort—unnoticed, until we've taken it too far. Our bewilderment doesn't mean we're believing in that person, place, thing, or activity *as* our Creator, but we're still trying to fill a void with something or someone *other* than God. Friend, we were created to place Jesus in this position! That is, if we want to unlock our destinies for being alive!

The Bible says, "For in him all things were created: things in heaven and on earth, visible and invisible, whether thrones or powers or rulers or authorities; all things have been created through him and for him. He is before all things, and in him all things hold together" (Colossians 1:16-17).

*In Him all things hold together!* Only a spiritual relationship with Jesus can hold your life together just right! This is *so* simple! It's so simple, it's almost too difficult to believe. But make no mistake, people who refuse to believe in Christ's deity, yet claim to believe in nothing at all, they will fight tooth and nail to prove they believe in nothing at all. That *fight* is called belief! That fight is their faith! We *can't* stop believing in *something* just like we can't stop our lungs from pumping oxygen in and out of our bodies! No matter how hard we try, we believe! We can't stop it!

For this reason, Stonehenge was built. For this reason, pyramids were erected. For this reason, witch doctors dance around fires at night—WE BELIEVE. The billion dollar question is: "Is what we believe the truth?"

If we don't believe in the truth, all bets are off. We can pretty much make up whatever belief system we want. Without a *particular* truth, even ISIS is just fine in what they are doing because that's *their* choice of truth.

"Matt, how can you say that?! They are beheading children in the streets and dipping live men and women in pools of acid! That's just wrong!"

"Says who?"

"Says me! Any normal person would know that just ain't right!"

"Okay, but says *who*? Who, or what, are you basing your truth on as normal? Who are you to say that's not the truth?"

My friend, without a precise truth, this world is simply an overgrown field of the Serengeti. Without an *exact* truth—something iron-clad—we are all just animals. The lion is not wrong for killing the zebra, just the same as the house cat is not wrong for eating the robin, just the same as Hitler would not be wrong for wiping out 6 million people from this planet. Be faster! Be smarter! Be *stronger*—or die! If there is no truth, then there are no guidelines to how we should live and treat others.

Without a singular truth, every aspect of life is simply *survival of the fittest*. Get rich, use others, push people out of your way, and do whatever makes you feel good—just don't get caught. Don't get eaten by a bigger animal. According to this incorrect logic, we are all just operating from our brains' synapses. *"Do what you want, when you want, because you want to—blindly. Repeat."*

Without truth, there is no such thing as spirituality, morals and ethics don't matter, love is not a real thing, and after death you simply cease to exist. You are annihilated. So if you want Mickey and Minnie Mouse to be your gods, suit yourself. You're allowed, of course, but that's not the real truth. And if truth is not real, then the word *truth* in itself is an oxymoron.

So what is the truth?! Jesus said, "I am the truth" (see John 14:6). Friend, it's up to *you* to believe that He actually *is* the truth! It's up to *you* to believe that what He *said* is the truth! The *real* truth of life on earth is that Jesus solved the mystery of truth for us, in person, and He did it with love!

So today, my friends, let me ask you this: Are you ready to believe in Jesus? If you are, absolutely everything about your life is about to change! Why? Because you will get a *new* life! You'll get Christ's life! I'm not talking about just having your sins removed—that's only one part of the gospel. I'm talking about you actually *receiving* Jesus' Spirit in your body—for good! The very *moment* you believe in the truth, that happens! You get Christ's life! Are you ready?!...Believe! (See Ephesians 1:13, Galatians 2:20, Philippians 1:21, Romans 6:6, 2 Corinthians 5:17).

**A prayer for you:** *Heavenly Father, today I want to thank you for revealing the truth to me about Jesus! Right now, I lift up all who are reading this, directly to you. For those who may or may not believe in Jesus as their Savior, I'm asking that you help them understand your grace on even deeper levels. Reveal the truth and give them the strength they need to overcome any doubts! We love you Lord, and we appreciate everything you do. In Christ's name I pray, amen.*

# DAY 58

## DON'T FORGET TO THANK JESUS

*"One of them, when he was healed, came back,*
*praising God in a loud voice. He threw himself*
*at Jesus' feet and thanked him..."*

LUKE 17:15-16

I sn't it amazing how we are quick to blame God when everything in our lives is falling apart, yet, when things are going well, we refuse to give Him any credit? That's exactly what happened one day as Jesus was traveling from town to town, on His way to Jerusalem.

There was a group of ten outcasts standing far from Him, shouting, "Jesus, Master, have pity on us!" (See Luke 17:13). They were yelling for help from a distance, because they had a skin disease called *leprosy*. People with this condition weren't allowed to be around others, they were castaways from society.

I've done some research on leprosy and this is a terrible disease! With a quick Google search, you can see that the images alone are horrendous! It's a disease which makes the skin all over your body bubble up like huge sunburn blisters, and it also impacts your respiratory system, nerves, and eyesight.

Wiki's information states: "Leprosy results in a lack of ability to feel pain and thus loss of parts of extremities due to repeated injuries or infection due to unnoticed wounds." That's bad! Losing body parts from infection because you can't feel yourself getting hurt?! Ouch!

To top it off, back in Jesus' day, anyone who had leprosy was not just physically hurting but also emotionally. Having this disease meant banishment from civilization! Adding insult to injury, these outcasts were deemed "unclean" by the legalistic Jews, as if God were punishing them *through* leprosy—which was not true.

Because of their disease, these ten men knew they weren't supposed to get next to Jesus. So in order to get their miracle, they stood at the treeline and yelled for Him to heal them...and...He did! Boom! Ten miracles at once, from far away! That's what Jesus does!

Afterwards, He immediately told them to go show themselves to the priests. Why? Because before they were healed, these people weren't allowed to be around priests due to the affliction on their bodies. Personally, I think Jesus wanted to show the self-righteous folk what He had just done for the "nasty people" these "Samaritans"—the ones whom the priests kept rejecting while using legalism as an excuse for their refusal to love everyone unconditionally.

One last thing I want to point out: only *one* of the healed men came back to thank Jesus! JUST ONE! Imagine that! Jesus had just completely changed these men's lives, and they *steal* the blessing and run away! Not even so much as a thumbs-up and smile! Just...gone! THEY STOLE IT, I TELL YOU!

I feel bad about this when I think about my past, just how much Jesus had done for me and I too ignored Him...I just kept on doing whatever the sin of my flesh and unrenewed mind wanted! *Blessing* after *blessing* after *blessing*, and I couldn't even do so much as get rid of my pride and say, "Thank you, Jesus. Thank you *so* much."

Oh how glad I am that I finally began to give Jesus all the credit He truly deserves! What a wonderful Savior! Thank you, Lord, for everything! You are good! SO GOOD!

**A prayer for you:** *Jesus, I want to thank you today, not just for all that you've done, but for all that you are. I appreciate you! Right now, I lift up everyone who is reading this, directly to you. For those who may have forgotten to thank you for what you've done for them, remind them that you are the giver of all good things. Remind them what you've done. Sometimes we get so excited about a blessing, we forget to stop and give you our gratitude. We love you! We thank you! Amen.*

# DAY 59

## DOES GOD HEAR MY PRAYERS?

*"Jesus told his disciples a parable to show them that*
*they should always pray and never give up."*

LUKE 18:1

D
o you ever feel like God doesn't hear your prayers? Friend, I'm here
to tell you today that God *does* hear your prayers. He is not only
listening to your spoken prayers, but He is also listening to the unspoken
prayers of your heart! (See Psalm 37:4, Romans 8:26). He knows more
about you than even *you* know about you, and...He answers *all* of your
prayers! He doesn't ignore a single one! God answers our prayers in one
of three ways:

1.  Yes.
2.  Yes, but wait, I'm still using this.
3.  No. I've got a better overall plan for my Kingdom.

I know it feels like your repeated prayers fall on deaf ears, but they do
not. I understand that sometimes you just want to give up and stop praying
completely, but don't! Your prayers are not only *heard* by God, but they

are *felt* by Him too (see Psalm 34:18, Hebrews 2:17:18). He is your *loving* Heavenly Father, and He only wants the best for all of His children (see Matthew 7:9-11).

In the book of Luke, chapter 18, Jesus told His disciples a parable to show them they should always pray and never give up. The story was about a widow who kept coming to an unjust judge for help. Even though he kept turning her away, she simply would *not* stop pestering him. The judge, however, was very arrogant and crooked. Jesus said that he "neither feared God, nor cared about men" (Luke 18:2), *both* are terrible qualities for any person in office to have.

This dirty and corrupt man kept overlooking the pleas of this woman. Her heartfelt cries fell flat due to the selfish power of this obstinate man who couldn't care less about her *or* her problems. However, because she would not stop persistently asking him for help, the judge finally said, "I will see that she gets justice so that she won't eventually wear me out!" (See Luke 18:5).

Jesus then explains to His disciples, "And will not God (who *is* loving and just) bring about justice for his chosen ones, those who cry out to him day and night? Will he keep putting them off?" The answer is no. "He will see that they get justice..." (see Luke 18:7-8, my note added).

Jesus makes it clear that there is something much more important than having every single prayer answered *exactly* how we want it: "You will get justice and quickly, however, when the Son of Man comes, *will he find faith on earth*?" (see Luke 18:8, my emphasis added).

Will He find faith on earth?...*Will He find faith on earth?!* Will He?! Or will we be like a nest full of baby birds with our mouths wide open, eyes closed, saying, "Gimme, gimme, gimme!"?

Why are we so focused on ourselves?! This life isn't *just* about us! It took me over 30 years to figure this out, and *yes* God wants to answer our prayers how we want, but He is much more interested in getting us from being spiritually *dead* to spiritually *alive*! And *then* He wants us to realize we are spiritually perfect for good! He is *not* our genie-in-a-bottle! He's our Dad! Good dads don't just give their kids anything and everything!

Good dads say, "No," sometimes. Good dads say, "Wait." Good dads think about their kid's future, and they think about their *other* kids too!

Friend, we must allow the attitude of Christ to come out of us (see Philippians 2:5). It's there, we just have to get it out (see Philippians 2:12). There is no law in prayer, but we should be praying prayers which have the aura of this: "God, you've heard me pray this a thousand times, and I still want it, but if you never give me what I'm asking for, I trust you. I know that *you know* what's best for me and others. So continue to do as you see fit, and help me to live out my spiritual perfection in this process of trusting you deeper. I love you, and I'm available to you."

There is no such thing as unanswered prayers. Realizing this fact will build up an unshakable confidence in you! Understanding that your Heavenly Daddy is looking out for you at all times *strengthens* you! You'll be able to enjoy your life no matter what is happening around you, and you'll *refuse* to fall into self-pity! This heavenly mindset also gives you tremendous enthusiasm and unconditional love for everyone! *This* is the relationship God longs to have with you—one that is authentic and trusting!

So today, my friends, know this: God loves you, and He hears your prayers. He is sovereign and incapable of being incorrect. Further, He doesn't just *hear* your prayers, but He's listening closely! He lives in us and He will never go away! He is a good *good* Father who loves us immeasurably! So keep praying! Keep trusting! Keep being your heaven-ready self! And most of all, enjoy your life as God's own child!

**A prayer for you:** *Dad, I want you to know how grateful I am for you. I want you to know how much I appreciate you making me your child forever. Thank you for your commitment to me. You are the real Promise Keeper. Right now, I lift up all who are reading this, directly to you. So many of them are hurting, Lord. So many have been praying to you for a very long time and they feel like it's not working. Speak to their hearts today and show them that their prayers ARE* *working. Please help these dear readers to develop a deeper relationship with you. Begin to teach them to trust you, to stand firm in your grace, and to keep praying! Teach them to ALWAYS communicate with you! In Christ's name I pray, amen.*

# DAY 60

## DOES GOD REALLY LOVE ME?

*"Are not two sparrows sold for a penny? Yet not one of them will fall to the ground outside your Father's care." ~Jesus*

### MATTHEW 10:29

I love that verse, "...yet not one (sparrow) will fall to the ground outside your Father's care." When Jesus said this, something so simple, the way I began to look at the birds that fly around my neighborhood was forever changed. While out on my morning run, I'd see a robin fly by and land on a tree branch, immediately I'd think to myself, "God knows about that *single* bird, and He cares for it. He actually loves *that* particular bird."

So amazing. So unfathomable. God is *so* big. He's doing "all of this" at once. All of what? Sustaining His Creation. On an even deeper level, God doesn't *just* know about that single bird in my subdivision's oak tree, but He also knows the molecular structure of that bird. He even causes that little bird's heart to beat...*these* were His ideas (see Genesis 1:21).

Just think about that for a moment, *everything* is in His hands, even our very own existence. The Bible says, "we live and move and have our being through Him" (see Acts 17:28). Life would not be happening without God wanting it to happen. Life would not be *possible* without His consent.

This is why Paul said, "He is before all things, and in him all things hold together" (Colossians 1:17). Paul was speaking of Jesus, who is a part of the Trinity: *Father, Son, Holy Spirit.* All three *together* equal God (see 1 John 5:7-8).

A hyper-critical person might say, "Yeah Matt, that's great. God is big, so what. Life still sucks." To that I'd say, "Oh, my friend, but *does* it?" What *if* this inconceivable God actually *loved* us? What if our Creator made this entire universe just so we could have a place to begin a personal relationship with Him? What if *that* was His big idea? Relationship? *Eternal* relationship?

What if our Designer loved us *so* much, He would actually *become* a part of His very own creation? What if He joined us in playing by His own created rules of physics and morals—and did so perfectly—on *our* behalf? What *if*, just to be fair to us, He took on the very notion of pain and death *for* us, to *help* us? That, my friend, is what happened in Jesus Christ!

So why is it we can't just "jump on in" and enjoy this relationship with such a loving God? Well, because God has allowed a *spiritual* enemy to join us on planet earth. "Matt, why would your so-called *loving* God do such a thing?! That sounds sadistic!"

To answer that question, I'd have to ask *you* a question: Have you ever tried to force someone to love you? How'd that work out?...It doesn't. It *never* works out. Forcing someone to love you is an impossibility. God knew this. He knew that a planet full of walking, talking, mannequins would never be able to genuinely love Him back, just the same as a sandbox full of army figurines can't love the boy back who is playing with them—no matter how he sets them up or "makes" them talk. In order to be able to love, we *have* to have free will. Therefore, God gave us the option to *not* love Him.

Our enemy, whom God has temporarily allowed to reside here with us, he is everything *opposite* of what God is. This idiot and his dark dorks only have three main goals: kill, steal, destroy (see John 10:10). Jesus said Satan is the father of lies and that he doesn't even have the *ability* to tell the truth (see John 8:44).

When the Holy Spirit began to point out this jack-wagon to me, He said, "Start fighting *him*, not people, and not yourself." Once I began to do this, my relationship with God went to a whole new level. Like Dorothy and her friends who could finally see behind the curtain at what the wizard *truly* looked like—a weak old man pressing buttons, trying to scare people and ruin their lives with loud noises and smoke—I, now knew the devil. My real enemy had been defined.

This moron not only wants us to doubt God, but he wants us to resent Him, ignore Him, be petrified of Him, feel condemned by Him, *and* he wants us to believe that God does *not* love us. "But Matt, how can God love me? I've done too many wrong things in my life for *anyone* to love me, let alone a perfect God."

Friend, I've been there. I can remember the days when I just wanted to die. I had believed the lies of the devil for *so long* that I honestly thought God was out to get me for my bad behavior and poor choices! I can even remember being afraid to pray! I'd squint and say, "God, I know I don't deserve it, but please, *help* me. I *need* your help."

I also remember thinking, "If I could *just* straighten my life out, *then* God would love me." These are lies from our enemy! These are falsities from our accuser! (See Revelation 12:10). He fights us *spiritually*, in our minds! (See Ephesians 6:10-17). We *must* begin to recognize that! God loves us as we are! Period! The Bible says, "God demonstrated his love for us in this: while we were still sinners, Christ died for us" (Romans 5:9).

Let me repeat that: WHILE WE WERE STILL SINNERS CHRIST DIED FOR US! So if we *were* sinners in our spirits, how did we become non-sinners in our spirits? How did we become saints? After all, that's what every Christian is, a *saint*. Some denominations have incorrectly awarded this title to only a handful of believers, but Paul said that *all* believers are saints! (See 1 Corinthians 1:2).

God has made the option of spiritual perfection—sainthood—easy: *believe Jesus has forgiven you of your sins and you will get a brand new holy spirit—one of your own—and it will be combined with God's Holy Spirit, forever* (see Ephesians 2:8-9, 2 Corinthians 5:17, Galatians 2:20, Romans 5:1, 6:6, Colossians 1:22, 3:3).

It is only through believing Jesus has completed your spiritual perfection *for* you, that you can become a child of God! (See John 1:12, Ephesians 1:5, Hebrews 10:14). Afterwards, Jesus keeps you saved—not you (see John 10:28). The only way you can become *un*-saved is if Jesus dies again, and that ain't happening (see Hebrews 7:25).

The Christian who doesn't understand their true identity in Christ will then beg the question, "What if I don't stop sinning completely, am I still saved?"

Well, did you stop sinning completely to *get* saved? No? Okay, so what did you do? You believed Jesus saved you, and He actually did! The Cross worked! So stop worrying about losing something that you aren't even maintaining! *Jesus* is maintaining your salvation, your amazing attitudes and actions are not! (See Hebrews 6:19, Philippians 3:8).

So today, my friends, know this: Absolutely nothing can separate you from the love of God, which is found in Jesus Christ! (See Romans 8:39). And yes, God *really* loves you! He loves you so much He formed this universe! He loves you so much He gave you life! He loves you so much He gave you Jesus! He loves you so much He decided to make His home in you forever! Enjoy this unconditional love and live it out each day!

**A prayer for you:** *Heavenly Father, thank you for your love. It has changed my entire life! Right now, I lift up all who are reading this, directly to you. So many of them don't realize just how much you love them, some are even scared of you. They've been incorrectly taught that your love is conditional. They've been taught to think you're mad at them, and you're not. The enemy has also embedded a tremendous amount of guilt in so many of their minds. Some even think you have too much going on to get involved with their "small" problems, and that's not true. Others believe they have to behave better before you'll pay any attention* *to them—teach them that is incorrect! I command any legalistic, religious spirit to stop pestering them!*

*Teach them about the power that lies within them—YOU! Break the chains on their minds of guilt, condemnation, addictions, and fear! Build up a new confidence in them! Reveal Satan's lies! Make him leave these good people alone! Strengthen them on such a level that they would no longer be passive, but instead, fighting hard through your grace! Teach them how to defeat hell with their words! Show them how to overcome evil with good, and hate with love! Use these awesome, heaven-ready people for great and mighty things! I know you will! In Jesus' powerful name I pray, amen.*

Dear friend,

Thank you so much for spending time with me through this book. I hope I was able to bring you a sense of peace and confidence in knowing more about what Christ has truly done. My prayer is for you to grow into even deeper revelations of your identity as a believer. Lastly, it would mean the world to me if you'd leave a kind review on Amazon.com, Goodreads.com, Barnes & Noble's website, or wherever you've purchased this book. Your opinion is very important and encouraging to me. I always look forward to reading reviews.

May God continue to bless you greatly, with even more knowledge, of His love for you through Jesus!

In Christ,
Matt

# 60 Days for Jesus, Volume 2: *Understanding Christ Better, Two Months at a Time*

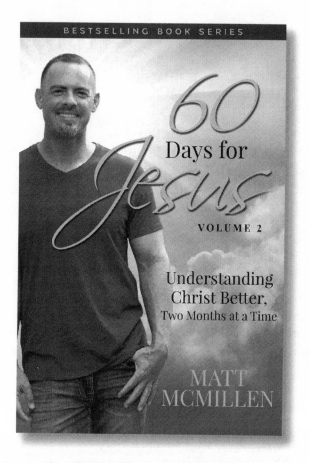

"This book is exactly what I needed to understand more about Jesus. I couldn't put it down. Thank you, Matt McMillen, for sharing your story to help strengthen others!" *-Amazon Customer*

# 60 Days for Jesus, Volume 3: *Understanding Christ Better, Two Months at a Time*

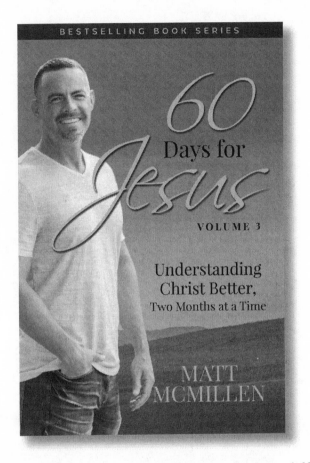

"Matt does an excellent job of providing clarity on many difficult issues every believer walks through on a daily basis. He does this by clearly articulating the scriptures to reveal the truth that really does set us free. This Volume, like the ones before, is an excellent devotional book to help any believer with their walk with God. Every page of this book is filled with the good news of God's unconditional love and grace. If you read one book this year, make it this one!" -*Amazon Customer*

# True Purpose in Jesus Christ: *Finding the Relationship for Which You Were Made*

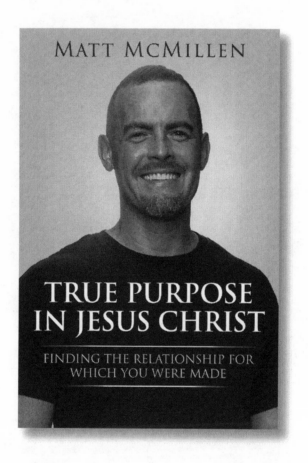

"One of the best books I've ever read! Matt's honesty about his life and what Jesus did to redeem him is amazing! He uses Scripture throughout his book to back up everything he talks about. I bought 20 books so I could share with the lost. Absolutely life changing! Thank you, Matt, for writing this book!" *-Amazon Customer*

# The Christian Identity, Volume 1: *Discovering What Jesus Has Truly Done to Us*

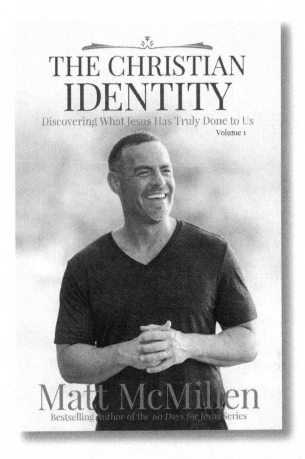

"Matt brilliantly explains the supernatural transformation that happens when we become believers in the finished work of the cross. His writing style makes this easy to understand as he answers some of the toughest questions that are on so many Christians' minds today." *-Amazon Customer*

# The Christian Identity, Volume 2: *Discovering What Jesus Has Truly Done to Us*

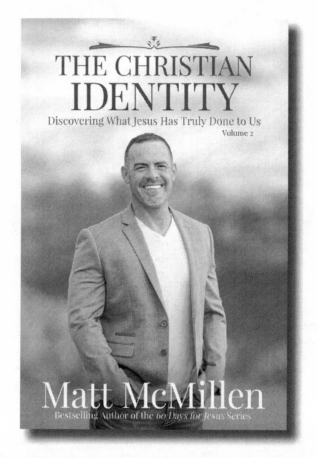

"Matt McMillen's books are amazing! You will learn so much and understand how to live your Christian li fe according to our Lord Jesus Christ. I've read all of his books and have shared them. I love his writing." -*Amazon Customer*

# The Christian Identity, Volume 3: *Discovering What Jesus Has Truly Done to Us*

"Just as I suspected, *The Christian Identity, Volume 3*, packed as much grace and freedom punch as the first two books in this series!" -*Amazon Customer*

Made in the USA
Columbia, SC
11 March 2022

57521055R00169